Paul's Kitchen

A collection of best loved recipes
using ingredients from your own garden

PAUL J. COVALESKY

ISBN: 1-4392-1532-4
ISBN-13: 9781439215326

DEDICATION

This book is dedicated to my beloved father,
Victor J. Covalesky, M.D., grandparents, and uncles
Joseph and Sylvester, who taught me a love for gardening.
And for my very first teacher in the kitchen who continues
to inspire me with her love and dedication, my mother.

INTRODUCTION

Born and raised on the farmlands of Pennsylvania Paul Covalesky learned at an early age the integral connection between the land and table. Not only did he have the experience of working on Sunday afternoon at his grandparents' farm, but also, he himself worked with his father and brothers to plant a harvest abundant with fresh vegetables, herbs and fruits every year. From his father, who was a well-renowned and well-beloved psychiatrist and neurologist, he developed a love of working with his hands, spending time outdoors and showing his hobby with his children. And it didn't end there. Processing this rich harvest, then past into the kitchen, where he watched how his mother would turn these fresh vegetables into scrumptious meals. Here he also learned her niche of trying new creations and experiment on her own to come up with something even better.

Paul has never stopped trying new recipes too. It has been this bold and creative approach that has brought him to make delicious dishes with his own unique twist.

Paul has worked with outstanding chefs, with such other unforgettable chefs as Julia Child at the Culinary Institute of America and experts like Paul Bocuse and Daniel Boulud.

And now these beloved recipes are enjoyable to you, when asked how long it took him to write this collection of recipes, Paul's response has been, "all my life." And, truly, that is the case for the journey of this Best Loved Collection of recipes has been a lifetime in the making.

Bon Appetite!

MEASUREMENT EQUIVALENTS

Liquid

1 cup	8 fluid ounces	½ pint	16 Tablespoons
2 cups	16 fluid ounces	1 pint	
4 cups	32 fluid ounces	2 pints	1 quart
4 quarts	128 fluid ounces	1 gallon	3.785 liters
8 quarts	one peck		
4 pecks	one bushel		
dash	less than ¼ teaspoonful		
1 teaspoon	0.667 fluid ounces	5 grams	
1 Tablespoon	½ fluid ounce	15 grams	3 teaspoons
2 Tablespoon	1 fluid ounce	30 grams	1/8 cup
8 Tablespoon	4 fluid ounce	¼ pint	½ cup

Dry

3 teaspoons	1 Tablespoon	½ ounce	
2 Tablespoons	1/8 cup	1 fluid ounce	
4 Tablespoons	¼ cup	2 fluid ounces	
5 1/3 Tablespoons	1/3 cup	2.6 fluid ounces	
8 Tablespoons	½ cup	4 ounces	
12 Tablespoons	¾ cup	6 ounces	0.375 pound
32 Tablespoons	2 cups	16 ounces	1 pound
64 Tablespoons	4 cups	32 ounces	2 pounds

CONTENTS

CHAPTER

1	BREADS	1
2	BEEF	11
3	CHICKEN	39
4	DESSERTS	
	CAKES	81
	CHEESECAKES	119
	COOKIES & SMALL DESSERTS	127
5	PIES & DOUGHS	139
6	DRESSINGS	151
7	DUCK	157
8	LAMB	163
9	APPETIZERS	177
10	PASTA	191
11	PORK	221
12	SALADS	231
13	SEAFOOD	241
14	SOUPS	313
15	VEAL	327
16	SEASONINGS	339
17	HOLIDAY COCKTAILS	349
18	INDEX	353

∽

BREADS

Blueberry Muffins Topped with Cinnamon Walnut Frosting
2
Carrot Muffins
3
Cinnamon Raisin Bread
4
French Bread Rye Braids
5
**Herb Brioche Stuffed with Brie Cheese and
Laced with Wild Flower Honey,
Garnished with Crushed Pecans**
6
Herb Style Pizza Bread
8
Pineapple and Cranberry Tea Scones
9

∽

∽

Blueberry Muffins Topped with Cinnamon Walnut Frosting

¼ c.	Crisco
½ c.	Sugar, granulated
1 ea.	Egg, whole
½ c.	Milk
1½ c.	All-Purpose Flour, sifted
¼ c.	Buckwheat Flour, sifted
1½ tsp.	Baking Powder
½ tsp.	Sea Salt
¼ tsp.	Nutmeg, ground
1 c.	Blueberries, fresh & freeze for one hour

Method:
1. In a mixing bowl, add the Crisco, sugar, eggs and milk. Add the flour, baking powder, salt and nutmeg and blend until mixture is smooth.
2. Fold in the blueberries and place in cupcake molds.
3. Bake in a 350°F oven for 10 to 15 minutes or until an inserted toothpick comes out clean.

Cinnamon Walnut Frosting:

½ c.	Sugar, granulated
1 tsp.	Cinnamon, ground
1 Tbl.	Walnuts, ground fine
½ c.	Butter, melted

Method:
1. Mix the sugar and cinnamon together.
   Add melted butter and mix thoroughly.
2. Drizzle mixture on cooled muffins.

∽

Carrot Muffins

1¾ c.	Extra Virgin Olive Oil
2 ea.	Eggs, whole
2 tsp.	Vanilla
1¾ c.	Sugar, granulated
1¾ c.	All-Purpose Flour, sifted
¼ c.	Buckwheat Flour, sifted
2 tsp.	Baking Powder
2 tsp.	Cinnamon, ground
1 tsp.	Sea Salt
¾ c.	Walnuts, coarsely chopped
2 c.	Carrots, peeled & finely grated
½ c.	Crushed Pineapple, drained
½ c.	Coconut Flakes

Method:
1. In a mixing bowl, add the oil, eggs, vanilla and sugar.
   Add the flour, baking powder, spices and blend until mixture is smooth.
2. Fold in the walnuts, carrots, pineapple and coconut.
   Place batter in cupcake molds.
3. Bake in a 350°F oven for 12 to 15 minutes or until an inserted toothpick comes out clean.

∽

Cinnamon Raisin Bread

½ c.	Milk, whole
½ c.	Water, cold
¼ c.	Wild Flower Honey
1½ pkg.	Dry Yeast
1 ea.	Egg, whole
½ tsp.	Sea Salt
3¾ c.	Bread Flour, sifted
¼ c.	Whole Wheat Flour, sifted
¼ c.	Buckwheat Flour, sifted
3 Tbl.	Butter, cold and cut into pieces
6 Tbl.	Cinnamon, ground
½ tsp.	Cardamom, ground
½ tsp.	Nutmeg, ground
2 c.	Raisins

Method:
1. Combine milk, water, sugar and yeast in a mixing bowl.
   Let yeast react for 3 to 5 minutes.
2. Add the rest of the ingredients.
   Knead on 1st speed for 3 minutes, and then place on 2nd speed for another 5 minutes.
3. Let proof in a warm place so dough triples in size.
   Punch down and turn dough over onto cutting board.
   Portion into loaf pans and let rise again until desired height is achieved.
4. Bake in a 400°F oven for 25 to 30 minutes.

∽

෧෨

French Bread Rye Braids

1½ c.	Water, warm
3 Tbl.	Extra Virgin Olive Oil
2 Tbl.	Wild Flower Honey
1 pkg.	Dry Yeast
2 tsp.	Sea Salt
3½ c.	Bread Flour, sifted
¼ c.	Dark Rye Flour, sifted
¼ c.	Buckwheat Flour, sifted

1. Place the water in the mixing bowl with the oil, sugar and yeast.
   Let yeast react for 3 to 5 minutes, and then add the salt and flour.
2. Knead on 1st speed for 3 to 5 minutes.
3. Let rise in a warm place so dough is triple in size.
   Punch down and turn dough over onto cutting board.
   Cut dough into two equal portions and roll out evenly.
   Pinch both end portions and lap over several times until it
   resembles a braid. Makes two loaves.
   Let rise again until desired height is achieved.
4. Place on oiled sheet pan and bake in a 400ºF oven until golden brown.

෧෨

∾

Herb Brioche Stuffed with Brie Cheese and Laced with Wild Flower Honey, Garnished with Crushed Pecans

3 oz.	Milk, heated
1 oz.	Wild Flower Honey
4 oz.	Bread Flour, sifted
1 oz.	Buckwheat Flour, sifted
1 pkg.	Dry Yeast

Method:
1. Combine milk, sugar and warm mixture, but do not simmer.
   Add the egg, flour and salt in bowl and add the warm mixture and yeast.
2. Mix on 1st speed for 3 to 5 minutes.
3. Place plastic wrap over the mixture and let rest for 1 hour.

2 ea.	Eggs, whole
10 oz	Bread Flour, sifted
2 oz.	Buckwheat Flour, sifted
2 oz.	Butter, whole & diced
½ tsp.	Sea Salt
¼ c.	Parsley, Chives and Cilantro, freshly chopped
As Needed	Bread Flour, sifted
16 oz.	Brie, round in size
3 Tbl.	Wild Flower Honey
¼ c.	Pecans, crushed

Method:

1. In the same mixing bowl, add the rest of the egg, flour, butter, salt and herbs.
2. Knead dough on 1st speed for 3 to 5 minutes.
3. Place in lightly oiled bowl, cover and set to proof for 1 hour until double in size.
   Punch down dough and roll out on floured surface.
4. Coat brie with honey and then place dough tightly around brie.
   Reserve some pieces of dough for garnish on top.
   Let rise until desired height is achieved.
5. Bake in 375ºF oven for 10 to 12 minutes.
6. Remove from oven and place on entrée plate.
   Garnish with pecans and wild flower honey.

∾

❧

Herb Style Pizza Bread

1¾ c.	Water, warm
1 Tbl.	Sugar, granulated
¼ c.	Extra Virgin Olive Oil
1 pkg.	Dry Yeast
1 tsp.	Sea Salt
4¼ c.	Bread Flour, Flour sifted
¼ c.	Whole Wheat Flour, sifted
¼ c.	Buckwheat Flour, sifted
5 Tbl.	Mozzarella cheese
2 Tbl.	Parmesan cheese
¼ tsp.	Garlic, minced
¼ tsp.	Basil, freshly chopped
¼ tsp.	Oregano, freshly chopped
¼ tsp.	Parsley, freshly chopped
¼ tsp.	Thyme, freshly chopped
8 ea.	Sun Dried Tomatoes, minced

Method:
1. In a mixing bowl, add the milk, sugar, oil and yeast.
    Let yeast react for 3 to 5 minutes, and then add the egg and salt.
    Add all ingredients to the mixing bowl with a dough hook.
2. Knead at 1st speed for 1 minute and 3 minutes on 2nd speed.
3. Proof in a warm place until dough triples in size.
    Punch down and proof one more time.
    Roll out onto floured surface and shape into two round portions.
    Portion into loaf pans and let rise until desired height is achieved.
4. Bake in a 400ºF oven for 20 to 25 minutes.

❧

∽

Pineapple and Cranberry Tea Scones

¼ c.	Butter, cold & cubed
1¾ c.	All-Purpose Flour, sifted
¼ c.	Buckwheat Flour, sifted
2 tsp.	Baking Powder
¼ tsp.	Sea Salt
2 Tbl.	Sugar, granulated
1 ea.	Egg, whole
½ c.	Milk, whole
3 Tbl.	Orange Zest
¼ c.	Cranberries, chopped
¼ c.	Pineapple, crushed

Method:
1. In a mixing bowl, combine the butter and flour.
   Mix ingredients until it resembles cornmeal.
2. Add baking powder, salt, sugar and egg.
   Slowly incorporate the milk.
   Add the orange zest, cranberries, pineapple and mix for 3 minutes.
3. Turn onto a floured board and roll into rounds with a pastry cutter.
   Arrange on a lightly floured baking sheet.
4. Bake at 400°F oven for 15 minutes or until golden brown.

∽

BEEF

Beef Wellington with Button Mushrooms and Eggplant Wrapped in a
Puff Pastry, Served with a Port Shitake Herb Cream Brown Sauce
13

Grilled Skewered Beef with Portabella, Shitake and Oyster Mushrooms,
Green and Yellow Zucchini, Served with Scallion Wild Rice
15

Grilled Beef Tornadoes and Shrimp, Served with an
Herb Scallop Champagne Sauce
17

Ground Sirloin Beef Chili with Red and White Beans
18

Marinated and Grilled Beef, Shrimp and Lobster,
Served with a Three Pepper Risotto
19

Marinated and Grilled London Broil with a Port Wild Mushroom Sauce,
Served with Parsley Red Bliss Potatoes and Brussels Sprouts
21

Prime Rib of Beef with Horseradish Au Jus, Served with Asparagus
And Twice Baked Stuffed Potato
23

Roasted Angus Beef Tenderloin and Veal Stuffed with Spinach,
Wild Mushroom Pine Nut Duxelle, Served with an
Herb Caper Hollandaise Sauce
25

Scaloppini of Angus Beef, Veal and Tuna, Served with an Italian Raspberry
Marmalade Vinaigrette and Accompanied with Eggplant and Zucchini
27

Tenderloin of Beef in a Chianti Herb Reduction,
Served with Grilled Wild Mushrooms and Asparagus
29

Tenderloin of Beef Medallions and Twin Jumbo Lobster with Lump
Crabmeat Stuffing Served with an Herb Tomato Hollandaise Sauce
31

**Tenderloin of Beef with a Thyme, Rosemary and Oregano Shiraz Sauce,
Served with Asparagus Butter**
33
Three Meat and Mushroom Meat Loaf
35
**Tortilla Wrap with Beef, Ham, Peppers, Black Beans,
Yellow Jack Cheese, Tomatoes and Wild Rice**
36

෨

◦◞

Beef Wellington with Button Mushrooms and Eggplant Wrapped in a Puff Pastry, Served with a Port Shitake Herb Cream Brown Sauce

1 each, use center cut only	Angus Beef Tenderloin, trimmed & sinew removed
2 Tbl.	Extra Virgin Olive Oil

Method:
1. Place olive oil in a large sauté pan and sear the beef tenderloin on all sides.
   Set aside and let cool for 20 minutes.

Mushroom Duxelle:

2#	Mushrooms, finely chopped
1 sm.	Eggplant, skin removed & diced small
¼ c.	Madeira Wine
1 Tbl.	Extra Virgin Olive Oil
1 clove	Garlic, minced
2 ea.	Shallots, minced
3 Tbl.	Parsley, freshly chopped
To Taste	Sea Salt
To Taste	Black Pepper, ground

Method:
1. Sauté mushrooms and eggplant with olive oil.
   Add garlic, shallots and reduce.
   Deglaze with Madeira wine.
   Add parsley and season to taste.
2. Set aside and let cool for 10 minutes.

1#	Puff Pastry, thawed & reserve 2 oz. for garnish
1 ea.	Egg, whipped with 2 Tbl. of water

Method:

1. Place Duxelle around the beef tenderloin until well coated and let rest in refrigerator.
   Wrap pastry around tenderloin with the ends pinched on the sides.
   Garnish with pastry leaves and grapes with remaining puff pastry.
   Egg wash entire surface.
2. Bake in a 350ºF oven for 30 minutes until golden brown.
3. Remove from oven and let rest for 20 minutes.
   Portion out 2 slices and arrange on entrée plate.
   Serve with a port shitake herb cream brown sauce.

Port Shitake Herb Cream Brown Sauce:

2 Tbl.	Extra Virgin Olive Oil, reserve 1 tablespoon for garnish
1 tsp.	Shallots, minced
½ tsp.	Garlic, minced
¼ c.	Shitake's, washed, cut medium diced & reserve 2 oz. for garnish
½ c.	Port
½ c.	Brown Stock, cold
1 Tbl.	Roux, warm
3 oz.	Heavy Cream
To Taste	Sea Salt
To Taste	Black Pepper, ground
1 Tbl.	Butter, whole
1 tsp.	Parsley, freshly chopped
½ tsp.	Oregano, freshly chopped
½ tsp.	Thyme, freshly chopped

Method:

1. Sweat the shallots and garlic in olive oil.
   Add mushrooms, wine and reduce by one-half.
   Stir in the brown stock and whisk in roux.
   Simmer for 5 minutes.
2. Add cream and simmer for another 5 minutes.
   Strain sauce, whisk in butter and add fresh herbs.
3. Separately in a sauté pan, add reserved shitake mushrooms with reserved olive oil.
   Sauté mushrooms for 5 minutes.
4. Place sliced portion on entrée plate, arrange sauce and garnish with shitake mushrooms.

෨

Grilled Skewered Beef with Portabella, Shitake and Oyster Mushrooms, Green and Yellow Zucchini, Served with Scallion Wild Rice

¼ c.	Soy Sauce
3 Tbl.	Oyster Sauce
3 Tbl.	Garlic, minced
1 Tbl.	Ginger, freshly grated
To Taste	Red Pepper Flakes
½ c.	Extra Virgin Olive Oil
3 ea.	Bay Leaf, cut in half
½#	Angus Top Butt, cut into large shapes
As Needed	Skewers, soaked in water for 20 minutes
2 Tbl.	Sesame Seeds, for garnish

Method:
1. In a steel bowl, add the soy sauce, oyster sauce, garlic, ginger, red pepper and bay leaf.
   Whisk in the olive oil a little at a time.
2. Skewer beef and set aside.
   Place beef skewer in dipping sauce and marinate for 1 hour.
3. Grill beef on both sides until desire doneness.
4. Sprinkle with sesame seeds on top and keep warm.

1 ea.	Portabella Mushrooms
3 ea.	Shitake Mushrooms
3 ea.	Oyster Mushrooms
5 oz.	Italian Vinaigrette
1 ea.	Green Zucchini, sliced thin
1 ea.	Yellow Zucchini, sliced thin
2 c.	Wild Rice, steamed
1 ea.	Scallions, chopped

Method:
1. Marinate mushrooms in the vinaigrette with the zucchini for 30 minutes.
   Grill zucchini and mushrooms until proper doneness.
2. Mix the scallions into the wild rice.
3. Arrange wild rice, zucchini, mushrooms and beef on oval plate.

1 Tbl.   Parsley, freshly chopped
2 Tbl.   Soy Sauce
1 tsp.   Wasabi Horseradish
1 tsp.   Rice Wine Vinegar
1 Tbl.   Extra Virgin Olive Oil

Method:
1. In a steel bowl, add the parsley, soy sauce, wasabi horseradish and rice wine vinegar.
Whisk in the olive oil.
2. Place mixture in small bowl for garnish and place next to oval plate.

໑ຯ

Grilled Beef Tornadoes and Shrimp, Served with an Herb Scallop Champagne Sauce

2-(6 oz.) each	Angus Beef Tenderloin, sinew & fat removed, cut into 2 portions
Pinch	Thyme, freshly chopped
Pinch	Oregano, freshly chopped
To Taste	Sea Salt
To Taste	Black Pepper, ground
3 ea.	Shrimp-peeled, de-veined & tails on

Method:
1. Season beef tenderloins with herbs, salt and pepper.
   Grill medium rare and keep warm.
   Butterfly shrimp, grill quickly and keep warm.
2. Place beef tenderloins and shrimp on entrée plate.
3. Arrange herb scallop champagne sauce appropriately.

Herb Scallop Champagne Sauce:

3 ea.	Scallop, diced small
3 Tbl.	Champange
½ tsp.	Lime Juice, freshly squeezed
1 cl.	Garlic, minced
1 ea.	Shallots, minced
1 Tbl.	Capers, small
¾ c.	Shrimp Stock, cold
1 Tbl.	Butter, whole
3 Tbl.	Cilantro & Parsley, freshly chopped
To Taste	Tabasco
To Taste	Sea Salt

Method:
1. In a sauce pot, add scallop, champagne, lime juice, garlic, shallots and capers.
   Bring to a simmer and let reduce.
2. Puree sauce, add shrimp stock, let simmer and whisk in whole butter.
   Add fresh herbs and season to taste.

໑ຯ

∽

Ground Sirloin Beef Chili with Red and White Beans

1#	Angus Sirloin Beef, ground
¼#	Angus Sirloin Beef tips, diced small
1 lg.	Onion, minced
2 tsp.	Garlic, minced
½ c.	Celery, diced medium
¼ tsp.	Thyme, freshly chopped
½ tsp.	Basil, freshly chopped
½ tsp.	Cumin, ground
¼ tsp.	Cayenne, ground
1 tsp.	Cilantro, freshly chopped
1 ea.	Bay Leaf, whole
1 tsp.	Chili Powder
½ tsp.	Oregano, freshly chopped
1½ tsp.	Sea Salt
1 Tbl.	Red Wine Vinegar
2 c.	Brown Stock, cold
1 ea.	Green Pepper, minced
1 qt.	Tomatoes, diced small
½ c.	Cornmeal, yellow
16 oz.	Red Kidney Beans, whole
16 oz.	White Navy Beans, cooked

Method:
1. Place sirloin beef in a large sauce pot and sauté to proper doneness. Drain the fat and discard.
2. Sauté the onion, garlic, spices, vinegar and add the tomato paste. Add the green peppers, stir in the tomatoes and simmer for 20 minutes.
3. Stir in the cornmeal and simmer for another 5 minutes.
4. Add the red kidney beans and simmer for another 3 minutes.

∽

Marinated and Grilled Beef, Shrimp and Lobster, Served with a Three Pepper Risotto

Three Pepper Risotto:

1 c.	Arborio Rice
2 Tbl.	Extra Virgin Olive Oil
1 cl.	Garlic, minced
2 ea.	Shallots, minced
1 ea.	Bay Leaf, whole
3¾ c.	Chicken Stock, cold
¼ ea.	Red Pepper, diced medium
¼ ea.	Yellow Pepper, diced medium
¼ ea.	Jalapeño Pepper, roasted
To Taste	Sea Salt
To Taste	Black Pepper, ground

Method:

1. Combine in a sauce pot the Arborio rice, olive oil, garlic, shallots and bay leaf.
   Add one third of chicken stock, bring to a boil and let simmer.
   Repeat twice with one third more of chicken stock and let reduce.
2. Add peppers and simmer for another 5 minutes.
3. Remove bay leaf and season to taste.

Marinade:

½ ea.	Orange, juice
1 Tbl.	Orange Zest
¼ c.	Extra Virgin Olive Oil
½ tsp.	Red Pepper Flakes
1 ea.	Bay Leaves, whole
½ tsp.	Oregano, freshly chopped
¼ tsp.	Thyme, freshly chopped
3 cl.	Garlic, minced
¼ c.	Cilantro, freshly chopped

Method:

1. Combine all ingredients in a steel bowl.

2-(4 oz.) each	Angus Beef Fillet, fat & sinew removed & sliced into 3 segments
4 ea.	Shrimp-peeled, de-veined & tails on
6 oz.	Lobster Tail, cut into medallions
4 Tbl.	Extra Virgin Olive Oil

1. Add beef, shrimp, lobster to marinade and place in refrigerator for 1 hour.
2. Brush grill with oil and cook beef medium rare.
   Grill seafood until proper doneness.
3. Arrange on an oval plate the beef, seafood and three pepper rice.

⌒⌒

Marinated and Grilled London Broil with a Port Wild Mushroom Sauce, Served with Parsley Red Bliss Potatoes and Brussels Sprouts

Port Wild Mushroom Sauce:

1 Tbl.	Extra Virgin Olive Oil
1 Tbl.	Shallots, minced
1 cl.	Garlic, minced
1 tsp.	Oregano, freshly chopped
½ tsp.	Marjoram, freshly chopped
¼ tsp.	Rosemary, freshly chopped
½ tsp.	Thyme, freshly chopped
½ tsp.	Parsley, freshly chopped
½ c.	Shitake Mushrooms, julienne
¼ c.	Port
2 c.	Beef Stock, cold
1 Tbl.	Roux, warm
To Taste	Sea Salt
To Taste	Black Pepper, ground

Method:
1. Sweat the shallots and garlic in olive oil.
   Add the herbs, mushrooms, wine and reduce until wine is almost gone.
2. Separately in a sauce pot, add the stock and bring to a boil.
   Whisk in the roux, let reduce and strain into the mushroom reduction.
3. Let sauce simmer to a proper consistency and season to taste.

Parsley Potatoes:

6 ea.	Red Bliss Potatoes, washed
To Taste	Sea Salt
To Taste	Black Pepper, ground
1 tsp.	Garlic Powder
3 Tbl.	Extra Virgin Olive Oil
3 Tbl.	Parsley, freshly chopped

Method:
1. Steam potatoes until 90 % done.
   Place oil on potatoes with seasoning and place in a 350ºF for 15 minutes.
2. Take out and sprinkle fresh parsley over potatoes.

Seasoned Brussels Sprouts:

1 bn.	Brussels Sprouts, ends removed & cut in half
½ tsp.	Thyme, freshly chopped
¼ tsp.	Parsley, freshly chopped

Method:
1. Steam brussels sprouts for 5 minutes and toss with fresh herbs.

Marinated Grilled London Broil:

3 lbs.	Angus Top Round, fat & sinew removed
1 pt.	Italian Vinaigrette
3 c.	Cabernet Sauvignon
1 cl.	Garlic, minced
1 tsp.	Oregano, freshly chopped
½ tsp.	Marjoram, freshly chopped
¼ tsp.	Rosemary, freshly chopped
½ tsp.	Thyme, freshly chopped
½ tsp.	Parsley, freshly chopped

Method:
1. Add vinaigrette, wine and herbs to meat in a square container with a tight fitting lid.
   Marinate beef in the refrigerator overnight.
2. Grill meat and score on both sides.
   Place in a 350ºF oven until beef is medium rare.
3. Remove beef from oven and rest for 15 minutes.
   Slice on the bias very thinly.
4. Arrange on oval plate the London broil and port wild mushroom sauce.
   Place potatoes and brussels sprouts on oval plate.

෴

❧

Prime Rib of Beef with Horseradish Au Jus, Served with Asparagus And Twice Baked Stuffed Potato

13#	Angus Rib Eye, fat & sinew removed
As Needed	Extra Virgin Olive Oil
As Needed	Sea Salt & Black Pepper, ground
As Needed	Oregano, Rosemary & Thyme, freshly chopped

Method:
1. Rub olive oil on rib eye, season with salt, pepper and fresh herbs.
2. Place in a 350°F oven until medium rare.
3. Remove from oven, let rest for 20 minutes and slice into 10 ounce portions.

Horseradish Au Jus:

2 oz.	Pan drippings, strained
As Needed	Oregano, freshly chopped
1 tsp.	Horseradish

Method:
1. Strain, remove grease, add fresh oregano and mix in horseradish.
2. Place horseradish au jus on the side.

Twice Baked Stuffed Potato:

1 ea.	Idaho Potato
As Needed	Olive Oil
As Needed	Garlic Powder
As Needed	Sea Salt & Black Pepper, ground
1 clove	Garlic, chopped & sautéed in oil
1 Tbl.	White Onions, finely diced
1 tsp.	Butter, whole
1 oz.	Milk, whole
2 tsp.	Sour Cream
½ tsp.	Parmesan Cheese, grated

> *1 ea.*   Pancetta, cooked & diced small
> *1 tsp.*   Chives, freshly chopped
> *To Taste* Sea Salt & White Pepper, ground
> *3 ea.*   Asparagus, peeled & steamed for
>   2 minutes.

Method:

1. Rub oil on potato, season with salt, pepper and garlic powder.
    Bake in a 425ºF oven until proper doneness.
2. Cut potato lengthwise and scoop out potato.
    Reserve skins, bake for 10 minutes, remove and set aside.
3. Place potato in a mixing bowl, add butter, garlic, onions and mix well
    until smooth.
    Add milk, mix thoroughly, then add the rest of the ingredients
    and mix well.
    In a piping bag with a star tip, pipe potato mixture inside potato skins.
    Bake again until golden brown.
4. Arrange prime rib, twice baked potato and asparagus on entrée plate.

☙

৵

Roasted Angus Beef Tenderloin and Veal Stuffed with Spinach, Wild Mushroom Pine Nut Duxelle, Served with An Herb Caper Hollandaise Sauce

Herb Caper Hollandaise Sauce:

1½ Tbl.	White Vinegar
1 ea.	Black Peppercorns, coarsely crushed
1 tsp.	Chardonnay
3 Tbl.	Cilantro & Parsley, freshly chopped
1 ea.	Egg Yolk
8 oz.	Clarified Butter, melted
1 Tbl.	Capers, small
To Taste	Tabasco
To Taste	Sea Salt

Method:

1. Place white vinegar, black peppercorns, wine, tarragon in a sauce pot and let reduce.
   Strain liquid in a steel bowl with egg yolks.
2. Whisk under a low flame until fluffy, being careful not to scramble egg yolks.
   Add the melted butter slowly, while still whisking rapidly.
3. Fold in capers and season to taste.

1#	Button Mushrooms, stems removed & tops diced medium
¼#	Portabella Mushrooms, stems removed & tops diced medium
6 oz.	Spinach, steamed & drained with no moisture & chopped
2 Tbl.	Extra Virgin Olive Oil
1 ea.	Shallots, minced
2 cl.	Garlic, minced
To Taste	Sea Salt

To Taste	Black Pepper, ground
¼ c.	Pine Nuts, coarsely crushed
1#	Veal, pound out flat
As Needed	Butchers Twine
3#	Angus Beef Tenderloin-sinew & fat removed & pounded out
1 tsp.	Oregano, freshly chopped
¼ tsp.	Thyme, freshly chopped

1. Sauté mushrooms in a sauté pan until all of the moisture is gone and mix with spinach.
   Separately, sauté the garlic, shallots with olive oil, season to taste and add to mixture.
2. Season veal and spread out mixture evenly with pine nuts.
   Roll up veal, tie with butchers twine, season to taste and brown on all sides until proper doneness.
   Cool stuffed veal, remove twine, place on beef tenderloin and roll up tightly.
3. Tie up tenderloin with butchers twine and sear until golden brown.
   Roast tenderloin in a 350°F oven until medium rare or proper doneness.
   Remove from oven, rest for 15 minutes and slice diagonally on entrée plate.
4. Serve with herb caper hollandaise sauce and garnish with fresh herbs.

෨

∾

Scaloppini of Angus Beef, Veal and Tuna, Served With an Italian Raspberry Marmalade Vinaigrette and Accompanied with Eggplant and Zucchini

2 oz.	Angus Beef Tenderloin, trimmed & sinew removed
2 oz.	Veal, trimmed & sinew removed
2 oz.	Yellowfin Tuna
As Needed	Sea Salt
As Needed	Black Pepper, ground
3 Tbl.	Extra Virgin Olive Oil

Method:
1. Season angus beef, veal and tuna.
2. Sauté angus beef and veal in olive oil, remove and keep warm.
3. Sauté yellowfin tuna very quickly on one side and arrange on entrée plate with beef and veal.

Italian Raspberry Marmalade Vinaigrette:

¾ c.	Raspberry Marmalade
½ tsp.	Oyster Sauce
2 Tbl.	Sherry
1 tsp.	Ginger, grated
1 cl.	Garlic, minced
1 ea.	Shallots, minced
1 tsp.	Parsley, freshly chopped
½ tsp.	Thyme, freshly chopped
½ tsp.	Oregano, freshly chopped
¼ c.	Italian Vinaigrette
¼ c.	Extra Virgin Olive Oil
To Taste	Sea Salt
To Taste	Black Pepper, ground

Method:
1. Combine all ingredients and rest for 20 minutes.

1 ea.	Eggplant, ends peeled & julienne
1 ea.	Yellow Zucchini, julienne
As Needed	Extra Virgin Olive Oil

Method:
1. Sauté eggplant and yellow zucchini very quickly in olive oil.
2. Arrange on entrée plate with Italian raspberry marmalade vinaigrette.

෨

~

Tenderloin of Beef in a Chianti Herb Reduction, Served with Grilled Wild Mushrooms and Asparagus

2-(4 oz.) each	Angus Beef Tenderloin, trimmed & sinew removed, cut into 2 portions
1 Tbl.	Shallots, minced
1 Tbl.	Garlic, minced
To Taste	Sea Salt
To Taste	Black Pepper, ground

Chianti Herb Reduction:

2 Tbl.	Extra Virgin Olive Oil
1 Tbl.	Carrot, diced medium
1 Tbl.	Onion, diced medium
1 Tbl.	Celery, diced medium
1 tsp.	Garlic, minced
1 tsp.	Oregano, freshly chopped
1 tsp.	Thyme, freshly chopped
½ tsp.	Basil, freshly chopped
¼ c.	Chianti Wine
1 c.	Veal Stock
To Taste	Sea Salt
To Taste	Black Pepper, ground
1 Tbl.	Butter, cold
1 tsp.	Thyme & Oregano, freshly chopped

Method:
1. Season beef tenderloin with shallots, garlic, salt and pepper. Grill beef tenderloin on both sides until medium rare.
2. In a sauté pan, sweat the vegetables and garlic in olive oil. Add herbs, deglaze with wine and reduce until almost gone. Stir in stock and reduce to a proper consistency.
3. Strain into another sauce pot and whisk in cold butter.

Grilled Wild Mushrooms and Asparagus:

8 oz.   Italian Vinaigrette
4 oz.   Wild Shitakes, stems removed
2 oz.   Portabella Mushrooms, sliced thick
3 ea.   Asparagus Spears, ends removed
1 ea.   Plum Tomato-skin, core & seeds removed, julienne

Method:
1. In a large steel bowl, add the vinaigrette, mushrooms, asparagus and marinate overnight.
    Grill mushrooms and asparagus until proper doneness.
2. Arrange tenderloin on entrée plate with grilled mushrooms and asparagus.
    Garnish with fresh tomatoes and fresh herbs.

ᦞ

⁓

Tenderloin of Beef Medallions and Twin Jumbo Lobster With Lump Crabmeat Stuffing Served with an Herb Tomato Hollandaise Sauce

Crabmeat Stuffing:

1 Tbl.	Extra Virgin Olive Oil
1 tsp.	Celery, finely chopped
1 Tbl.	Red Pepper, finely chopped
1 tsp.	Chives, freshly chopped
1 tsp.	Parsley, freshly chopped
¼ c.	Pinot Grisgio
3 oz.	Lump Crabmeat
¼ c.	Lobster Stock, cold
2 Tbl.	Cream Cheese
To Taste	Old Bay Seasoning
To Taste	Sea Salt
To Taste	White Pepper, ground
As Needed	Bread Crumbs

Method:
1. In a sauté pan, sweat celery and red pepper in olive oil.
    Add herbs, deglaze with wine and reduce until liquid is almost gone.
    Let mixture cool and add in a steel bowl.
2. Add crabmeat, stock, cream cheese, bread crumbs and mix well.
    Season appropriately and form into four round shapes.

Herb Tomato Hollandaise Sauce:

3 oz.   Hollandaise Sauce
3 Tbl.   Cilantro & Parsley, freshly chopped

Method:
1. In a steel bowl, fold in herbs with hollandaise sauce.

2-(4 oz.) each   Angus Beef Tenderloin, trimmed & sinew removed, cut into 2 portions
2 ea.   Jumbo Lobster Tail, cut into rounds
½ c.   Shrimp stock, cold
½ tsp.   Oregano, freshly chopped
½ tsp.   Parsley, freshly chopped
1 ea.   Plum Tomato-skin, core & seeds removed, julienne

Method:
1. Grill tenderloin on both sides until medium rare. Remove and keep warm.
2. Poach lobster rounds with shrimp stock until proper doneness. Remove and keep warm.
3. Place tenderloins on entrée plate with crabmeat and lobster. Arrange tomatoes and herb hollandaise sauce on entrée plate. Garnish with fresh herbs.

∽

Tenderloin of Beef with a Thyme, Rosemary and Oregano Shiraz Sauce, Served with Asparagus Butter

Asparagus Juice:

3 ea. Asparagus, peeled and roughly chopped
½ c. Water, cold

Method:
1. Place asparagus and water in a sauce pot.
   Bring to a boil and simmer for 3 minutes.
2. Strain into a sauce pot and simmer again until liquid is almost gone.
3. Cool asparagus in refrigerate for 20 minutes.

Asparagus Butter:

1 oz. Asparagus Juice
4 oz. Whole Butter, softened
1 tsp. Thyme & Parsley, freshly chopped

Method:
1. In a steel bowl, add the asparagus juice and butter.
   Blend to a smooth consistency, roll onto plastic wrap and place in freezer for 20 minutes.
2. Remove from freezer, roll asparagus butter onto fresh herbs and cut into desired shapes.

2-(4 oz.) each Angus Beef Tenderloin-trimmed & sinew removed, cut into 2 portions
1 Tbl. Olive Oil
1 c. Shiraz
1 Tbl. Shallots, minced
½ Tbl. Garlic, minced
½ tsp. Thyme, freshly chopped
½ tsp. Rosemary, freshly chopped
½ tsp. Oregano, freshly chopped

½ ea.	Bay Leaf, whole
½ c.	Brown Sauce, hot
¼ c.	Veal Stock, cold
To Taste	Sea Salt
To Taste	Black Pepper, ground
1 Tbl.	Thyme, Rosemary & Oregano-freshly chopped

Method:

1. Rub olive oil on beef tenderloin and grill on both sides until medium rare.
   Remove and keep warm.
2. Deglaze with wine, add shallots, garlic and reduce by one-half.
   Add herbs, brown sauce, veal stock and reduce by one-half again.
   Strain sauce and season appropriately.
3. Arrange tenderloin of beef on entrée plate with sauce.
   Place asparagus butter on beef tenderloin at service.
   Garnish with fresh herbs.

∽

᠀

Three Meat and Mushroom Meat Loaf

1½#	Angus Beef Sirloin, ground
¼#	Pork, ground
¼#	Veal, ground
3 cl.	Garlic, minced
1 ea.	Onion, diced medium
1 ea.	Green Pepper, diced medium
½ ea.	Celery, chopped
1 tsp.	Basil, freshly chopped
½ tsp.	Oregano, freshly chopped
½ tsp.	Thyme, freshly chopped
1 tsp.	Parsley, freshly chopped
3 Tbl.	Parmesan Cheese, grated
3 oz.	Mushrooms, diced medium
6 ea.	Fresh Bread, cut into cubes with ends removed
¼ c.	Milk, soaked with the bread
¼ c.	Ketchup
1 Tbl.	Dijon Mustard
2 tsp.	Sea Salt
1 tsp.	Black Pepper, ground
4 ea.	Eggs, whole
1½ c.	Tomato Juice

Method:
1. Combine all ingredients to a steel bowl and mix thoroughly. Grease a baking dish and place mixture in the pan.
2. Bake in a 350ºF oven for 1½ hours. Remove from oven and let rest for 15 minutes.
3. Remove meat loaf from pan and slice thinly on oval plate.

᠀

∽

Tortilla Wrap with Beef, Ham, Peppers, Black Beans, Yellow Jack Cheese, Tomatoes and Wild Rice

1 ea.	Red Pepper, diced medium
2 ea.	Green Pepper, diced medium
2 Tbl.	Extra Virgin Olive Oil
1 c.	Onions, diced medium
2 cl.	Garlic, minced
1 tsp.	Cilantro, freshly chopped
1½ tsp.	Thyme, freshly chopped
1 tsp.	Cumin, ground
2 tsp.	Parsley, freshly chopped
½ tsp.	Chili Powder, ground
½ ea.	Jalapeño Pepper, seeds removed & diced small
To Taste	Soy Sauce
To Taste	Sea Salt
To Taste	Black Pepper, ground
1#	Ham, medium diced
1½#	Angus Beef Sirloin, ground
4 c.	Wild Rice, cooked
1 cn.	Black Beans
1 ea.	Plum Tomato-skin, core & seeds removed, diced medium
½#	Yellow Sharp Cheese, grated
1 cn.	Refried Beans
8 ea.	Tortillas, warm
2 oz.	Salsa
3 Tbl.	Cilantro, freshly chopped

Method:

1. In a sauté pan, sweat the peppers, onion and garlic in olive oil.
    Stir in herbs, ham and keep warm.
2. In a separate sauté pan, add ground beef and cook until
    proper doneness.
    Retain fat and discard.
    Add wild rice, black beans and mix appropriately.
3. Mix both mixtures in a steel bowl and keep warm.
4. Grill tortilla wrap on both sides.
    Place some of the mixture on the tortilla wrap with the
    refried beans, tomatoes and cheese.
    Fold appropriately, cut in half and place on salad plate.
5. Serve with salsa and chopped cilantro.

CHICKEN

Breast of Chicken Saltimbocca Stuffed with Spinach,
Proscuitto Ham and Two Cheeses, Breaded and Deep Fried,
Served with a Garlic Herb Sherry Cream Sauce
41

Chicken Almond Crusted Tenders
43

Chicken Breast with a Sausage Sage Stuffing Enclosed in a
Pine Nut Crust, Served with a Basil Shiraz Cream Sauce
44

Chicken Tenderloins with Garden Fresh Vegetables and Cashews,
Served with Wild Rice
46

Chicken Roulade Stuffed with Mango and Vanilla Bean
47

Chicken Scaloppini with Artichokes, Roasted Garlic and Tomato Sauce,
Served with Piped Red Bliss Potatoes
49

Chicken Tenderloins with Button Mushrooms and Puff Pastry Rounds
Laced With a Sun Dried Tomato Port Cream Sauce
51

Chicken Tenderloins with Green and Hot Peppers,
Served with Sliced Chive Potatoes
53

Chicken and Veal Dumplings in an Herb Lime Vodka Cream Brown Sauce
55

Chicken Wellington with a Wild Mushroom Stuffing wrapped in Puff
Pastry and Served with an Almond Garlic Sherry Cream Sauce
57

Grilled Chicken Breast Wrapped in Asparagus with Sautéed Spinach And
Diced Roasted Red Peppers, Served with a Lemon Caper Reduction and
Portabella Mushrooms
59

Coconut Chicken Tenders with Pineapple Mango Mint Chutney
61

Grilled Chicken Breasts Smothered in a
Button Mushroom Three Pepper Herb Cream Sauce
62

*Marinated Dijon Mustard Grilled Chicken with
Herb Risotto and Served with Asparagus*
63
*Marinated Grilled Chicken Breast over Lettuce Greens,
Served with a Warm Vinaigrette*
65
*Marinated Grilled Chicken Tenderloins with Lump Crabmeat, Roasted
Yellow Peppers And Sun Dried Tomatoes, Served with Black Beans*
66
Marinated Strips of Chicken with Oriental Vegetables
68
*Roasted Chicken Breast with Apple Bread Stuffing,
Served with a Tomato Herb Brown Sauce, Grilled Zucchini and Polenta*
70
*Roasted Half Chicken and Garlic Red Bliss Potatoes
With Pan Gravy and Toasted Pine Nuts, Served with a
Corn, Cucumber, Roasted Red Pepper and Cilantro Salsa*
72
*Roasted Herb Chicken with a Roasted Garlic, Leek and Artichoke Sauce,
Served with Herb Idaho Mashed Potatoes*
75
*Sautéed Chicken Breast with a Pepper, Olive and Tomato Salsa,
Served with Fresh Asparagus*
77
Sautéed Chicken Breast with a Wild Mushroom Garlic Cream Sauce
79

❧

∾

Breast of Chicken Saltimbocca Stuffed with Spinach, Proscuitto Ham and Two Cheeses, Breaded and Deep Fried, Served with a Garlic Herb Sherry Cream Sauce

Garlic Herb Sherry Cream Sauce:

2 Tbl.	Extra Virgin Olive Oil
1 ea.	Shallots, minced
4 cl.	Garlic, minced
¼ c.	Sherry
2 Tbl.	Parsley, freshly chopped
1 Tbl.	Thyme, freshly chopped
2 c.	Chicken Velouté, hot
To Taste	Sea Salt
To Taste	White Pepper, ground

Method:
1. In a sauté pan, sweat the shallots and garlic in olive oil. Deglaze with wine, add herbs and reduce until liquid is almost gone. Add Velouté and simmer for 5 minutes.
2. Strain sauce and season to taste.

4-(10 oz.) each	Chicken Breast, remove skin & trim fat
2 oz.	Spinach-steamed, drained & chopped
2 oz.	Proscuitto Ham, sliced thin
4 ea.	Mozzarella Cheese, sliced thin
4 ea.	Provolone Cheese, sliced thin
To Taste	Sea Salt
To Taste	White Pepper, ground
To Taste	Sage, finely chopped
As Needed	Buckwheat Flour, sifted
2 ea.	Eggs, with 2 Tbl. of Water
2 c.	Bread Crumbs
3 Tbl.	Parsley, freshly chopped
As Needed	Olive Oil

Method:
1. Pound chicken out slightly on both sides.
    Season and add one slice of Proscuitto and one slice of
    Mozzarella Cheese, then spinach.
    Roll up chicken and freeze for 1 hour.
2. In a steel bowl, mix together the bread crumbs and parsley.
    Place chicken in flour, then egg wash and finally parsley bread mixture.
3. Deep fry chicken until golden brown and drain on paper towel.
    Bake chicken in a 350ºF oven until proper doneness.
4. Remove from oven, let cool and slice diagonally.
    Arrange chicken and sauce on entrée plate.

෨

Chicken Almond Crusted Tenders

¼ c.	Bread Crumbs
¼ c.	Sliced Almonds, toasted
3 Tbl.	Graham Cracker Crumbs
1 tsp.	Sugar, granulated
2 Tbl.	Parsley, freshly chopped
As Needed	Buckwheat Flour, sifted
2 ea.	Eggs, scrambled in a little water
8-(6 oz.) each	Chicken Tenderloins, sinew removed & pounded out
As Needed	Olive Oil

Method:
1. In a steel bowl, mix the bread crumbs, almonds, graham cracker crumbs, sugar and parsley.
   Place chicken in flour and dust off excess.
   Dip chicken in egg wash and then crumb almond mixture.
   Freeze chicken for 1 hour.
2. Remove from freezer and deep fry until golden brown.
3. Bake chicken in a 350ºF oven until proper doneness.

∽

Chicken Breast with a Sausage Sage Stuffing Enclosed in a Pine Nut Crust, Served with a Basil Shiraz Cream Sauce

Basil Shiraz Cream Sauce:

1 Tbl.	Extra Virgin Olive Oil
1 ea.	Shallots, minced
½ cl.	Garlic, minced
1 tsp.	Basil, freshly chopped
¼ tsp.	Thyme, freshly chopped
Pinch	Cayenne Pepper, ground
¼ c.	Shiraz
¼ c.	Chicken Stock, cold
¼ c.	Heavy Cream, hot
1 Tbl.	Roux, warm
To Taste	Sea Salt
To Taste	Black Pepper, ground

1. In a sauté pan, sweat the onions and garlic in olive oil. Add herbs, deglaze with wine and reduce by one-half. Stir in stock and reduce by one-half again.
2. Add hot cream and whisk in warm roux to a smooth consistency.
3. Strain sauce and season to taste.

Sausage Sage Stuffing:

3 Tbl.	Extra Virgin Olive Oil
¼ c.	Onions, finely chopped
¼ c.	Celery, finely chopped
½ tsp.	Thyme, freshly chopped
½ tsp.	Sage, freshly chopped
To Taste	Sea Salt
To Taste	Black Pepper, ground
½ tsp.	Poultry Seasoning, ground
½ c.	Chicken Stock, cold
¼ c.	Sausage-cooked, drained & minced
8 ea.	White Bread, crusts removed & cubed
4-(8 oz.) each	Chicken Breasts, skin off & pounded out lighted

Method:
1. In a sauté pan, sweat the onions and celery in olive oil.
   Stir in the herbs, sausage, stock and let cool.
   In a steel bowl, add sauté mixture, cubed bread and mix thoroughly.
   Season with salt, black pepper and poultry seasoning.
2. Place stuffing in the middle of chicken breast and roll up tightly.
3. Cover chicken breasts with plastic wrap and freeze for 1 hour.

For the Deep Frying:

1 c.	Corn Flake Crumbs
½ c.	Bread Crumbs
¼ c.	Pine Nuts, coarsely chopped
¼ c.	Buckwheat Flour, sifted
2 ea.	Eggs, with 2 Tbl. of Water
As Needed	Olive Oil

1. In a steel bowl, mix together the corn flake crumbs, bread crumbs and pine nuts.
   Place chicken in flour, then egg wash and finally the pine nut crumb mixture.
2. Deep fry chicken until golden brown and drain on paper towel.
   Bake chicken in a 350°F oven until proper doneness.
3. Let chicken cool and slice diagonally.
4. Arrange chicken and basil Shiraz cream sauce on entrée plate.

∽

Chicken Tenderloins with Garden Fresh Vegetables And Cashews, Served with Wild Rice

3 Tbl.	Extra Virgin Olive Oil
1 tsp.	Ginger, grated
1 cl.	Garlic, minced
¼ c.	Leeks, white only & julienne
½ c.	Savoy Cabbage, julienne
½#	Snow Peas, julienne
¼#	Orange Peppers, diced small
¼#	Yellow Peppers, diced small
¼ c.	Baby Corn, cut on bias
¼ c.	Straw Mushrooms, cut in half lengthwise
¼ c.	Chicken Stock, cold
To Taste	Soy Sauce
To Taste	Duck Sauce
½ tsp.	Red Pepper Flakes
¼#	Cashews, toasted
1#	Chicken Tenderloins-pounded, cut into strips & season with white pepper
3 c.	Wild Rice, cooked

Method:
1. Heat olive oil into a medium high wok.
   Sauté ginger, garlic and leeks.
   Add the cabbage, peas and peppers.
   Toss in the corn, mushrooms, remove vegetables and set aside.
2. Using the same wok, add chicken and sauté until proper doneness.
   Deglaze with chicken stock, add soy sauce, duck sauce, red pepper flakes and cashews.
   Add vegetables with chicken and toss lightly.
3. Arrange chicken and vegetables on entrée oval plate with wild rice.

∽

༄

Chicken Roulade Stuffed with Mango and Vanilla Bean

2-(6 oz.) ea.	Chicken Breast, skin & fat removed
2-(4 oz.) ea.	Chicken Tenderloins, sinew & fat removed & diced medium
1 Tbl.	Extra Virgin Olive Oil
1 ea.	Shallots, minced
1 cl.	Garlic, minced
¼ tsp.	Mint, freshly chopped
¼ tsp.	Thyme, freshly chopped
3 Tbl.	Chardonnay
¼ c.	Mango, diced small
1 ea.	Egg, whole

4 oz.	Half & Half, cold
1 ea.	Vanilla Bean, seeds only
As Needed	White or Wheat Bread-crusts removed, toasted & cut into small rounds
3 leaves	Basil, julienne
¼ ea.	Roasted Red Pepper, skin removed & julienne
¼ ea.	Mango, diced small

Method:

1. Place chicken breast's on plastic wrap, pound flat and leave in refrigerator until needed.
2. In a sauté pan, sweat the shallots, garlic, herbs in olive oil and deglaze with wine.
   Add mango, reduce for 2 minutes, take off heat and let cool.
3. Place tenderloins in a Cuisinart and chop until smooth.
   Add the mango mixture, egg and blend well.
   Slowly add the half & half while mixing and blend to a smooth consistency.
   Remove mixture, place in a steel bowl and fold in vanilla bean seeds.
4. Place mixture in a pastry bag with no star tip.
   Pipe mixture on chicken and roll firmly with plastic wrap.
   Place another wrap on the chicken and wrap tightly again.
   Wrap tightly with foil around chicken and place in poaching container.
5. Poach in chicken stock to an internal temperature of 150ºF.
   Let cool in chicken stock and place in refrigerator overnight.
6. Unwrap chicken roulade, slice thinly and place on toast rounds.
   Garnish with chopped basil, roasted red pepper and mango.

⁊

∾

Chicken Scaloppini with Artichokes, Roasted Garlic and Tomato Sauce, Served with Piped Red Bliss Potatoes

For the Chicken:

2-(10 oz.) each	Chicken Breast, fat & sinew removed, slice in half lengthwise & pounded out
To Taste	Sea Salt
To Taste	White Pepper, ground
As Needed	Buckwheat Flour, sifted
3 Tbl.	Extra Virgin Olive Oil
1 Tbl.	Cilantro & Parsley, freshly chopped

Method:
1. Season chicken, dredge in flour, shake off excess and sauté on both sides in olive oil.
Remove chicken from sauté pan and keep warm.
2. Arrange chicken, potatoes and sauce on entrée plate.
3. Garnish with fresh herbs.

Piped Red Bliss Potatoes:

6 ea.	Red Potatoes-skin on, diced large & cooked in boiling salted water
¼ c.	Milk
2 Tbl.	Butter, whole
To Taste	Sea Salt
To Taste	White Pepper, ground

Method:
1. Drain potatoes and place in oven to dry out.
2. Place through a ricer into a steel bowl, add butter and slowly add the milk.
Mash potatoes until a smooth consistency and season to taste.

Artichoke, Roasted Garlic and Tomato Sauce:

1 ea.	Shallots, minced
3 Tbl.	Extra Virgin Olive Oil
5 cl.	Roasted Garlic
½ tsp.	Thyme, freshly chopped
½ tsp.	Parsley, freshly chopped
¼ c.	Chardonnay
¼ c.	Chicken Stock, cold
4 ea.	Artichokes, quartered
6 ea.	Capers
2 oz.	Plum Tomatoes-skin, core & seeds removed, diced small
To Taste	White Pepper, ground
2 Tbl.	Butter, whole

Method:

1. In the same pan, remove fat, and sweat the shallots in olive oil.
   Add garlic, herbs, deglaze with wine, stir in chicken stock and reduce by one-half.
   Toss in artichokes, capers, tomatoes and season to taste.
2. Whisk in whole butter.

❧

୬

Chicken Tenderloins with Button Mushrooms and Puff Pastry Rounds Laced With a Sun Dried Tomato Port Cream Sauce

For the Puff Pastry:

     As Needed Puff Pastry

Method:
1. Cut pastry into shapes and place on a sheet pan for baking. Place sesame seeds on top and bake in a 350ºF oven for 9 minutes or until golden brown.
2. Remove puff pastry from the oven and keep warm.

10 oz.	Chicken Tenderloins, sinew removed
To Taste	Sea Salt
To Taste	Black Pepper, ground
As Needed	Buckwheat Flour, sifted
As Needed	Extra Virgin Olive Oil
2 Tbl.	Onions, minced
½ cl.	Garlic, minced
¼ tsp.	Thyme, freshly chopped
¼ tsp.	Basil, freshly chopped
¼ c.	Port
2 ea.	Sun Dried Tomatoes, julienne
½ c.	Chicken Stock, cold
½ c.	Half & Half, hot
1 Tbl.	Roux, warm
3 ea.	Button Mushrooms, stems removed & quartered
¼ ea.	Red Pepper, diced small
¼ ea.	Yellow Pepper, diced small
1 tsp.	Lime Juice, freshly squeezed
To Taste	Sea Salt
To Taste	Black Pepper, ground
3 Tbl.	Parsley, freshly chopped

Method:
1. Season chicken, dredge in flour and shake excess off.
   Sauté chicken until golden brown on both sides.
   Remove tenderloins and cut on the bias.
2. In the same pan, sauté shallots and garlic in olive oil.
   Add fresh herbs, deglaze with wine, add sun dried tomatoes and reduce until wine is almost gone.
3. In a separate sauce pot, add the chicken stock, half & half and reduce by one-half.
   Whisk in roux, bring to a boil and simmer for 10 minutes.
4. Strain sauce into the sun dried tomato mixture.
   Add mushrooms, peppers, lime juice and simmer for 10 minutes.
   Stir in chicken, season to taste and add fresh parsley.
5. Arrange chicken, sun dried tomato port cream sauce and puff pastry on entrée plate.

෨෧

∽

Chicken Tenderloins with Green and Hot Peppers, Served with Sliced Chive Potatoes

6-(8 oz.) each	Chicken tenderloins, pounded out slightly
As Needed	Buckwheat Flour, sifted
3 Tbl.	Extra Virgin Olive Oil

For the Sauce:

1 Tbl.	Olive Oil
1 tsp.	Garlic, minced
1 ea.	Shallots, minced
½ tsp.	Thyme, freshly chopped
½ tsp.	Tarragon, freshly chopped
¼ tsp.	Basil, freshly chopped
3 Tbl.	Chardonnay
½ c.	Chicken Stock, cold
1 tsp.	Roux, warm
¼ ea.	Green Pepper, sliced
¼ ea.	Red Pepper, sliced
1 ea.	Red Hot Pepper, split in half & seeds removed
½ ea.	Onions, sliced
½ tsp.	Dijon Mustard
To Taste	Sea Salt
To Taste	Black Pepper, ground
1 ea.	Red Potatoes, sliced thin
As Needed	Chives, whole
As Needed	Olive Oil

Method:

1. Dredge chicken in flour, shake off excess and sauté on both sides in
    olive oil.
    Sauté the garlic and shallots in olive oil, add herbs and deglaze
    with wine.
    Add stock and reduce by one-half.
    Whisk in roux, add peppers, onions, mustard and let simmer
    for 5 minutes.
2. Place one slice of potato on work surface, then chives and another
    slice of potato.
    Freeze potatoes for 20 minutes and deep fry in olive oil until
    golden brown.
3. Place chicken on oval plate with potatoes around the sides standing up.

෴

∾

Chicken and Veal Dumplings in an Herb Lime Vodka Cream Brown Sauce

4 oz.	Veal, ground
4 oz.	Chicken, ground
10 oz.	Spinach, fresh & medium chopped
3 Tbl.	Extra Virgin Olive Oil
½ c.	Parmesan Cheese, grated
½ tsp.	Oregano, freshly chopped
½ tsp.	Mint, freshly chopped
½ tsp.	Thyme, freshly chopped
1 tsp.	Parsley, freshly chopped
1 tsp.	Chives, freshly chopped
¾ c.	Bread Crumbs
2 ea.	Eggs, whole
To Taste	Sea Salt
To Taste	Black Pepper, ground
As Needed	Chicken Stock, hot

Method:
1. Combine all ingredients together and mix thoroughly.
    Roll into small dumplings and place in refrigerator for 1 hour.
2. Place dumplings in boiling chicken stock and simmer until proper doneness.

Herb Lime Vodka Cream Brown Sauce:

1 tsp.	Extra Virgin Olive Oil
1 tsp.	Shallots, minced
½ tsp.	Garlic, minced
¼ c.	Shitake Mushrooms, sliced thin
¼ c.	Lime Vodka
½ c.	Brown Stock, cold
1 tsp.	Roux, warm
½ c.	Heavy Cream, hot
To Taste	Sea Salt
To Taste	Black Pepper, ground
1 tsp.	Parsley, freshly chopped
½ tsp.	Oregano, freshly chopped
½ tsp.	Thyme, freshly chopped

Method:

1. In a sauté pan, sweat the shallots and garlic in olive oil.
   Add mushrooms, deglaze with Vodka and reduce.
2. Stir in brown stock, let boil and bring to a simmer.
   Whisk in roux, add cream and simmer for 10 minutes.
   Strain sauce into another sauce pot.
3. Place dumplings in sauce and let simmer for 2 minutes.
   Arrange dumplings and sauce on entrée plate.
   Garnish with fresh herbs.

෴

∾

Chicken Wellington with a Wild Mushroom Stuffing Wrapped in Puff Pastry and Served with an Almond Garlic Sherry Cream Sauce

Almond Garlic Sherry Cream Sauce:

As Needed	Extra Virgin Olive Oil
2 Tbl.	Shallots, minced
2 cl.	Garlic, minced
¼ tsp.	Thyme, freshly chopped
¼ tsp.	Basil, freshly chopped
¼ tsp.	Parsley, freshly chopped
¼ c.	Sherry
¼ c.	Chicken Stock, cold
½ c.	Heavy Cream, hot
1 Tbl.	Roux, warm
Season	Sea Salt & Black Pepper, ground
4 oz.	Almonds, toasted & reserve
	½ oz. for Garnish

Method:

1. Sweat shallots and garlic in olive oil, add fresh herbs and deglaze with wine.
   Add stock, cream and reduce by one-half.
   Whisk in roux and reduce to a medium consistency.
2. Medium grind toasted almonds, add to sauce, simmer for 7 minutes and strain sauce.

For the Chicken Wellington:

4-(10 oz.) each	Chicken Breasts, with skin on
3 Tbl.	Extra Virgin Olive Oil
¼ c.	Onions, finely chopped
¼ c.	Celery, finely chopped
8 oz.	Shitake, Straw, Oyster Mushrooms-diced medium
Pinch	Thyme, freshly chopped
Pinch	Poultry Seasoning, ground
¼ c.	Chardonnay
Pinch	Sea Salt & Black Pepper, ground
8 ea.	White Bread, crusts removed & cubed
¾ c.	Chicken Stock, cold
4 sheets	Puff Pastry

Method:
1. Sauté onions and celery in olive oil.
   Add mushrooms, herbs, deglaze with wine and reduce.
   In a steel bowl, add sauté mixture, bread, stock and mix thoroughly.
2. Separate mixture into four equal amounts.
   Place mixture on chicken breasts and fold sides inward.
   Wrap chicken in plastic wrap and freeze for 40 minutes.
3. Remove chicken from freezer, roll puff pastry out slightly and wrap around chicken breast.
   Place chicken on sheet pan and bake in a 350°F oven until proper doneness.
4. Arrange chicken and almond garlic cream sauce on entrée plate.

◦∾

❦

Grilled Chicken Breast Wrapped in Asparagus With Sautéed Spinach And Diced Roasted Red Peppers, Served with a Lemon Caper Reduction and Portabella Mushrooms

10 oz.	Chicken Breasts, skin removed & pounded out thin
To Taste	Poultry Seasoning
To Taste	Sea Salt
4 ea.	Asparagus, Marinated in Italian Vinaigrette Overnight
As Needed	Butcher's Twine
To Taste	Black Pepper, ground
To Taste	Sea Salt
As Needed	Extra Virgin Olive Oil

Method:
1. Season chicken with poultry seasoning and sea salt.
   Place 4 asparagus on chicken and wrap up tightly with butcher's twine.
2. Grill on all sides in olive oil until golden brown.
   Place in a 350°F oven until proper doneness.
3. Remove from oven and keep warm.

Lemon Caper Reduction:

1 Tbl.	Extra Virgin Olive Oil
1 cl.	Garlic, minced
2 ea.	Shallots, minced
½ tsp.	Lemon Zest
2 tsp.	Lemon juice, freshly squeezed
¼ c.	Chicken Stock, cold
1 Tbl.	Capers, drained
2 tsp.	Parsley, freshly chopped
1 tsp.	Thyme, freshly chopped
1 tsp.	Butter, whole
To Taste	Sea Salt
To Taste	Black Pepper, ground

Method:
1. Sweat the garlic and shallots in olive oil.
   Add lemon zest, lemon juice, chicken stock and reduce by one-half.
2. Stir in the capers, herbs, whisk in butter and season to taste.

3 oz.	Spinach, whole & sautéed quickly in olive oil
4 ea.	Portabella Mushrooms, sliced & sautéed in olive oil
1 Tbl.	Roasted Red Peppers, diced small

Method:
1. Unwrap chicken and slice diagonally.
2. Arrange spinach, chicken and roasted red peppers on entrée plate.
   Add lemon caper reduction and portabella mushrooms on entrée plate.

☙

∾

Coconut Chicken Tenders with Pineapple Mango Mint Chutney

¼ c.	Bread Crumbs
¼ c.	Coconut Flakes
8 ea.	Chicken Tenderloins, sinew removed & pound out slightly
To Taste	Sea Salt
To Taste	White Pepper, ground
As Needed	Buckwheat Flour, sifted
2 ea.	Eggs, scrambled in a little water
As Needed	Olive Oil

Method:
1. In a steel bowl, add bread crumbs, coconut flakes and mix thoroughly.
2. Season chicken, dredge in flour and dust off excess.
   Place chicken in egg wash.
   Add the crumb coconut mixture and press down to coat both sides.
   Place chicken on sheet pan lined with waxed paper and freeze for 30 minutes.
3. Deep fry in olive oil until golden brown and drain on paper towel.
   Finish cooking in a 350°F oven until proper doneness.
4. Serve with pineapple mango mint chutney.

Pineapple Mango Mint Chutney:

½ c.	Mango, diced small
½ c.	Pineapple, diced small
1 tsp.	Mint, freshly chopped

Method:
1. Reserve three tablespoonfuls of mango.
   Place diced mango and pineapple in blender and mix well.
2. Fold mango and fresh mint into mixture.

∾

〜

Grilled Chicken Breasts Smothered in a Button Mushroom Three Pepper Herb Cream Sauce

2-(10 oz.) each   Chicken Breasts-skin, fat removed & pounded out
2 Tbl.   Extra Virgin Olive Oil

Method:
1. Rub chicken in olive oil before grilling.
   Grill chicken on both sides until proper doneness and keep warm.

Button Mushroom Three Pepper Herb Sauce:

10 ea.   Button Mushrooms, stems removed & sliced
2 Tbl.   Extra Virgin Olive Oil
2 cl.   Roasted Garlic, minced
2 Tbl.   Chardonnay
1 tsp.   Parsley, freshly chopped
½ tsp.   Thyme, freshly chopped
½ ea.   Green Pepper, diced medium
½ ea.   Red Pepper, diced medium
½ ea.   Jalapeño Pepper, minced
1 c.   Chicken Stock, cold
1 c.   Heavy Cream, hot
8 oz.   Cream Cheese, cut into pieces
To Taste   Cayenne Pepper, ground
To Taste   Sea Salt
To Taste   Black Pepper, ground
1 ea.   Scallions, cut on the bias
½ tsp.   Parsley, Tarragon & Chives, finely chopped

Method:
1. Sauté mushrooms in olive oil and add roasted garlic.
   Deglaze with wine, add herbs and peppers.
2. Stir in chicken stock, bring to a boil, add heavy cream and reduce by one-half.
   Whisk in bits of cream cheese a little at a time. Season to taste.
3. Garnish with scallions and fresh herbs.
4. Arrange chicken and button mushroom three pepper herb sauce on entrée plate.

〜

∽

Marinated Dijon Mustard Grilled Chicken with Herb Risotto and Served with Asparagus

2-(10 oz.) each	Chicken Breasts-skin, fat removed & pounded out
3 Tbl.	Dijon Mustard
2 oz.	Italian Vinaigrette
3 Tbl.	Extra Virgin Olive Oil
1 cl.	Garlic, minced
½ tsp.	Thyme, freshly chopped
½ tsp.	Parsley, freshly chopped
½ tsp.	Cilantro, freshly chopped

Method:
1. Combine in a steel bowl the Dijon mustard, Italian vinaigrette, olive oil, garlic and herbs.
   Pound out chicken slightly on both sides and marinate for 30 minutes.
2. Grill chicken on both sides until proper doneness.
3. Set aside and keep warm.

1 cl.	Garlic, minced
½ c.	Onion, medium diced
1 Tbl.	Extra Virgin Olive Oil
3 Tbl.	Chardonnay
½ tsp.	Thyme, freshly chopped
½ tsp.	Parsley, freshly chopped
¼ c.	Yogurt, plain
3 Tbl.	Dijon Mustard
To Taste	Sea Salt
To Taste	White Pepper, ground
2 ea.	Havarti Cheese, sliced thin & cut into strips
½ c.	Risotto- cooked, add 3 Tbl. herbs of Cilantro, Thyme and Basil 2 minutes at the end
8 ea.	Asparagus, peeled & blanched
½ tsp.	Parsley & Cilantro, freshly chopped

Method:
1. Sweat the garlic and onions in olive oil.
   Add herbs and deglaze with wine.
2. In a steel bowl, combine the mixture, herbs, sour cream and mustard.
   Season to taste and mix thoroughly.
3. Spread 2 tablespoonfuls of mixture on chicken and havarti cheese
   on top.
   Broil until cheese melts.
4. Arrange chicken, herb risotto and fresh asparagus on entrée plate.
   Garnish with fresh herbs.

∾

∾

Marinated Grilled Chicken Breast over Lettuce Greens, Served with a Warm Vinaigrette

As Needed	Extra Virgin Olive Oil
2-(10 oz.) each	Chicken Breasts-skin, fat & sinew removed & pounded out
2 oz.	Italian Vinaigrette
To Taste	Black Pepper, cracked
½ tsp.	Poultry Seasoning, ground
1 ea.	Bay Leaf, whole
½ tsp.	Thyme, freshly chopped
½ tsp.	Oregano, freshly chopped

Method:
1. Combine the vinaigrette in a steel bowl with spices and add chicken. Marinate chicken for 30 minutes in refrigerator.
2. Grill chicken on both sides until proper doneness. Set aside and keep warm.

Lettuce Greens with warm Vinaigrette:

¼ c.	Green Oak Leaf Lettuce, washed & cut
¼ c.	Romaine, washed & cut
¼ c.	Radicchio, washed & cut
½ ea.	Belgium Endive, washed & cut
1 oz.	Italian Vinaigrette, warm

Method:
1. Place salad greens on plate.
2. Cut chicken into strips and arrange on greens.
3. Heat vinaigrette until warm. Drizzle vinaigrette on top.

∾

∾

Marinated Grilled Chicken Tenderloins with Lump Crabmeat, Roasted Yellow Peppers And Sun Dried Tomatoes, Served with Black Beans

3-(3 oz.) each	Chicken Tenderloins-skin, fat & sinew removed & pounded out
2 oz.	Italian Vinaigrette
2 Tbl.	Extra Virgin Olive Oil
1 cl.	Garlic, minced
2 ea.	Shallots, sliced
¼ c.	Riesling
1 tsp.	Rosemary, freshly chopped
½ tsp.	Thyme, freshly chopped
¼ tsp.	Cilantro, freshly chopped
¼ c.	Chicken Stock, cold

1 Tbl.	Yellow Pepper-roasted, skin & seeds removed, cut into strips
2 ea.	Sun Dried Tomatoes, cut into strips
To Taste	Sea Salt
To Taste	White Pepper, ground
4 oz.	Black Beans
1 Tbl.	Parsley, freshly chopped
½ tsp.	Thyme, freshly chopped
4 oz.	Jumbo Lump Crabmeat
As Needed	Thyme Flowers, freshly chopped

Method:

1. Marinate chicken in vinaigrette for 30 minutes.
   Grill chicken on both sides until proper doneness, set aside and keep warm.
2. In a sauté pan, sweat the garlic and shallots in olive oil.
   Deglaze with wine, add herbs, chicken stock and reduce by one-half.
   Add yellow peppers, sun dried tomatoes, salt, white pepper and toss on low heat.
3. Heat black beans separately in a sauté pot.
   Fold in fresh parsley, thyme and remove from stove.
4. Arrange black beans, chicken, sauce and crabmeat on entrée plate.
   Garnish with fresh herbs.

෴

⁓

Marinated Strips of Chicken with Oriental Vegetables

14 oz.	Chicken Breast-skin, fat removed & pounded out
½ oz.	Soy Sauce
2 oz.	Sesame Oil
2 c.	Wild Rice, cooked
2 pk.	Cellophane Noodles, boiled in salted water for 3 minutes
3 Tbl.	Sesame Seeds, garnish

Method:
1. Marinate chicken in soy sauce, sesame oil and place in refrigerator for 30 minutes.
2. Grill chicken until proper doneness, cut into strips, set aside and keep warm.

Oriental Vegetables:

2 Tbl.	Extra Virgin Olive Oil
1 ea.	Carrots, peeled & sliced thin
1 rib	Celery, sliced thin
½ ea.	Bok Choy, sliced thin
1 ea.	Green Zucchini, bias cut
1 ea.	Yellow Squash, bias cut
1 bn.	Broccoli Florets
½ bn.	Cauliflower Florets
½#	Shitake Mushrooms, sliced thin
½ ea.	Red Pepper, bias cut
1 cn.	Water Chestnuts
4 oz.	Bean Sprouts
2 Tbl.	Ginger, grated
3 Tbl.	Soy Sauce
½ c.	Hoisin Sauce
2 Tbl.	Oyster Sauce
Pinch	Red Pepper Flakes

Method:

1. In a wok, sauté vegetables in olive oil.
   Add mushrooms, red pepper, water chestnuts, bean sprouts and sauté quickly.
   Remove vegetables and keep warm.
2. Sauté the ginger, add soy sauce, hoisin sauce, oyster sauce and red pepper flakes to taste.
   Reserve oriental sauce and keep warm.
3. Arrange chicken, noodles, vegetables and wild rice on oval entrée plate.
   Drizzle oriental sauce on chicken and vegetables.
   Garnish with sesame seeds.

∾

Roasted Chicken Breast with Apple Bread Stuffing, Served with a Tomato Herb Brown Sauce, Grilled Zucchini and Polenta

4-(10 oz.) each	Chicken Breasts, with skin on
3 Tbl.	Extra Virgin Olive Oil
¼ c.	Onions, minced
¼ c.	Celery, minced
¼ tsp.	Thyme, freshly chopped
¼ tsp.	Poultry Seasoning, ground
To Taste	Sea Salt
To Taste	Black Pepper, ground
1 ea.	Apple-cored, peeled & diced small
8 ea.	White bread, crusts removed & cubed
½ c.	Chicken Stock, cold
To Taste	Thyme, Poultry Seasoning, Paprika, Sea Salt & Black Pepper
1 ea.	Grilled Zucchini, sliced thin
2 ea.	Grilled Polenta, cut in rounds

Method:
1. In a sauté pan, sweat the onions, celery in olive oil, add seasonings and let cool.
   In a steel bowl, mix the sautéed mixture, bread, apples and stock.
2. Separate mixture into four equal amounts onto chicken breasts and wrap tightly.
   Season chicken with thyme, poultry seasoning, paprika, salt and black pepper.
3. Place in a 350ºF oven until chicken is done and skin is golden brown.
4. Remove chicken, let rest for 10 minutes and slice chicken on the bias.

Tomato Herb Brown Sauce:

2 Tbl.	Extra Virgin Olive Oil
2 Tbl.	Shallots, minced
2 cl.	Garlic, minced
1 Tbl.	Parsley, freshly chopped
1 tsp.	Thyme, freshly chopped
½ tsp.	Basil, freshly chopped
½ tsp.	Cilantro, freshly chopped
3 Tbl.	Chardonnay
¼ c.	Plum Tomatoes-skin, core & seeds removed, diced small
1 c.	Brown Sauce, hot
To Taste	Sea Salt
To Taste	Black Pepper, ground
1 Tbl.	Parsley & Chives, freshly chopped

Method:
1. Sauté the garlic, shallots in olive oil, add herbs and deglaze with wine. Add tomatoes, brown sauce and simmer for 5 minutes.
2. Arrange on plate the sliced chicken, tomato herb brown sauce, grilled zucchini and polenta.
   Garnish with fresh herbs.

∾

∽

Roasted Half Chicken and Garlic Red Bliss Potatoes With Pan Gravy and Toasted Pine Nuts, Served with a Corn, Cucumber, Roasted Red Pepper and Cilantro Salsa

Roasted Chicken:

1½#	Chicken, whole
To Taste	Sea Salt
To Taste	Black Pepper, ground
To Taste	Thyme, freshly chopped
To Taste	Poultry Seasoning, ground
1 ea.	Lemon Juice, freshly squeezed
1 ea.	Apple, seeds removed & cut in half
1 ea.	Parsley stems
1 ea.	Thyme, sprig

Method:
1. Season with salt, pepper, thyme, poultry seasoning and lemon juice. Place lemon rind, apple, parsley and thyme inside the chicken.
2. Roast chicken in a 300°F oven until proper doneness and let rest for 15 minutes.
   Remove chicken, split in half and keep warm.

Pan Gravy and Toasted Pine Nuts:

1 ea.	Chicken Neck
3 c.	Water, cold
¼ c.	Onion, diced small
1 ea.	Bay leaf, whole
¼ c.	Thyme, freshly chopped
1 Tbl.	Parsley, freshly chopped
To Taste	Sea Salt
To Taste	Black Pepper, ground
As Needed	Pan Drippings from Chicken
¼ c.	Chardonnay

3 oz.   Roux, warm

1 oz.   Pine nuts, toasted & ground

Method:

1. Place neck, water, onion, herbs, salt and black pepper in a sauce pot. Let boil and simmer for 10 minutes.
2. From the roasting pan, remove fat and deglaze with wine. Add pan drippings to sauce pot.
3. Whisk in roux and add toasted pine nuts.
4. Simmer for another 3 minutes Strain sauce into another sauce pot.

Garlic Mashed Red Bliss Potatoes:

2 ea.   Red Bliss Potatoes, half of the skin on & diced medium

To Taste   Sea Salt

To Taste   Black Pepper, ground

¼ tsp.   Parsley, freshly chopped

1 tsp.   Butter, whole

2 cl.   Garlic, roasted

1 oz.   Milk, whole

Method:

1. Cook potatoes in boiling salted water until proper doneness. Place in oven to dry out potatoes.
2. Place through a ricer and add in a steel bowl. Add parsley, butter, garlic and blend well. Slowly add milk, mix until smooth and season to taste.
3. Place in pastry bag and shape on plate.

Corn, Cucumber, Celery, Roasted Red Pepper and Cilantro Salsa:

1 oz.   Corn, steam for 2 minutes

1 oz.   Cucumber, no seeds & diced medium

1 oz.   Celery, diced medium

1 Tbl.   Roasted red pepper, diced medium

½ tsp.   Cilantro, freshly chopped

½ tsp.   Mint, freshly chopped
½ tsp.   Thyme, freshly chopped
To Taste   Sea Salt
To Taste   Black Pepper, ground
2 Tbl.   Italian vinaigrette

Method:
1. Add ingredients in a steel bowl and mix thoroughly.
    Refrigerate for 20 minutes.
2. Arrange chicken, potatoes, salsa and pan gravy on entrée plate.

∽

$\backsim$

Roasted Herb Chicken with a Roasted Garlic, Leek and Artichoke Sauce, Served with Herb Idaho Mashed Potatoes

1½# Chicken, whole

Herb Butter:

¼# Butter, softened
2 Tbl. Parsley & Thyme, freshly chopped
¼ tsp. Poultry Seasoning, ground
To Taste Black Pepper, ground
To Taste Sea Salt

Method:
1. Combine butter, parsley, thyme, and mix well until smooth. Spread herb butter over chicken, season with poultry seasoning, black pepper and salt.
2. Roast chicken in a 350ºF oven until proper doneness and let rest for 15 minutes.
Remove chicken, split in half and keep warm.

Herb Idaho Mashed Potatoes:

2 ea. Idaho Potatoes, peeled & medium diced
1 tsp. Parsley, freshly chopped
1 tsp. Butter, whole
1 oz. Milk, whole
To Taste Sea Salt
To Taste White Pepper, ground

Method:
1. Cook potatoes in boiling salted water until proper doneness and drain. Place in oven to dry out potatoes and place through a ricer.
2. In a steel bowl, add potatoes, parsley, butter, garlic and blend well. Slowly add milk, mix until smooth and season to taste.

Roasted Garlic, Leek and Artichoke Sauce:

1 Tbl.	Leeks, sliced
1 Tbl.	Extra Virgin Olive Oil
1 tsp.	Roasted Garlic
½ tsp.	Thyme, freshly chopped
½ tsp.	Parsley, freshly chopped
½ tsp.	Tarragon, freshly chopped
¼ c.	Chardonnay
½ c.	Artichoke Hearts, cut into quarters
¼ c.	Plum Tomatoes-skin, core & seeds removed, diced medium
1 c.	Chicken Stock, cold
To Taste	Sea Salt
To Taste	Black Pepper, ground

Method:
1. In a sauté pan, sweat the leeks in olive oil, add roasted garlic, herbs and deglaze with wine.
   Add artichokes, tomatoes, stock and reduce.
2. Remove from stove, place in blender and mix to a smooth consistency.
3. Arrange on plate the Idaho potatoes, split chicken and artichoke sauce.

෨

∾

Sautéed Chicken Breast with a Pepper, Olive and Tomato Salsa, Served with Fresh Asparagus

10 oz.	Chicken Breasts-skin, fat removed & pounded out
As Needed	Buckwheat Flour, sifted
2 Tbl.	Extra Virgin Olive Oil
8 ea.	Asparagus, steamed

Method:
1. Dredge chicken in flour and dust off excess.
   Sauté chicken in olive oil until golden brown, remove and keep warm.
2. Steam asparagus and keep warm.

Pepper, Olive and Tomato Salsa:

1 Tbl.	Extra Virgin Olive Oil
2 Tbl.	Shallots, minced
2 cl.	Garlic, minced
3 Tbl.	Vodka
Pinch	Red Pepper Flakes
½ ea.	Red Pepper, diced small
½ ea.	Yellow Pepper, diced small
3 ea.	Plum Tomatoes-skin, core & seeds removed, diced small
¼ c.	Black Olives, pitted & sliced lengthwise
1 tsp.	Capers, whole
1 tsp.	Cilantro, freshly chopped
1 tsp.	Thyme, freshly chopped
½ tsp.	Basil, freshly chopped
½ c.	Beef Stock, cold
2 Tbl.	Butter, cold
As Needed	Parsley, whole
As Needed	Chives, whole

Method:
1. In the same sauté pan, remove fat, sweat the shallots and garlic in olive oil.
   Deglaze with vodka, add peppers, tomatoes, olives, capers, herbs and red pepper flakes.
   Stir in stock and reduce by one-half.
2. Remove from stove and whisk in cold butter.
3. Arrange chicken, salsa and asparagus on entrée plate.
   Garnish with fresh herbs.

∽

∾

Sautéed Chicken Breast with a Wild Mushroom Garlic Cream Sauce

2-(10 oz.) each	Chicken Breasts-skin, fat removed & pounded out
To Taste	Poultry Seasoning, ground
As Needed	Buckwheat Flour, sifted
2 Tbl.	Extra Virgin Olive Oil

Method:
1. Season chicken with poultry seasoning.
   Dredge chicken in flour and dust off excess.
2. Sauté chicken on both sides until proper doneness.
3. Remove from pan and keep warm.

Wild Mushroom Roasted Garlic Cream Sauce:

2 Tbl.	Extra Virgin Olive Oil
2 Tbl.	Shallots, minced
2 cl.	Garlic, roasted
1 Tbl.	Parsley, freshly chopped
1 tsp.	Thyme, freshly chopped
½ tsp.	Basil, freshly chopped
½ tsp.	Oregano, freshly chopped
¼ c.	Portabella Mushrooms, cut into strips
¼ c.	Chardonnay
2 Tbl.	Buckwheat Flour, sifted
½ c.	Chicken Stock, cold
¼ c.	Half & Half, hot
To Taste	Sea Salt
To Taste	Black Pepper, ground
1 Tbl.	Scallions, freshly chopped

Method:

1. In the same sauté pan, remove fat, sweat the shallots, garlic, herbs and mushrooms in olive oil.
   Deglaze with wine, and incorporate flour.
   Whisk in chicken stock and reduce by one-half.
2. Stir in half & half and reduce to proper consistency.
   Season to taste.
3. Arrange chicken and wild mushroom roasted garlic cream sauce on entrée plate.
   Garnish with fresh scallions.

~~

CAKES

Apple Crisp with Cinnamon, Oats and Walnuts
83
Banana Cake with Cream Cheese and Coconut Frosting
84
Blackberry Forest Cake
85
Black Walnut and Hazelnut Cake
86
Blueberry Cake
87
Carrot Cake with Pineapple, Coconut and Walnuts,
Served with a Lemon Cream Cheese Frosting
88
Carrot Cake with Pineapple, Raisins and Pecans
89
Chocolate Black Walnut Brownies, Served with Chocolate
Almond Marsala Sabayon
90
Chocolate Hazelnut Oil Cake, with a Chocolate Whipped Frosting,
Covered with Hazelnuts
92
Chocolate Walnut Soufflés
93
Coconut Orange Cake with an Orange Cream Cheese Frosting
94
Coffee Cake with a Cream Cheese, Pineapple and Mango Filling
95
Coffee Cake Laced with a Walnut Pistachio Filling
97
Coffee Cake with a Pecan Walnut Topping
99
Dark Chocolate Coconut Godiva Sabayon Cake
100
Disaronno Liqueur Sponge Cake Filled with Layers of Fruit
And Whipped Cream
102

German Chocolate Orange Cake, with a Chocolate Whipped Cream Frosting,
Covered with Dark Chocolate Shavings
103
Hazelnut and Pecan Chocolate Cake with a Dark Chocolate Ganache,
Covered with Dark Chocolate Curls and Raspberries
104
Moist Chocolate Brazil Nut Coffee Cake with White Icing
105
Old Fashioned Pumpkin Walnut Cake
107
Orange Kahlua Cocoa Cake with a Rich Chocolate Kahlua Frosting
108
Pear Cinnamon Walnut Cake
110
Poppy Seed Cake
111
Pumpkin and Acorn Squash Cake with Orange Lemon Frosting
112
Rhubarb Cake
113
Two Berry Sponge Cake
114
Walnut Cinnamon Apple Cake
115
Winter Persimmon Nut Cake
116
Yellow Peach and Papaya Upside Down Cake
117
Zucchini Cake
118

∾

Apple Crisp with Cinnamon, Oats and Walnuts

3 Tbl. Crisco

4 c. Apples-peeled, cored and sliced thin

¾ tsp. Cinnamon, ground

3 Tbl. Sugar, granulated

Method:
1. Rub Crisco into and around mini baking dish.
2. Toss in steel bowl the apples, cinnamon and sugar.
   Place contents into baking dish.

½ c. Buckwheat Flour, sifted

¼ c. Oatmeal, finely chopped

¼ c. Walnuts, coarsely chopped

¾ c. Light Brown Sugar, lightly packed

3 oz. Butter, cut into 1-inch cubes

Method:
1. Mix ingredients thoroughly in a steel bowl until mealy texture is formed.
   Place coarsely on top of apples.
2. Bake in a 350ºF oven for 45 minutes.
3. Remove from oven, let cool for 10 minutes and serve.

∽

Banana Cake with Cream Cheese and Coconut Frosting

Cream Cheese and Coconut Frosting:

16 oz.	Cream Cheese
4 c.	Sugar, confectioner's
6 Tbl.	Butter, whole
1 tsp.	Vanilla
2 Tbl.	Lemon Zest
1 c.	Coconut Flakes

Method:
1. Cream all ingredients in a mixing bowl and blend to a smooth consistency.

½ c.	Crisco
½ c.	Extra Virgin Olive Oil
3 c.	Sugar, granulated
½ tsp.	Sea Salt
2 tsp.	Vanilla
3 c.	Banana's, ripe
4 ea.	Egg Yolks
1 c.	Buttermilk
1 tsp.	Baking Soda
2 tsp.	Baking Powder
¼ tsp.	Nutmeg, ground
Dash	Cinnamon, ground
3¼ c.	All-Purpose Flour, sifted
½ c.	Buckwheat Flour, sifted
4 ea.	Egg Whites, stiff peaks

Method:
1. Place in a mixing bowl the Crisco, oil, sugar, salt, vanilla and blend well on 2nd speed.
   Add banana's and mix again until smooth.

2. Slowly add yolks one at a time, add buttermilk and mix well.
   Incorporate the baking soda, baking powder, spices and both
   all-purpose and buckwheat flour's.
   Blend to a smooth consistency.
3. Fold egg whites into the mixture.
   Pour batter into a greased and floured 10-inch pan.
4. Bake in a 350ºF oven for 30 to 35 minutes or until an inserted toothpick
   comes out clean.

Blackberry Forest Cake

1 ea.	Chocolate Cake, 10" Round Sponge
¼ c.	Grand Marnier
¼ c.	Simple Syrup
3 c.	Chocolate Whipped Cream
12 oz.	Blackberries, preserved
Garnish	Chocolate Shavings
Garnish	Blackberries, preserved
Garnish	Chocolate Cake Crumbs

Method:
1. Slice chocolate sponge so you have three layers.
   Soak all layers with Grand Marnier and simple syrup.
2. Pipe rings of chocolate cream on the first layer of the sponge and
   smooth out.
   Place blackberries on the inside middle layer of cake.
3. Place second layer sponge on top and pipe again the chocolate cream.
   Place third layer sponge on top and layer the chocolate cream on top
   as well as the sides.
   Place blackberries around the cake and chocolate shavings
   in the middle.
4. Cover half of the bottom sides with cake crumbs.

∾

Black Walnut and Hazelnut Cake

½ c.	Butter, whole
½ c.	Crisco
2 c.	Sugar, granulated
5 ea.	Egg Yolks
1 c.	Buttermilk
1 tsp.	Vanilla
1 tsp.	Baking Soda
2 tsp.	Baking Powder
1¾ c.	All-Purpose Flour, sifted
¼ c.	Buckwheat Flour, sifted
1½ c.	Black Walnuts, finely chopped
½ c.	Hazelnuts, finely chopped
3 oz.	Coconut Flakes
5 ea.	Egg Whites, stiff peaks

Method:
1. In a mixing bowl, combine butter, Crisco and sugar. Mix well to a smooth consistency on 2nd speed.
2. Slowly add yolks one at a time, add buttermilk and blend. Add vanilla, baking soda, baking powder, flour and blend well.
3. Fold in the walnuts, hazelnuts, coconut flakes and egg whites. Pour into a greased and floured 10-inch baking pan.
4. Bake in a 350ºF oven for 25 to 30 minutes or until an inserted toothpick comes out clean.

∾

∽

Blueberry Cake

¾ c.	Crisco
1¼ c.	Sugar, granulated
1 tsp.	Sea Salt
1 tsp.	Vanilla
4 ea.	Egg yolks
½ c.	Orange Juice
3 tsp.	Baking Powder
2¾ c.	All-Purpose Flour, sifted
¼ c.	Buckwheat Flour, sifted
4 ea.	Egg Whites, stiff peaks
1 qt.	Blueberries, fresh & freeze for 30 minutes

Method:
1. In a mixing bowl, add Crisco, sugar, salt and vanilla. Mix well to a smooth consistency on 2nd speed.
2. Slowly add egg yolks one at a time, add orange juice and blend well. Add baking powder, flour and blend to a smooth consistency.
3. Fold in egg whites and blueberries. Pour into a greased and floured baking pan.
4. Bake in a 350ºF oven for 25 to 30 minutes or until an inserted toothpick comes out clean.

∽

Carrot Cake with Pineapple, Coconut and Walnuts, Served with a Lemon Cream Cheese Frosting

Lemon Cream Cheese Frosting:

6 oz.	Cream Cheese
3 c.	Sugar, confectioners
6 Tbl.	Butter, whole
1 tsp.	Vanilla
3 Tbl.	Lemon Zest

Method:
1. Cream all ingredients in a mixing bowl and blend to a smooth consistency.

3 ea.	Eggs Yolks
1½ c.	Extra Virgin Olive Oil
1 tsp.	Vanilla
2 c.	Sugar, granulated
½ tsp.	Sea Salt
1 tsp.	Baking Soda
2 tsp.	Cinnamon, ground
½ tsp.	Nutmeg, ground
1¾ c.	All-Purpose Flour, sifted
¼ c.	Buckwheat Flour, sifted
2 c.	Carrots, grated
1 c.	Pineapple, crushed & drained
1 c.	Coconut Flakes
1 c.	Walnuts, coarsely chopped
3 ea.	Egg Whites, stiff peaks

Method:
1. Combine in a mixing bowl the yolks, oil, vanilla, sugar, salt, baking soda and spices.
   Mix well on 1st speed and slowly add the flour.
   Add carrots and blend to a smooth consistency.
2. Fold in the pineapple, coconut, walnuts and egg whites.
   Pour into a greased and floured baking pan.
3. Bake in a 350ºF oven for 40 to 50 minutes or until an inserted toothpick comes out clean.

∾

Carrot Cake with Pineapple, Raisins and Pecans

3 ea.	Egg Yolks
1½ c.	Extra Virgin Olive Oil
1 tsp.	Vanilla
2 c.	Sugar, granulated
1 tsp.	Sea Salt
1 tsp.	Baking Soda
2 tsp.	Baking Powder
2 tsp.	Cinnamon, ground
½ tsp.	Nutmeg, ground
3 oz.	Buttermilk, cold
2¾ c.	All-Purpose Flour, sifted
¼ c.	Buckwheat Flour, sifted
2 c.	Carrots, grated
8 oz.	Pineapple, crushed & drained
½ c.	Dark Raisins
1 c.	Pecans, coarsely chopped
3 ea.	Egg Whites, stiff peaks

Method:
1. Combine in a mixing bowl the yolks, oil, vanilla and sugar.
   Add the salt, baking soda, baking powder, spices and mix well on 1st speed.
2. Slowly add the buttermilk and incorporate the flour to a smooth consistency.
   Add carrots and blend thoroughly.
3. Fold in pineapple, raisins, pecans and egg whites.
   Pour into a greased and floured baking pan.
4. Bake in a 350ºF oven for 40 to 50 minutes or until an inserted toothpick comes out clean.

∾

൭

Chocolate Black Walnut Brownies, Served with Chocolate Almond Marsala Sabayon

Chocolate Almond Marsala Sabayon:

6 ea.	Egg Yolks
3 oz.	Sugar, granulated
4 oz.	Marsala Liquor
6 oz.	Dark Chocolate (85% cocoa), melted
1 c.	Heavy Cream, whipped
¼ c.	Almonds, finely ground

Method:
1. Combine the yolks, sugar and marsala in a steel bowl.
   Whip under low heat until ribbon stage is achieved.
2. Heat melted chocolate and let cool to room temperature.
   Whisk in chocolate to sabayon mixture.
3. Let cool completely and fold in whipped cream.

2½ c.	Sugar, granulated
1 c.	Butter, melted
2 Tbl.	Water, cold
1½ Tbl.	Espresso Coffee
6 oz.	Semi-Sweet Chocolate, coarsely chopped
2 oz.	Dark Chocolate (85% cocoa), coarsely chopped
5 ea.	Eggs, whole
1 Tbl.	Vanilla
1¼ c.	All-Purpose Flour, sifted
¼ c.	Buckwheat Flour, sifted
¼ tsp.	Sea Salt
1 c.	Black Walnuts, coarsely chopped

Method:
1. Combine sugar, butter, water and coffee in a sauce pot.
   Cook over low heat stirring constantly and bring to a boil.
   Remove from heat and add the chocolate chips until melted.

2. Stir in the eggs, salt and vanilla.
3. Fold in the flour, salt and walnuts.
   Pour into a greased and floured baking pan.
4. Bake in a 350ºF oven for 25 to 30 minutes or until an inserted toothpick comes out clean.
   Remove, let cool and cut into desired shapes.
   Serve with chocolate marsala sabayon.

෧෨

∽

Chocolate Hazelnut Oil Cake, with a Chocolate Whipped Frosting, Covered with Hazelnuts

2 c.	All-Purpose Flour, sifted
¼ c.	Buckwheat Flour, sifted
2 tsp.	Baking Soda
1½ tsp.	Sea Salt
¾ c.	Cocoa Powder, sifted
¼ c.	Hazelnuts, finely chopped
1¾ c.	Sugar, granulated
3 ea.	Eggs, whole
¾ c.	Extra Virgin Olive Oil
1½ tsp.	Vanilla
1½ c.	Buttermilk
2 c.	Chocolate Whipped Cream
1 c.	Hazelnuts, finely chopped

Method:
1. In a mixing bowl, add flour, baking soda, salt, cocoa powder, hazelnuts and sugar.
   Mix ingredients on 1st speed for 1 minute.
2. Slowly add eggs one at a time.
   Add in the oil, vanilla and blend well.
3. Slowly add the buttermilk on 1st speed and then mix on 2nd speed to a smooth consistency.
   Pour into a greased and floured baking pan.
4. Bake in a 350ºF oven for 25 to 30 minutes or until an inserted toothpick comes out clean.

∽

Chocolate Walnut Soufflés

As Needed	Butter, softened
As Needed	Sugar, granulated
3 ea.	Egg Yolks
¼ c.	Sugar, granulated
½ tsp.	Vanilla
2 Tbl.	Butter, melted
1 tsp.	Cornstarch, sifted
¼ c.	Cocoa, sifted
¼ c.	Walnuts, finely ground
3 Tbl.	Coffee Liqueur
¼ c.	Dark Chocolate (85% Cocoa), finely chopped
6 ea.	Egg Whites, soft peaks
As Needed	Powdered Sugar, sifted

Method:
1. Rub butter around soufflé cups, sprinkle sugar inside and place in refrigerator for 5 minutes.
2. In a mixing bowl, add egg yolks, sugar and whip to a fluffy stage. Add vanilla, melted butter and fold in cornstarch, cocoa, walnuts, coffee liqueur and dark chocolate.
3. Fold in the egg whites to a smooth consistency and place in soufflé cups.
4. Bake in a 375ºF oven for 20 minutes.
5. Remove from oven, let cool and place powdered sugar on top.

ငာ

Coconut Orange Cake with an Orange Cream Cheese Frosting

Orange Cream Cheese Frosting:

6 oz.	Cream Cheese
3 c.	Sugar, confectioners
6 Tbl.	Butter, whole
1 tsp.	Vanilla
3 Tbl.	Orange Zest

Method:
1. Cream all ingredients in a mixing bowl.
2. Blend to a smooth consistency.

½ c.	Butter, whole
1½ c.	Sugar, granulated
1 tsp.	Vanilla
½ tsp.	Sea Salt
4 ea.	Egg Yolks
2 tsp.	Baking Powder
2 c.	All-Purpose Flour, sifted
¼ c.	Buckwheat Flour, sifted
1 c.	Milk, whole
4 c.	Coconut Flakes
3 Tbl.	Orange Zest
4 ea.	Egg Whites, stiff peaks

Method:
1. In a mixing bowl, add butter, sugar, vanilla, salt and mix on 2nd speed.
2. Slowly add eggs one at a time until well incorporated.
   Add the baking powder, flour and blend well.
3. Slowly add the milk and blend well.
   Add the coconut, orange zest and blend to a smooth consistency.
4. Fold in egg whites.
   Pour into a greased and floured baking pan.
5. Bake in a 350ºF oven for 30 to 35 minutes or until an inserted toothpick comes out clean.

ငာ

෨෨

Coffee Cake with a Cream Cheese, Pineapple and Mango Filling

¼ c.	Water, warm
1 c.	Milk, warm
½ c.	Sugar, granulated
2 pkg.	Dry Yeast
1 tsp.	Sea Salt
¼ c.	Crisco
¼ c.	Butter, whole
4¼ c.	All-Purpose Flour, sifted & reserve ½ c.
¾ c.	Buckwheat Flour, sifted
2 ea.	Eggs, whole
Dash	Cardamom, ground
Dash	Nutmeg, ground
Dash	Cinnamon, ground

Method:
1. In a mixing bowl, combine the water, milk, yeast, sugar and let rest for a few minutes.
   Add the salt, Crisco, butter, flour, eggs and spices.
2. With a dough hook, mix on 1st speed for 3 minutes.
   Add reserved flour and mix on 1st speed for another 2 minutes.
3. Proof dough in a warm place for 1 hour.

Cream Cheese Filling for Coffee Cake:

½ c.	Golden Raisins
3 Tbl.	Cognac Liquor
1#	Cream Cheese
½ c.	Sugar, granulated
¼ c.	Butter, whole
3 Tbl.	Buckwheat Flour, sifted
¼ c.	Sour Cream
2 tsp.	Lemon Zest
1 tsp.	Vanilla
4 oz.	Pineapple, crushed & drained
4 oz.	Mango, blended
As Needed	Cream of Wheat
1 ea.	Egg, whip with 1 Tbl. water
¼ c.	Sugar, granulated
1 tsp.	Cinnamon, ground

Method:
1. In a small bowl, combine raisins, cognac, cover with plastic wrap and let sit overnight.
2. Combine in a mixing bowl, the cream cheese, sugar, butter, flour and mix to a smooth consistency.
   Add the sour cream, lemon, vanilla and blend thoroughly.
3. Fold in raisins, crushed pineapple and mango.
4. Roll out dough thinly and fill with some of the cream cheese mixture in the middle.
   Place on a sheet pan with cream of wheat on the bottom.
   Egg wash on top and sprinkle with cinnamon sugar mixture.
5. Bake in a 350ºF oven for 30 to 35 minutes until golden brown.

∽

ᘒ

Coffee Cake Laced with a Walnut Pistachio Filling

¼ c.	Water, warm
1 c.	Milk, warm
½ c.	Sugar, granulated
2 pkg.	Dry Yeast
1 tsp.	Sea Salt
¼ c.	Crisco
¼ c.	Butter, whole
4¼ c.	All-Purpose Flour, sifted & reserve ½ c.
¾ c.	Buckwheat Flour, sifted
2 ea.	Eggs, whole
Dash	Cardamom, ground
Dash	Nutmeg, ground
Dash	Cinnamon, ground

Method:
1. In a mixing bowl, combine the water, milk, yeast, sugar and let rest for a few minutes.
   Add the salt, Crisco, butter, flour, eggs and spices.
2. With a dough hook, mix on 1st speed for 3 minutes.
   Add reserved flour and mix on 1st speed for another 2 minutes.
3. Proof dough in a warm place for 1 hour.

Walnut Filling:

¼#	Butter, whole
1 c.	Sugar, granulated
1 c.	Honey
1 tsp.	Sea Salt
½ c.	Milk, whole
2#	Walnuts, finely ground
1#	Pistachios, finely ground
2 ea.	Eggs, whole
3 Tbl.	Orange Zest
As Needed	Cream of Wheat
1 ea.	Egg, whip with 1 Tbl. water
¼ c.	Sugar, granulated
1 tsp.	Cinnamon, ground

Method:
1. Add butter, sugar, honey, salt and milk to a sauce pot.
   Heat mixture to a simmer and stir occasionally until sugar has dissolved.
2. Mix in the walnuts, pistachios and orange zest.
   Let cool, stir in the eggs and let rest in refrigerator for 30 minutes.
3. Roll out dough thinly and fill with some of the mixture in the middle.
   Cut dough on each side into strips and place one on top of the other,
   so end result looks laced.
   Place on a sheet pan with cream of wheat on the bottom.
   Egg wash on top and sprinkle with cinnamon sugar mixture.
4. Bake in a 350ºF oven for 30 to 35 minutes until golden brown.

೧

Coffee Cake with a Pecan Walnut Topping

½ c.	Butter, whole
1¼ c.	Sugar, granulated
2 ea.	Eggs, whole
1½ c.	All-Purpose Flour, sifted
¼ c.	Buckwheat Flour, sifted
1½ tsp.	Baking Powder
1 tsp.	Baking Soda
½ tsp.	Sea Salt
1¼ c.	Sour Cream
1 tsp.	Vanilla

Pecan Topping:

¼ c.	Sugar, granulated
1½ tsp.	Cinnamon, ground
½ c.	Pecans, finely chopped
½ c.	Walnuts, finely chopped

Method:
1. In a mixing bowl, blend the butter and sugar on 2nd speed.
2. Slowly add eggs one at a time until well incorporated.
    Add flour, baking powder, baking soda, salt and blend until smooth.
    Mix in the sour cream and vanilla until well incorporated.
3. Pour into a greased and floured baking dish.
    Combine sugar, cinnamon and nuts and sprinkle evenly over the top of the cake.
4. Bake in a 350ºF oven for 45 minutes or until an inserted toothpick comes out clean.

೧

~

Dark Chocolate Coconut Godiva Sabayon Cake

Chocolate Sabayon:

9 ea.	Egg Yolks
4 oz.	Sugar, granulated
2 oz.	Godiva Liqueur
1 tsp.	Cocoa Powder
2 c.	Chocolate Whipped Cream

Method:
1. Combine yolks, sugar, liqueur and cocoa powder in a steel bowl.
   Whip under low heat until ribbon stage is achieved.
   Let cool completely.
2. Fold in chocolate whipped cream.

Chocolate Whipped Cream:

| 2 c. | Heavy Cream |
| ¼# | Dark Chocolate (85% cocoa), chips |

Method:
1. Heat heavy cream on stove.
   Melt chocolate in a double boiler and let cool.
2. Whisk in heavy cream a little at a time until well incorporated.
   Let cool completely in refrigerator.
3. Place mixture in mixing bowl and whip on 3rd speed until soft peaks form.

1 each (10" round)	Chocolate Sponge Cake, cut into 3 Even layers
¼ c.	Simple Syrup
¼ c.	Godiva Liqueur
2½ c.	Chocolate Sabayon
1½ c.	Chocolate Whipped Cream
Garnish	Chocolate Cake Crumbs
Garnish	Dark Chocolate Shavings
Garnish	Coconut Flakes

Method:
1. Soak all layers of chocolate sponge with simple syrup and Godiva Liqueur.
   Place sabayon on the first layer of chocolate sponge.
   Repeat with layers of sabayon and sponge.
2. Place third layer of sponge on top.
3. Frost the top and sides of cake with chocolate whipped cream.
   Cover one third of the bottom sides with cake crumbs.
4. Garnish on the top of cake with chocolate shavings and coconut around the sides.

ے

಄

Disaronno Liqueur Sponge Cake
Filled with Layers of Fruit
And Whipped Cream

1 ea.	Sponge Cake, cut into 4 layers
2 oz.	Disaronno Liqueur
3 oz.	Simple Syrup, cooled
3 c.	Heavy Cream, whipped to stiff peaks
1 qt.	Strawberries, sliced
6 ea.	Kiwi fruit, outer skin removed and sliced thin
½ ea.	Pineapple-skins & core removed, sliced thin
Garnish	Strawberries, stem on

Method:
1. Mix together the Disaronno Liqueur and simple syrup in a steel bowl. Soak sponge cakes with mixture.
2. Place a cake layer and frost with whipped cream. Arrange strawberry slices on first cake layer.
3. Place second cake layer on top, whipped cream and arrange kiwi slices.
   Place third cake layer on top, whipped cream and arrange pineapple slices.
   Place fourth cake layer on top and whipped cream top layer and sides of entire cake.
4. Decorate top of cake with whole strawberries on the outer edge. Make a second inner circle with kiwi slices.
   Arrange pineapple slices in the center circle and refrigerate.

಄

∽

German Chocolate Orange Cake, with A Chocolate Whipped Cream Frosting, Covered with Dark Chocolate Shavings

4 oz.	Dark Chocolate (85% Cocoa), coarsely chopped
2½ oz.	Water, cold
½ c.	Butter, whole
1 c.	Sugar, granulated
½ tsp.	Sea Salt
1 tsp.	Vanilla
3 ea.	Egg Yolks
½ c.	Buttermilk, cold
1½ c.	All-Purpose Flour, sifted
¼ c.	Buckwheat Flour, sifted
1 tsp.	Baking Soda
3 ea.	Egg Whites, stiff peaks
½ c.	Orange Zest
2 c.	Chocolate Whipped Cream
½ c.	Dark Chocolate Shavings

Method:
1. Heat the chocolate and water in a double boiler until melted.
2. In a mixing bowl add the butter, sugar, salt and vanilla, and blend on 2nd speed.
3. Slowly add the egg yolks one at a time and then the buttermilk on 1st speed.
   Add the flour, baking soda and blend well.
   Slowly add the melted chocolate and blend to a smooth consistency.
4. Fold in egg whites and orange zest.
   Pour into a greased and floured baking pan.
5. Bake in a 350ºF oven for 30 to 35 minutes or until an inserted toothpick comes out clean.

∽

ᢍ

Hazelnut and Pecan Chocolate Cake with a Dark Chocolate Ganache, Covered with Dark Chocolate Curls and Raspberries

1 ea.	Chocolate Cake, cut into three layers
1 oz.	Hazelnut Liqueur
1 oz.	Simple Syrup
½ c.	Hazelnuts, finely ground
½ c.	Pecans, finely ground
¼ c.	Raspberry Jam
2 c.	Dark Chocolate Ganache, with 1 Tbl. of strong coffee
As Needed	Dark Chocolate (85% cocoa), cut into curls
¾ c.	Raspberries, garnish

Method:
1. Combine the hazelnut liqueur and simple syrup together. Soak all layers of the chocolate cake.
2. Place first layer on bottom and layer with whipped cream, then some of the hazelnuts on top.
   Add raspberry jam to the second layer on both sides, then chocolate whipped cream on top.
3. Place hazelnuts on top of chocolate whipped cream.
   Place raspberry jam on the bottom of the third cake layer and place on top.
4. Cover entire cake with chocolate Ganache and refrigerate for one hour.
   Place dark chocolate curls in the center.
   Arrange raspberries around cake.

ᢍ

᠗

Moist Chocolate Brazil Nut Coffee Cake with White Icing

White Icing:

1 c.	Milk, whole
3 Tbl.	All-Purpose Flour, sifted
2 Tbl.	Buckwheat Flour, sifted
½ c.	Butter, whole
½ c.	Crisco
1 c.	Sugar, confectioners
1 tsp.	Vanilla

Method:
1. In a sauce pot, add the milk and flour.
   Heat on a low flame and stir to for 5 minutes.
   Cool completely in refrigerator.
2. In a mixing bowl, whip the butter, Crisco, sugar, vanilla and blend well.
   Add the milk and flour mixture and blend to a smooth consistency.

1¾ c.	All-Purpose Flour, sifted
¼ c.	Buckwheat Flour, sifted
1 tsp.	Sea Salt
1 tsp.	Baking Powder
2 tsp.	Baking Soda
¾ c.	Cocoa Powder, sifted
2 c.	Sugar, granulated
2 ea.	Egg Yolks
1 c.	Extra Virgin Olive Oil
1 tsp.	Vanilla
1 c.	Coffee, cold
1 c.	Buttermilk, cold
2 ea.	Egg Whites, stiff peaks
½ c.	Brazil Nuts, finely ground

Method:
1. In a mixing bowl, add the flour, salt, baking soda and powder, cocoa, vanilla and sugar.
   Blend ingredients together on 1st speed.
2. Slowly add the egg yolks one at a time.
   Add the olive oil, vanilla, coffee and mix well.
   Slowly add the buttermilk on 1st speed and then mix on 2nd speed to a smooth consistency.
3. Fold in the egg whites and brazil nuts.
   Pour into a greased and floured baking pan.
4. Bake in a 350ºF oven for 25 to 30 minutes or until an inserted toothpick comes out clean.

☙

∽

Old Fashioned Pumpkin Walnut Cake

2 ea.	Eggs, whole
1¼ c.	Pumpkin, blended
1 c.	Sugar, granulated
1 c.	Milk, whole
2 Tbl.	Extra Virgin Olive Oil
1¾ c.	All-Purpose Flour, sifted
¼ c.	Buckwheat Flour, sifted
2 tsp.	Baking Powder
½ tsp.	Baking Soda
2 tsp.	Cinnamon, ground
1 tsp.	Ginger, ground
½ tsp.	Cloves, ground
½ tsp.	Sea Salt
½ c.	Walnuts, finely chopped

Method:
1. Beat eggs, pumpkin, sugar, milk olive oil in a mixing bowl and blend well for 2 minutes.
   Add baking powder, baking soda, spices, salt and blend well.
   Incorporate the flour, walnuts and blend to smooth consistency.
2. Pour into a greased and floured baking pan.
3. Bake in a 350ºF oven for 40 to 50 minutes or until an inserted toothpick comes out clean.

∽

∾

Orange Kahlua Cocoa Cake with a Rich Chocolate Kahlua Frosting

Rich Chocolate Kahlua Frosting:

6 Tbl.	Butter, whole
1 Tbl.	Crisco
3 Tbl.	Cocoa Powder, sifted
1#	Sugar confectioners'
3 Tbl.	Kahlua Liqueur
3 Tbl.	Coffee, cold
¼#	Dark Chocolate (85% cocoa), cut into chips, melted & then cooled

Method:
1. Place ingredients in a mixing bowl.
   Blend to a smooth consistency, and then slowly add the dark chocolate while mixing.

Orange Kahlua Cocoa Cake:

¾ c.	Sugar, granulated
½ c.	Crisco
1 c.	Light Brown Sugar
3 ea.	Egg Yolks
1 tsp.	Baking Soda
1½ tsp.	Baking Powder
½ c.	Cocoa Powder, sifted
2 c.	All-Purpose Flour, sifted
¼ c.	Buckwheat Flour, sifted
¾ c.	Strong Coffee, cooled
¾ c.	Kahlua Liqueur
3 ea.	Egg Whites, stiff peaks
½ c.	Orange Zest
¼ c.	Almonds, finely chopped
¼ c.	Hazelnuts, finely chopped

Method:
1. In a mixing bowl, add the Crisco, sugar and blend on 2nd speed.
2. Slowly add the egg yolks one at a time on 1st speed.
   Add the baking soda, baking powder, cocoa powder and flour.
3. Slowly add the coffee, kahlua and blend to a smooth consistency.
   Add the almonds, hazelnuts and blend well.
4. Fold in the egg whites and orange zest.
   Pour into a greased and floured baking pan.
5. Bake in a 350°F oven for 25 to 30 minutes or until an inserted toothpick comes out clean.

∽

Pear Cinnamon Walnut Cake

1½ c.	Sugar, granulated
4 oz.	Butter, whole
1 oz.	Crisco
¼ tsp.	Sea Salt
½ tsp.	Cinnamon, ground
¼ tsp.	Nutmeg, ground
2 ea.	Eggs, whole
1½ c.	All-Purpose Flour, sifted
¼ c.	Buckwheat Flour, sifted
1¼ tsp.	Baking Powder
¾ tsp.	Baking Soda
¾ c.	Milk, whole
¼ c.	Walnuts, finely chopped
1#	Pears-peeled, cored & diced small

Method:
1. In a mixing bowl, add the sugar, Crisco, butter, salt, spices and blend well on 2nd speed.
2. Incorporate eggs one at a time.
   Add the flour, baking powder, baking soda and blend well.
   Slowly incorporate the milk on 1st speed and then on 2nd speed.
3. Fold in the walnuts, pears and mix to a smooth consistency.
   Pour into a greased and floured baking pan.
4. Bake in a 350ºF oven for 30 to 35 minutes or until an inserted toothpick comes out clean.

∽

༈

Poppy Seed Cake

¾ c.	Poppy Seed Filling
1 c.	Buttermilk
1½ c.	Extra Virgin Olive Oil
2 c.	Sugar, granulated
4 ea.	Egg Yolks
3½ c.	All-Purpose Flour, sifted
½ c.	Buckwheat Flour, sifted
1 tsp.	Baking Soda
2 tsp.	Baking Powder
4 ea.	Egg Whites, stiff peaks

Method:
1. In a mixing bowl, add poppy filling, buttermilk, olive oil, sugar and blend well on 1st speed.
   Add the yolks one at a time until well incorporated.
   Incorporate flour, baking soda and baking powder.
2. Mix well on 2nd speed to a smooth consistency.
3. Fold in the egg whites.
   Pour mixture into a greased and floured baking pan.
4. Bake in a 350ºF oven for 25 to 30 minutes or until an inserted toothpick comes out clean.

༈

〜

Pumpkin and Acorn Squash Cake with Orange Lemon Frosting

Orange Lemon Frosting:

1#	Cream Cheese
½#	Butter, whole
2 Tbl.	Lemon Juice, freshly squeezed
3 Tbl.	Lemon Zest
2 Tbl.	Orange Juice
3 Tbl.	Orange Zest
3 Tbl.	Buckwheat Flour, sifted
½#	Sugar, confectioners

Method:
1. Mix all ingredients together until smooth.

2 ea.	Eggs, whole
8 oz.	Sugar, granulated
¾ c.	Pumpkin, blended
¾ c.	Acorn Squash, blended
2 tsp.	Cinnamon, ground
½ tsp.	Nutmeg, ground
2¼ tsp.	Baking Powder
1½ tsp.	Baking Soda
2 c.	All-Purpose Flour, sifted
¼ c.	Buckwheat Flour, sifted
6 oz.	Butter, melted

Method:
1. In a mixing bowl, add eggs, sugar and heat on stove while whipping to a temperature of 110ºF.
   Remove from stove and whip mixture on 3rd speed.
   Whip until ribbon stage is formed, approximately 3 minutes.
2. Add pumpkin, acorn squash, cinnamon, nutmeg, baking powder and baking soda. Incorporate the flour and blend well.
   Slowly add the melted butter and blend to a smooth consistency.
3. Pour mixture into a greased and floured baking pan.
4. Bake in a 350ºF oven for 25 to 30 minutes or until an inserted toothpick comes out clean.

〜

∽

Rhubarb Cake

1½ c.	Sugar, granulated
½ c.	Crisco
2 ea.	Egg Yolks
1 tsp.	Baking Soda
1 tsp.	Cinnamon, ground
¼ tsp.	Cloves, ground
¼ tsp.	Allspice, ground
½ tsp.	Sea Salt
3 oz.	Milk, cold
1¾ c.	All-Purpose Flour, sifted
¼ c.	Buckwheat Flour, sifted
2 c.	Rhubarb, skin removed & diced small
2 ea.	Egg Whites, stiff peaks
¾ c.	Walnuts, finely ground
1½ tsp.	Cinnamon, ground
¾ c.	Light Brown Sugar

Method:
1. In a mixing bowl, add the sugar, Crisco and mix on 2nd speed.
2. Slowly add the yolks one at a time until well incorporated.
   Add the baking soda, spices, salt, milk and blend well.
   Incorporate the flour, rhubarb and then mix on 2nd speed to a smooth consistency.
3. Fold in the egg whites.
   Pour into a greased and floured baking pan.
4. Combine the walnuts, cinnamon, light brown sugar in a steel bowl and mix together.
   Place crumb mixture on top of cake.
5. Bake in a 350ºF oven for 30 to 35 minutes or until an inserted toothpick comes out clean.

∽

∽

Two Berry Sponge Cake

6 ea.	Eggs, whole
¾ c.	Sugar, granulated
4 oz.	Raspberries, whole
2 oz.	Strawberries, sliced
¾ c.	All-Purpose Flour, sifted
¼ c.	Buckwheat Flour, sifted
¼ c.	Cornstarch, sifted
3 oz.	Butter, melted
1 tsp.	Vanilla

Method:
1. In a mixing bowl, add eggs, sugar and heat on stove while whipping to a temperature of 110°F.
   Remove from stove and whip mixture on 3rd speed.
   Whip until ribbon stage is formed, approximately 3 minutes.
2. Add raspberries, strawberries and mix for 30 seconds more.
   Incorporate the flour and cornstarch together and mix well.
   Fold in butter and vanilla.
3. Pour mixture into a greased and floured baking pan.
4. Bake in a 350°F oven for 20 to 25 minutes or until an inserted toothpick comes out clean.

∽

෩

Walnut Cinnamon Apple Cake

¼ c.	Crisco
1 c.	Sugar, granulated
1 tsp.	Cinnamon, ground
¼ tsp.	Nutmeg, ground
1 tsp.	Vanilla
1 ea.	Egg Yolk
1 c.	All-Purpose Flour, sifted
¼ c.	Buckwheat Flour, sifted
½ tsp.	Baking Soda, sifted
1 tsp.	Baking Powder, sifted
5 ea.	Apples-core removed, peeled & diced small
1 c.	Walnuts, finely chopped
1 ea.	Egg White, stiff peaks

Method:
1. In a mixing bowl, add the Crisco, sugar, spices and vanilla.
   Mix on 2nd speed to a smooth consistency.
2. Incorporate egg yolk into mixture.
   Add flour, baking soda, baking powder and blend well.
   Mix in the apples and walnuts.
3. Fold in the egg whites.
   Pour batter into a greased and floured baking dish.
4. Bake in a 350ºF oven for 25 to 30 minutes or until an inserted toothpick comes out clean.

෩

∽

Winter Persimmon Nut Cake

4 oz.	Butter, whole
1 c.	Sugar, granulated
1 tsp.	Vanilla
4 ea.	Egg Yolks
½ c.	Milk, whole
1¼ c.	All-Purpose Flour, sifted
¼ c.	Buckwheat Flour, sifted
2 tsp.	Baking Powder
¼ tsp.	Sea Salt
2 ea.	Persimmon's, peeled & chopped fine
¼ c.	Pecans, chopped
¼ c.	Hazelnuts, chopped
¼ c.	Golden Raisins
4 ea.	Egg Whites, stiff peaks

Method:
1. In a mixing bowl, add the butter, sugar, vanilla and mix on 2nd speed to a smooth consistency.
2. Add the yolks one at a time until well incorporated.
   Incorporate milk into mixture alternately with the flour until smooth.
   Add baking powder, salt, persimmons and blend well.
   Mix in the pecans, hazelnuts and raisins.
3. Fold in the egg whites.
   Pour into a greased and floured baking pan.
4. Bake in a 350ºF oven for 25 to 30 minutes or until an inserted toothpick comes out clean.

∽

∽

Yellow Peach and Papaya Upside Down Cake

2 c.	All-Purpose Flour, sifted
½ c.	Buckwheat Flour, sifted
2½ tsp.	Baking Powder
½ tsp.	Sea Salt
1½ c.	Sugar, granulated
½ c.	Light Brown Sugar
½ c.	Crisco
2 ea.	Eggs, whole
2 tsp.	Vanilla
1 c.	Milk, cold
½ c.	Butter, melted
¼ tsp.	Nutmeg, ground
4 ea.	Yellow Peaches-peeled, cored & sliced
¾ c.	Papaya, skin removed & sliced

Method:
1. In a mixing bowl, add the flour, baking powder, salt, sugar and Crisco. Mix until mixture resembles course meal.
2. Slowly add the eggs one at a time until well incorporated. Add vanilla, milk, butter, nutmeg and mix well to a smooth consistency.
3. Place peaches and papaya on the bottom of a greased and floured baking pan. Pour batter mixture on top.
4. Bake in a 350ºF oven for 25 to 30 minutes or until an inserted toothpick comes out clean.
5. Let cake cool completely and invert upside down.

∽

෨

Zucchini Cake

2 c.	Zucchini, grated
2 c.	Sugar, granulated
½ tsp.	Sea Salt
1½ tsp.	Baking Soda
2 tsp.	Baking Powder
1 c.	Extra Virgin Olive Oil
2 tsp.	Vanilla
1½ tsp.	Cinnamon, ground
½ tsp.	Nutmeg, ground
½ tsp.	Ginger, ground
4 ea.	Egg Yolks
3 c.	All-Purpose Flour, sifted
½ c.	Buckwheat Flour, sifted
¾ c.	Walnuts, chopped
¾ c.	Dark Raisins
4 ea.	Egg Whites

Method:

1. In a mixing bowl, add the zucchini, sugar, salt, baking soda, baking powder, oil, vanilla and spices.
   Mix on 1st speed and blend well.
2. Add egg yolks one at a time and incorporate the flour into the mixture on 1st speed.
   Mix in the walnuts and raisins.
3. Fold in the egg whites.
   Pour into two well greased and floured cake pans.
4. Bake at 350ºF for 50 minutes or until an inserted toothpick comes out clean.

෨

CHEESECAKES

Baked Mango Cheesecake with a Graham Cracker and Pecan Crust, Served with Blended Mango and Mixed Berries
120

Berry Jam Cheesecake Topped with Mixed Berries
121

Delicate Chocolate Cheesecake
122

Lime and Mandarin Orange Cheesecake
123

Mini Royal Persimmon Cheesecakes
124

Peach Ricotta Cheesecake
125

꙰

Baked Mango Cheesecake with a Graham Cracker and Pecan Crust, Served with Blended Mango and Mixed Berries

Graham Cracker Crust:

1 c.	Graham Crackers, ground
1 c.	Pecans, ground
¼ c.	Butter, melted
¼ c.	Sugar, granulated
¼ tsp.	Cinnamon, ground
¼ tsp.	Nutmeg, ground

Method:
1. Combine all ingredients in a steel bowl and mix thoroughly. Place on bottom and sides of a spring form baking pan.

1½#	Cream Cheese, cut into bits
1¼ c.	Sugar, granulated
¾ c.	Sour Cream
1½ c.	Mango, seed removed & blended
1½ tsp.	Vanilla
½ c.	Buckwheat Flour, sifted
¼ tsp.	Sea Salt
3 ea.	Eggs, whole
As Needed	Mango, diced medium
As Needed	Assorted Mixed Berries

Method:
1. In a mixing bowl, add cream cheese, sugar, sour cream, mango, vanilla, flour and salt.
   Mix on 2nd speed and blend to a smooth consistency.
2. Add slowly the eggs one at a time and blend well.
   Pour into a graham cracker and pecan crust.
3. Bake in a 350ºF oven for 40 to 50 minutes or until an inserted toothpick comes out clean.
4. Remove from oven and let cool completely in refrigerator.
   Serve with diced mango and assorted mixed berries.

꙰

Berry Jam Cheesecake Topped with Mixed Berries

3#	Cream Cheese, cut into bits
¾#	Sugar, granulated
6 ea.	Eggs, whole
¾#	Sour Cream
3 oz.	Heavy Cream
6 oz.	Milk, whole
¼ c.	Buckwheat Flour, sifted
1 tsp.	Vanilla
1 ea.	Graham Cracker Crust
1 c.	Raspberry & Strawberry Jam
As Needed	Raspberries, whole
As Needed	Blueberries, whole
1 oz.	Simple Syrup

Method:
1. In a mixing bowl, combine the cream cheese, sugar and mix until smooth on 2nd speed.
2. Slowly add the eggs one at a time and blend well.
   Add heavy cream, milk, flour, vanilla, sour cream and blend to a smooth consistency.
   Pour into a graham cracker crust bottom spring form pan.
3. Drizzle jam in circles and swirl in the mixed berry jam.
4. Bake at 350ºF in a 160ºF water bath for 1 hour and 15 minutes.
5. Remove from oven and let cool completely.
   Top cheesecake with berries and brush with simple syrup.

∽

Delicate Chocolate Cheesecake

3#	Cream Cheese
1#	Sugar, granulated
4 oz.	Cornstarch, sifted
2 oz.	Buckwheat Flour, sifted
1 tsp.	Sea Salt
1 oz.	Heavy Cream
1½ tsp.	Vanilla
4 ea.	Eggs, whole
4 oz.	Butter, melted
2 oz.	Cocoa Powder, sifted
4 oz.	Dark Chocolate Chips (85% cocoa), melted
1 ea.	Graham Cracker Crust

Method:
1. In a mixing bowl, combine cream cheese, sugar, cornstarch, flour and salt.
   Mix to smooth consistency on 2nd speed.
   Add heavy cream, vanilla and blend until smooth.
2. Slowly add the eggs until well incorporated.
   Add slowly the melted butter, cocoa powder and melted chocolate.
   Pour into a graham cracker crust bottom spring form pan.
3. Bake at 275ºF in a 160ºF water bath for 1 hour and 45 minutes.
4. Remove from oven and let cool completely in refrigerator.

∽

∽

Lime and Mandarin Orange Cheesecake

3 #	Cream Cheese
¾ #	Sugar, granulated
6 ea.	Eggs, whole
12 oz.	Sour Cream
3 oz.	Heavy Cream
6 oz.	Milk, whole
3 oz.	Lime Juice, freshly squeezed
2 oz.	Buckwheat Flour, sifted
1 tsp.	Vanilla
1 c.	Mandarin Orange Jam
1 ea.	Graham Cracker Crust

Method:
1. In a mixing bowl, combine the cream cheese, sugar and mix until smooth on 2nd speed.
2. Incorporate the eggs one at a time.
   Slowly add the heavy cream, milk, vanilla, sour cream and mix to a smooth consistency.
   Add the lime juice, flour and blend until smooth.
3. Pour into a graham cracker crust bottom spring form pan.
   Swirl in the mandarin orange jam.
4. Bake at 350ºF in a 160ºF water bath for 1 hour and 15 minutes.
   Remove from oven and let cool completely in refrigerator.

∽

∾

Mini Royal Persimmon Cheesecakes

As Needed	Butter, whole
3 Tbl.	Cinnamon, ground
¼ c.	Sugar, granulated
3#	Cream Cheese
1#	Sugar, granulated
4 oz.	Cornstarch, sifted
2 oz.	Buckwheat Flour, sifted
1 tsp.	Sea Salt
1 oz.	Heavy Cream
1½ tsp.	Vanilla
3 ea.	Eggs, whole
3 ea.	Persimmon, skin removed & blended
4 oz.	Butter, melted
2 oz.	Lemon Juice, freshly squeezed
1 oz.	Lime Juice, freshly squeezed

Method:
1. Rub butter around mini baking pans.
   Combine the sugar, cinnamon in a steel bowl and cover sides of pan with the mixture.
2. In a mixing bowl, combine cream cheese, sugar, cornstarch, flour, salt and mix well on 2nd speed.
   Add heavy cream, vanilla and blend until smooth.
3. Slowly add the eggs until well incorporated.
   Fold in melted butter, lemon and lime.
   Pour into baking pans.
4. Bake at 275°F in a 160°F water bath for 50 minutes or until an inserted toothpick comes out clean.
   Remove from oven and let cool completely in refrigerator.

∾

∾

Peach Ricotta Cheesecake

1#	Cream Cheese
1½ c.	Sugar, granulated
½ ea.	Lemon Juice, freshly squeezed
2#	Ricotta Cheese
1 tsp.	Vanilla
4 ea.	Egg Yolks
5 Tbl.	Cornstarch, sifted
6 oz.	Sour Cream
4 oz.	Butter, melted
½ c.	Peaches, blended
4 ea.	Egg Whites, firm peaks
1 ea.	Graham Cracker Crust

Method:
1. In a mixing bowl, combine the cream cheese, sugar, lemon, ricotta cheese and vanilla.
   Mix on 1st speed and blend to a smooth consistency.
2. Slowly add the yolks one at a time until mixture is well incorporated.
   Add the cornstarch, sour cream and blend until smooth.
   Slowly add the melted butter, peaches and blend to a smooth consistency.
3. Fold in the egg whites into the mixture.
   Pour into a graham cracker crust bottom spring form pan.
4. Bake at 275ºF in a 260ºF water bath for 1 hour and 45 minutes.
   Remove from oven and let cool completely in refrigerator.

Topping:

½ c.	Sugar, granulated
3 Tbl.	Cinnamon, ground
½ tsp.	Nutmeg, ground

Method:
1. Mix together and add on top of cheesecake before serving.

∾

COOKIES & SMALL DESSERTS

Cream Cheese Raspberry Cookies
128
Honey Wheat Chocolate Chip Cookies
129
Crème Caramel with Caramelized Orange Sugar
130
Crepe Berry Turnovers with Vanilla Nutmeg Sauce,
Served with Vanilla Bean Ice cream
131
Hazelnut Chocolate Soufflés with a Chocolate Sabayon
133
Peach Papaya Cobbler, Served with Vanilla Bean Ice Cream
134
Puff Pastry with Poppy Cream Cheese
135
Rice Pudding Laced with Dark Sweet Raisins and Orange Zest
136
Strawberries Filled with Orange Cream Cheese, Garnished with Pecans
137

∾

∾

Cream Cheese Berry Cookies

¾ c.	Butter, whole
4 oz.	Cream Cheese
¾ c.	Sugar, confectioners'
2 tsp.	Lemon Juice, freshly squeezed
1 tsp.	Vanilla
1¾ c.	All-Purpose Flour, sifted
¼ c.	Buckwheat Flour, sifted
As Needed	Raspberry/Strawberry/Blueberry/Orange Marmalade/Blackberry Jams
As Needed	Coconut, finely ground
As Needed	Sugar, confectioners'

Method:
1. In a mixing bowl, add the butter, cream cheese, sugar, lemon and vanilla.
    Blend to a smooth consistency, add flour and mix thoroughly.
2. Place on a sheet pan into desired shapes and add one-half teaspoon of berry jam on top.
3. Bake in a 350ºF oven for 9 minutes or until lightly brown.
4. Mix equal parts coconut and sugar in a bowl.
    Sprinkle with coconut and confectioners' sugar on each cookie.

∾

∽

Honey Wheat Chocolate Chip Cookies

¾ c.	Butter, whole
¼ c.	Crisco
¾ c.	Sugar, granulated
½ c.	Light Brown Sugar, packed
½ tsp.	Sea Salt
1 tsp.	Vanilla
2 ea.	Eggs, whole
1¾ c.	All-Purpose Flour, sifted
¼ c.	Buckwheat Flour, sifted
1 tsp.	Baking Soda
¾ c.	Honey Wheat Germ/Oatmeal, finely ground
½ c.	Walnuts, coarsely chopped
¼ c.	Dark Sweet Raisins
½ c.	Semi-Sweet Chocolate Chips
1½ c.	Dark Chocolate (85% cocoa) Chips

Method:
1. In a mixing bowl, add butter, Crisco, sugar, salt and vanilla. Blend to a smooth consistency.
2. Incorporate the eggs one at a time and mix thoroughly. Slowly add the flour, baking soda and mix well. Add the honey wheat germ or oatmeal, walnuts, raisins and chocolate chips.
3. Place one tablespoonful of mixture on sheet pan.
4. Bake in a 325ºF oven for 9 minutes.

∽

‿

Crème Caramel with Caramelized Orange Sugar

Caramelized Orange Sugar:

1 c.	Sugar, granulated
¼ tsp.	Lemon Juice, freshly squeezed
3 Tbl.	Water, cold
As Needed	Orange marmalade

Method:
1. Rub butter in ramekins and refrigerate for 10 minutes.
2. In a heavy sauce pot, add sugar, lemon juice and water.
   Boil until sugar caramelizes on medium heat.
3. Take out ramekins and place a small amount of caramelized sugar on bottom.
   Let cool and place one teaspoonfuls of orange marmalade in center of ramekin.

3 ea.	Eggs, whole
2 ea.	Egg Yolks
4 oz.	Sugar, granulated
To Taste	Vanilla
2 c.	Milk, whole

Method:
1. In a steel bowl, add eggs, sugar and vanilla and mix well.
   In a sauce pot, bring the milk to a boil and add to the egg mixture, while whisking constantly.
   Place egg mixture back to the pot and let cool.
2. Pour into the caramelized orange ramekins.
3. Bake at 350°F in a 160°F water bath for 30 to 35 minutes.
4. Remove from oven and let cool overnight.
   Place ramekin upside down on desert plate and serve.

‿

∾

Crepe Berry Turnovers with Vanilla Nutmeg Sauce, Served with Vanilla Bean Ice cream

Vanilla Nutmeg Sauce:

1 c.	Half & Half, cold
1 ea.	Vanilla Bean, skin & seeds
2 oz.	Sugar, granulated
3 ea.	Egg Yolks
As Needed	Nutmeg, ground

Method:
1. In a sauce pot, add the half & half, vanilla and bring to a simmer.
2. In a steel bowl, add the sugar, yolks and whisk to a cold ribbon stage. Slowly pour the hot liquid into the yolk and sugar mixture, while whisking constantly.
3. Strain into a container and let cool in an ice bath to stop the cooking. Sprinkle with nutmeg on top and refrigerate until ready to use.

Crepes:

8 ea.	Eggs, whole
¼ tsp.	Sea Salt
1 Tbl.	Sugar, granulated
2 c.	Milk, whole
1¾ c.	All-Purpose Flour, sifted
¼ c.	Buckwheat Flour, sifted
Dash	Nutmeg, ground
1 c. or less	Water, cold

Method:
1. Place the eggs, salt, sugar, milk in a bowl and mix well.
2. Whisk in the flour, add nutmeg and mix thoroughly. Add the water to thin the mixture to a smooth consistency.
3. Place a thin layer in a hot sauté pan with no oil and spread out. Brown on both sides and let cool.

As Needed   Mixed Berries-blackberries, blueberries, raspberries, strawberries
As Needed   Vanilla Bean Ice cream
As Needed   Vanilla Sauce

1. Place Berries on crepe and roll to desired shape.
2. Shape vanilla ice cream on desert plate.
3. Pour vanilla nutmeg sauce over crepe.

ᔐ

Hazelnut Chocolate Soufflés with a Chocolate Sabayon

Hazelnut Chocolate Soufflés:

1 oz.	Butter, soft
1 oz.	Sugar, granulated
2 Tbl.	Buckwheat Flour, sifted
3 Tbl.	Cocoa Powder, sifted
½ oz.	Hazelnuts, finely chopped
6 oz.	Milk, whole & warm
½ tsp.	Vanilla
3 ea.	Egg Yolks
3 ea.	Egg Whites, stiff peaks
As Needed	Butter, whole

Method:
1. In a mixing bowl, add the butter, sugar and mix until creamy.
   Add flour, cocoa powder, hazelnuts and mix thoroughly.
2. Slowly add the heated milk and vanilla.
   Add yolks one at a time until well incorporated.
3. Fold egg whites into mixture a little at a time.
4. Rub butter in ramekins and refrigerate for 10 minutes.
   Bake at 425°F in a 160°F water bath for 15 minutes.

Chocolate Sabayon:

3 ea.	Egg Yolks
1¼ oz.	Sugar, granulated
1 tsp.	Vanilla
3 oz.	Marsala wine
2 oz.	Dark Chocolate Chips (85% cocoa), melted
¾ c.	Heavy Cream, whipped

Method:
1. Place the yolks, sugar, vanilla and wine in a steel bowl.
   In a double boiler, place steel bowl on top.
   Whisk until ribbon stage is formed under low heat.
2. Cool mixture completely and whisk in the cooled melted chocolate.
   Fold in the whipped cream.
3. Serve with hazelnut chocolate soufflés.

∽

Peach Papaya Cobbler, Served with Vanilla Bean Ice Cream

4 ea.	Peaches, peeled & cut into slices
1 ea.	Papaya, peeled & cut into slices
8 Tbl.	Butter, whole
1½ c.	Sugar, granulated
¾ c.	All-Purpose Flour, sifted
¼ c.	Buckwheat Flour, sifted
1½ Tbl.	Baking Powder
½ c.	Milk, whole
As Needed	Butter, whole
As Needed	Vanilla Bean Ice Cream
As Needed	Walnuts, coarsely chopped

Method:

1. Melt 4 tablespoons of butter in a medium saucepan.
   Add the fruit and one-half cup sugar.
   Stir in 2 tablespoonfuls of flour and simmer for 5-7 minutes,
   until fruit is soft and juice is syrupy.
2. In a medium steel bowl, combine the remaining cup of sugar, flour
   and baking powder.
   Whisk in the milk and mix to a smooth consistency.
   Add 4 tablespoonfuls of melted butter.
3. Rub butter into a baking dish.
   Pour in the batter, reserving about one-third of a cup for the top layer.
   Pour the peach papaya mixture over the top of the batter.
   Lightly pour the reserved batter over fruit mixture and spread
   around evenly to cover.
4. Bake in a 350ºF oven for 50 to 60 minutes or until an inserted
   toothpick comes out clean.
   Remove from oven and let cool overnight.
   Serve with Vanilla Bean Ice cream and chopped walnuts.

∽

Puff Pastry with Poppy Cream Cheese

1 sheet Puff Pastry
4 oz. Cream Cheese
3 Tbl. Poppy Seed Butter
½ tsp. Lemon Juice, squeezed

Method:
1. Cut puff pastry into desired diamond shapes.
2. Place in a 400ºF oven until brown, remove from oven and let cool completely.
3. Place cheese, poppy butter, lemon in a mixer and blend until smooth. Fill contents in pastry bag with a star tip and pipe out mixture. Serve on platter.

∾

Rice Pudding Laced with Dark Sweet Raisins and Orange Zest

6 c.	Milk, whole
2 c.	Water, cold
1 c.	White Rice, medium grain
4 oz.	Butter, whole
1½ c.	Sugar, granulated
1 tsp.	Vanilla
¼ c.	Dark Sweet Raisins
1 Tbl.	Orange Zest
Dash	Cinnamon, ground
Dash	Nutmeg, ground
½ c.	Whipped Cream

Method:
1. Combine the milk, water, white rice, butter, sugar, and vanilla into a sauce pot.
   Bring to a boil and simmer until rice is cooked.
2. Incorporate raisins and orange zest into mixture.
   Pour into a dish pan.
3. Sprinkle cinnamon and nutmeg on top.
   Let cool overnight and fold in whipped cream.

∾

⁀∽

Strawberries Filled with Orange Cream Cheese, Garnished with Pecans

8 oz.	Cream Cheese
½ tsp.	Orange Zest
½ tsp.	Parsley, freshly chopped
½ tsp.	Orange Liquor
1 pt.	Strawberries, stems on, washed & slit
As Needed	Pecans, finely chopped

Method:
1. In a mixing bowl, add cream cheese, orange zest, parsley, orange liquor and mix until smooth.
   Place mixture in a pastry bag with a star tip.
2. Stuff strawberries with mixture.
3. Sprinkle chopped pecans on strawberries.
   Serve on desired platter.

⁀∽

PIES

Acorn Squash Pie, Served with Whipped Cream
140
Lime Mint Cream Pie
141
Mini Apple and Orange Marmalade Crust Pies
142
Sour Cream Apple Pie, Served with Disaronno Sauce
144
Wild Blackberry Crust Pie, Served with Whipped Cream
146

DOUGHS

Pie Dough with Essence of Pecans
147
Pizza Dough with Fresh Oregano
148
Braided Sugar Raised Doughnuts
149

୦〜୨

Acorn Squash Pie, Served with Whipped Cream

30 oz.	Acorn Squash, cut in half & seeds removed
2 ea.	Pie Shells
4 ea.	Eggs, whole
1¼ c.	Sugar, Granulated
½ c.	Light Brown Sugar
½ tsp.	Sea Salt
2 tsp.	Cinnamon, ground
1 tsp.	Ginger, ground
½ tsp.	Cloves, ground
24 oz.	Milk, whole
As Needed	Whipped Cream
As Needed	Nutmeg, freshly ground

Method:

1. Place acorn with skin side up and add one-half cup of water on bottom of pan.
   Bake acorn squash in a 350°F oven for 50 minutes and let cool completely.
   Remove acorn squash from inside and discard shell.
2. Beat eggs lightly in large steel bowl.
   Whisk in the sugar, spices, acorn squash and milk.
   Pour mixture into pie shells.
3. Bake in a 350°F oven for 55 to 60 minutes or until an inserted toothpick comes out clean.
4. Let cool overnight and top with whipped cream.
   Sprinkle nutmeg on top of pie.

୦〜୨

Lime Mint Cream Pie

9-inch	Pie crust
¾ c.	Half & Half, cold
¼ c.	Mint, freshly chopped
¼ c.	Lime Juice, freshly squeezed
½ c.	Sugar, granulated
¼ c.	Cornstarch, sifted
3 ea.	Eggs, whole
As Needed	Whipped Cream
As Needed	Mint Leaves, garnish

Method:
1. In a sauce pot, heat the half & half, mint, lime and sugar.
   Strain and reserve one third of the mixture.
2. In a large steel bowl, beat the eggs, cornstarch and the reserved mixture.
   Temper heated mixture into the reserved mixture.
3. Pour into pie crust and bake in 350ºF oven for 30 to 40 minutes.
   Remove from oven and let cool overnight.
4. Place whipped cream on top.
   Garnish with mint leaves.

∾

Mini Apple and Orange Marmalade Crust Pies

Pastry:

¼ c.	Butter, whole & cut into small pieces
½ c.	Crisco
2 c.	All-Purpose Flour, sifted
¼ c.	Buckwheat Flour, sifted
¼ tsp.	Sea Salt
½ c. or more	Water, cold

Method:
1. Place the butter, flour and salt in a food processor.
   Pulse chop for 5 seconds.
2. Add water and process until a ball is formed.
   Place in refrigerator for one-half hour.
3. Shape dough into pie molds and refrigerate for 5 minutes.

Apple Orange Marmalade Filling:

½ c.   Orange Marmalade
2 tsp. Water
3 ea.   Cortland Apples-cored, peeled & sliced thin
½ c.   Sugar, granulated
1 Tbl. Butter, cut into shavings
2 Tbl. Orange Zest

1. Heat the orange marmalade with 2 teaspoons of water in a small saucepot.
2. Arrange overlapping apple slices to form a circle around pie dough. Place the sugar on top, then shavings of butter, then drip orange marmalade on top of the apples.
   Cover with double layer foil wrap and place in oven.
3. Bake in a 350ºF oven for 25 to 30 minutes.
4. Remove from oven and sprinkle pies with orange zest.

∾

Sour Cream Apple Pie, Served with Disaronno Sauce

Graham Cracker Crust:

½ c.	Graham Cracker, Crumbs
½ c.	Walnuts, finely chopped
¼ c.	Butter, melted
¼ c.	Sugar, granulated
¼ tsp.	Cinnamon, ground
¼ tsp.	Nutmeg, ground

Method:
1. Combine all ingredients in a steel bowl and blend well.
2. Place on bottom and sides of a pie pan.

2 ea.	Eggs, whole
8 oz.	Sour Cream
1 c.	Sugar, granulated
2 Tbl.	Buckwheat Flour, sifted
1 tsp.	Vanilla
¼ tsp.	Sea Salt
3 c.	Apples-skin & core removed, sliced thin
4 Tbl.	All-Purpose Flour, sifted
3 Tbl.	Butter, cold
¼ c.	Walnuts, coarsely chopped
¼ c.	Light Brown Sugar
1 ea.	Pie Shell

Method:
1. In a steel bowl, add eggs, sour cream, sugar, flour, vanilla and salt.
   Mix thoroughly and fold in the apples.
   Pour into a walnut graham cracker crust pie shell.
2. For the topping, add flour, cold butter, walnuts and light brown sugar.
   Mix until mixture resembles course meal and place on top pie mixture.
3. Bake in a 350ºF oven for 35 to 40 minutes.

Disaronno Sauce:

3 ea. Egg Yolks
½ c. Sugar, granulated
1 oz. Disaronno Liqueur
1 c. Whipped Cream

Method:
1. Whisk the yolks, sugar and Liqueur to a ribbon stage over a double boiler.
   Remove from stove and let cool completely.
2. Fold in whipped cream into the mixture.
3. Slice pie on dessert plate and serve with Disaronno sauce.

∽

Wild Blackberry Crust Pie, Served with Whipped Cream

Pastry:

¼ c.	Butter, whole & cut into small pieces
½ c.	Crisco
2 c.	All-Purpose Flour, sifted
¼ c.	Buckwheat Flour, sifted
¼ tsp.	Sea Salt
½ c. or more	Water, cold

Method:
1. Place the butter, flour and salt in a food processor.
   Pulse chop for 5 seconds.
2. Add water and process until a ball is formed.
   Place in refrigerator for one-half hour.
3. Shape dough into 9-inch pie mold and refrigerate for 5 minutes.

Wild Blackberry Filling:

5 c.	Wild Blackberries
1¼ c.	Sugar, granulated
½ c.	Cornstarch, sifted
1 tsp.	Minute Tapioca
1 Tbl.	Butter, cut into shavings
As Needed	Whipped Cream, soft peaks
As Needed	Mint Leaves, whole

Method:
1. Place in a steel bowl, wild blackberries, sugar and cornstarch.
2. Remove pie dough from refrigerator and spread out minute tapioca
   on the bottom.
3. Add wild blackberries and butter shavings on top.
   Shape another pie dough flat with a one-inch hole in the middle
   of pie and place on top.
4. Bake in a 375ºF oven for 45 to 50 minutes.
   Remove from oven, let cool and serve with whipped cream.
   Garnish with mint leaves.

∽

∽

Pie Dough with Essence of Pecans

1½ c.	All-Purpose Flour, sifted
¼ c.	Buckwheat Flour, sifted
½ c.	Pecans, finely chopped
¾ c.	Crisco
½ tsp.	Sea Salt
¾ c.	Water, cold

Method:
1. In a cuisinart, add the flour, pecans, Crisco and salt.
   Pulse mixture a few times until mixture forms a mealy texture.
2. Add water until a ball is formed.
   Place in refrigerator for one-half hour.
3. Roll out into desired shapes.

∽

∾

Pizza Dough with Fresh Oregano

1¼ c.	Water, warm
¼ c.	Milk, whole
2½ tsp.	Honey
1 pkg.	Yeast
5 Tbl.	Extra Virgin Olive Oil
1½ tsp.	Sea Salt
3 c.	Bread Flour, sifted
¼ c.	Rye Flour, sifted
¼ c.	Wheat Flour, sifted
3 Tbl.	Oregano, freshly chopped
½ tsp.	Parsley, freshly chopped
¼ tsp.	Thyme, freshly chopped
As Needed	Bread Flour, sifted

Method:
1. In a mixer, add the water, honey and sprinkle yeast on top.
   Let rest until bubble action occurs, approximately 10 minutes.
2. Add oil and salt.
   Add the rest of the ingredients in the mixer.
   Mix on 1st speed with dough hook until a ball is formed and mix
   another 3 minutes.
3. Let rise for one-half to one hour, punch dough down and let
   rise again for another 15 minutes.
4. Dust with bread flour and roll out into desired shapes.

∾

∾

Braided Sugar Raised Doughnuts

1 c.	Milk, warm
¼ c.	Water, warm
1 c.	Light Brown Sugar
1 pkg.	Dry Yeast
2 ea.	Eggs, whole
½ c.	Butter, softened
½ c.	Crisco
4¾ c.	All-Purpose Flour, sifted
¾ c.	Buckwheat Flour, sifted
1 tsp.	Sea Salt
1 tsp.	Cinnamon, ground
½ tsp.	Cardamom, ground
½ tsp.	Nutmeg, ground
As Needed	Olive Oil
As Needed	Sugar, granulated
As Needed	Cinnamon, ground

Method:
1. In a mixing bowl add milk, water, light brown sugar and sprinkle yeast on top.
   Let rest until bubble action occurs, approximately 10 minutes.
2. Add eggs, butter, Crisco, flour, salt and spices.
   Reserve one-half cup flour.
   Mix on 1st speed with dough hook, until ball is formed.
   Add reserved flour if dough is too wet.
3. Let rise for one hour, punch dough down and let rise again.
   Punch down again and cut into desired shapes.
4. Deep fry in olive oil until golden brown on both sides and drain on paper towel.
   Mix together the sugar and cinnamon.
   Sprinkle the sugar and cinnamon on top.

∾

∾

DRESSINGS

Balsamic Vinaigrette
152
Caesar Vinaigrette
153
Lemon Anchovy Vinaigrette
154
Raspberry Vinaigrette
155

∾

Balsamic Vinaigrette

8 oz.	Balsamic Vinegar
2½ oz.	White Wine Vinegar
2½ oz.	Red Wine Vinegar
½ oz.	Garlic, minced
½ oz.	Sea Salt
½ tsp.	Black Pepper, ground
1 tsp.	Dill, freshly chopped
1 tsp.	Basil, freshly chopped
1 tsp.	Oregano, freshly chopped
1 tsp.	Parsley, freshly chopped
½ oz.	Lemon Juice, freshly squeezed
½ oz.	Sugar, granulated
2½ oz.	Water, cold
10½ oz.	Extra Virgin Olive Oil

Method:
1. Add all ingredients in a steel bowl, except the olive oil.
   Whisk for 3 minutes until sugar is dissolved.
2. Slowly mix in the olive oil a few drops at a time.
3. Continue to add olive oil until vinaigrette is completely emulsified.

⁓

Caesar Vinaigrette

5 Tbl.	Garlic, minced
2 Tbl.	Scallions, white only & finely chopped
1 c.	Mayonnaise
½ c.	Mustard
2 c.	Water, cold
¼ c.	White Wine Vinegar
½ c.	Lemon Juice, squeezed
¼ oz.	Soy Sauce
3 oz.	Anchovy Fillets, mashed
1 tsp.	Parsley, freshly chopped
3 c.	Extra Virgin Olive Oil

Method:
1. Sauté garlic, onions in 1 tablespoon of olive oil and let cool.
2. Combine all ingredients in a steel bowl, except the olive oil. Blend thoroughly making a paste like mixture.
3. Whisk ingredients together while slowly adding the olive oil to a smooth consistency.
   Keep refrigerated until ready to use.

⁓

∽

Lemon Anchovy Vinaigrette

1 ea.	Egg Yolk
½ oz.	Anchovies, mashed
½ tsp.	Dijon Mustard
1 ea.	Shallots, minced
½ tsp.	Sour Cream
2 Tbl.	Lemon-juice, freshly squeezed
1 tsp.	Lemon Zest
¼ c.	Extra Virgin Olive Oil

Method:
1. Combine all ingredients in a steel bowl, except the olive oil. Blend thoroughly making a paste like mixture.
2. Whisk ingredients together while slowly adding the olive oil to a smooth consistency.
3. Keep refrigerated until ready to use.

∽

∾

Raspberry Vinaigrette

1 oz.	Red Wine Vinegar
¼ oz.	Raspberry Vinegar
2 Tbl.	Water, cold
10 ea.	Fresh Raspberries-whole & puree
1 tsp.	Sugar, granulated
1 Tbl.	Parsley, freshly chopped
¼ c.	Extra Virgin Olive Oil
To Taste	Sea Salt
To Taste	Black Pepper, ground

Method:

1. In a steel bowl, add the vinegar, water, raspberry puree, sugar and parsley.
   Whisk for 3 minutes until sugar is dissolved.
2. Slowly mix in the olive oil a few drops at a time.
   Continue to add olive oil until vinaigrette is completely emulsified.
3. Season to taste.

∾

∽

DUCK

Duck Cordon Bleu with Proscuitto Ham and Smoked Gouda Cheese,
Breaded and Deep Fried with a Garlic Herb Port Cream Sauce
158
Breast of Duck with a Ginger and Wild Mushroom Brown Sauce
160
Roasted Duck with an Orange Velouté Brown Sauce
161

∽

∾

Duck Cordon Bleu with Proscuitto Ham and Smoked Gouda Cheese, Breaded and Deep Fried with a Garlic Herb Port Cream Sauce

Garlic Herb Port Cream Sauce:

2 Tbl.	Vidalia Onions, minced
2 Tbl.	Extra Virgin Olive Oil
1 cl.	Garlic, minced
¼ tsp.	Thyme, freshly chopped
¼ tsp.	Basil, freshly chopped
¼ c.	Port
¼ c.	Chicken Stock, cold
¼ c.	Half & Half, hot
1 Tbl.	Roux, warm

1. Sauté onions, garlic in olive oil, then add herbs.
   Deglaze with wine and reduce by one-half.
2. Add chicken stock and reduce by one-half again.
   Stir in half & half and simmer for 15 minutes.
3. Whisk in roux to a smooth consistency and simmer for another
   10 minutes.
4. Strain sauce into another sauce pot.

4-(8 oz.) each	Duck Breast, skin off & fat removed
To Taste	Sea Salt
To Taste	Black Pepper, ground
To Taste	Thyme, freshly chopped
2 oz.	Proscuitto Ham, sliced thin
4 ea.	Gouda Cheese, sliced thin
As Needed	Buckwheat Flour, sifted
2 ea.	Eggs, whole
3 c.	Bread Crumbs
½ c.	Parmesan Cheese, grated
1 Tbl.	Parsley, finely chopped
As Needed	Olive Oil

Method:

1. Pound duck out on both sides.
   Season and add one slice of Proscuitto and one slice of Gouda
   Cheese, then fold sides inward.
   Plastic wrap duck and place in freezer for one hour.
2. In a steel bowl, mix together the bread crumbs, parmesan cheese
   and parsley.
   Place duck in flour and shake excess off, egg wash and then the
   bread mixture.
3. Deep fry duck until golden brown and drain on paper towel.
   Place duck in a 350ºF oven for 25 to 30 minutes.
4. Serve with garlic herb port cream sauce.

∾

∽

Breast of Duck with a Ginger and Wild Mushroom Brown Sauce

2 ea.	Duck Breast, with skin on & pounded out slightly
As Needed	Buckwheat Flour, sifted
1 Tbl.	Extra Virgin Olive Oil
½ tsp.	Ginger, freshly grated
1 tsp.	Shallots, minced
1 cl.	Garlic, minced
3 Tbl.	Brandy
¼ c.	Portabella Mushrooms, julienne
¼ c.	Chanterelle Mushrooms, cut in quarters
¾ c.	Brown Stock, cold
1 Tbl.	Roux, warm

Method:
1. Dredge duck in flour and shake excess off.
   Sauté duck in olive oil on both sides and finish in a 350ºF oven until proper doneness.
   Remove duck from oven, let rest for 15 minutes and keep warm.
2. In the same sauté pan, drain fat, add olive oil, ginger, shallots, garlic and sweat.
   Deglaze with brandy and sauté mushrooms.
3. Add brown stock and bring to a boil.
   Whisk in roux to a smooth consistency and simmer for another 7 minutes.
4. Slice duck on the bias and serve with sauce.

∽

∾

Roasted Duck with an Orange Velouté Brown Sauce

Duck Smear:

½ tsp.	Basil, dried
½ tsp.	Thyme, dried
½ tsp.	Marjoram, dried
½ tsp.	Tarragon, dried
½ tsp.	Sage, dried
½ tsp.	Poultry Seasoning, ground
2 tsp.	Black Pepper, ground
1 tsp.	Sea Salt
¼ c.	Extra Virgin Olive Oil

Method:
1. Combine all ingredients to a steel bowl and mix thoroughly.
2. Place in refrigerator overnight.

1 ea.	Duck, whole
As Needed	Duck Smear
1 ea.	Orange, cut into quarters
1 ea.	Onion, cut into quarters
1 ea.	Apple, cut into quarters
As Needed	Butchers Twine

Method:
1. Stuff duck with the orange, onion and apple.
   Squeeze some of the juice of the orange on top.
2. Tightly wrap with butchers twine.
   Rub duck smear around duck.
3. In a roasting pan with a grill on the bottom, place duck on top.
   Place in a 375ºF oven for 1½ hours or until done and skin is crispy.
4. Remove from oven, let rest for 15 minutes, remove contents inside duck and discard.

∾

⌒〜

Orange Velouté Brown Sauce:

1 cl.	Garlic, minced
1 ea.	Shallot, minced
1 Tbl.	Extra Virgin Olive Oil
¼ c.	Grand Marnier
1 Tbl.	Parsley, freshly chopped
½ tsp.	Thyme, freshly chopped
¼ c.	Orange Juice
1½ Tbl.	Orange Zest, julienne
½ c.	Brown Sauce, hot
½ c.	Chicken Velouté, hot

Method:
1. Sauté the garlic and shallots in olive oil.
   Deglaze with Grand Marnier.
   Add herbs, orange juice, orange rind and simmer until almost gone.
2. Stir in the brown sauce, velouté, bring to a boil and simmer for
   5 minutes.
3. Strain sauce and serve with duck.

⌒〜

~∾

LAMB

Lamb Carpaccio, Smoked Salmon and Avocado with a Dijon Mint
Horseradish Sauce, Served with Fresh Seasonal Greens
164
Lamb Pot Roast with Big Carrots, Creamy Rutabaga Potatoes
And Pot Roast Brown Sauce
166
Marinated Lamb Shanks with a White Bean and Tomato Garlic Puree,
Served with a Mango Apple Sauce
168
Mini Lamb Shanks with Rosemary Mint Sauce and White Beans
170
Roasted Lamb with Mint Hollandaise Sauce,
Served with Parsley Couscous and Grilled Asparagus
172
Sautéed Lamb Cutlets, Served with Bacon and Savoy Cabbage
174

~∾

∾

Lamb Carpaccio, Smoked Salmon and Avocado With a Dijon Mint Horseradish Sauce, Served with Fresh Seasonal Greens

Dijon Mint Horseradish Sauce:

¼ c.	Horseradish, fresh
¼ c.	Sour Cream
¼ c.	Mayonnaise
2 Tbl.	Dijon Mustard
¼ tsp.	Dry Mustard
2 Tbl.	Mint Jelly
½ tsp.	Garlic Powder
½ tsp.	Parsley, freshly chopped
To Taste	Sea Salt
To Taste	White Pepper, ground

Method:
1. Combine ingredients in a steel bowl and mix well.

1 ea.	Lamb, trimmed & boneless
¼ c.	Extra Virgin Olive Oil
As Needed	Sea Salt
As Needed	Black Pepper, cracked
As Needed	Thyme, freshly chopped
As Needed	Oregano, freshly chopped
1 ea.	Avocado, sliced
2 oz.	Smoked Salmon
As Needed	Seasonal Greens
As Needed	Italian Vinaigrette
Garnish	Chives, cut ½ inch

Method:
1. Rub olive oil over entire area of the lamb.
   Mix all spice ingredients together and coat lamb.
   Sear on all sides and keeping lamb very rare.
2. Place in the freezer until ready to use.
   Remove from freezer, slice thinly.
3. Arrange lamb, avocado, smoked salmon and seasonal greens with vinaigrette on salad plate.
4. Serve with dijon horseradish sauce and garnish with chives.

∾

Lamb Pot Roast with Big Carrots, Creamy Rutabaga Potatoes And Pot Roast Brown Sauce

3#	Lamb, trimmed & boneless
To Taste	Sea Salt
To Taste	Black Pepper, ground
As Needed	Buckwheat Flour, sifted
As Needed	Extra Virgin Olive Oil
1 c.	Shiraz
1 ea.	Tomato, cut in quarters
2 ea.	Bay Leaf, whole
2 Tbl.	Thyme, freshly chopped
2 Tbl.	Oregano, freshly chopped
1 Tbl.	Rosemary, freshly chopped
1 Tbl.	Parsley, freshly chopped
1 tsp.	Marjoram, freshly chopped
3 cl.	Garlic, whole
1 ea.	Onion, quartered large
2 ea.	Celery ribs, cut into large pieces
5 ea.	Carrots, peeled with ends removed & cut in half on the bias
1¼ gal.	Beef Stock, cold

Method:
1. Season lamb, flour on all sides and dust off excess.
   Add oil to a large roasting pot and sear on all sides.
2. Remove lamb and deglaze with wine.
   Add lamb and the rest of the ingredients and bring to a boil.
   Place a lid on roasting pot, reduce heat and let simmer for 2 hours or until lamb is tender.
3. Remove lamb, carrots and strain the broth.
   Reserve 1 quart broth for pot roast brown sauce.

3 ea.	Lamb, sliced
4 oz.	Creamy Rutabaga Potatoes
3 ea.	Carrots, peeled & cut on bias

Method:
1. Arrange on oval plate the sliced lamb, creamy rutabaga potatoes and big carrots.
2. Place pot roast brown sauce on the side.

Creamy Rutabaga Potatoes:

2 c. Potatoes, peeled & diced large
1 c. Rutabaga, diced small
1 cl. Garlic, minced
½ ea. Onion, diced small
¼ tsp. Thyme, freshly chopped
1 tsp. Sea Salt

Method:
1. Add all ingredients in a pot with water to cover.
   Bring to a boil and simmer until rutabaga is done.
2. Drain well and mash in ricer.
   Place in mixing bowl, add butter and mix well.
3. Slowly add the milk and blend to a smooth consistency.

Pot Roast Brown Sauce:

¼ c. Shiraz
½ tsp. Thyme, freshly chopped
½ tsp. Oregano, freshly chopped
½ tsp. Parsley, freshly chopped
1½ qts. Broth from stew, strained
2 oz. Roux, warm
To Taste Sea Salt
To Taste Black Pepper, ground

Method:
1. Add wine and herbs into a sauce pot.
   Bring to a simmer and reduce until wine is almost gone.
2. Add broth, bring to a boil and simmer for 15 minutes.
   Whisk in roux and simmer for another 10 minutes.
3. Strain sauce and season to taste.

∾

Marinated Lamb Shanks with a White Bean and Tomato Garlic Puree, Served with a Mango Apple Sauce

2 cl.	Garlic, minced
2 Tbl.	Parsley, freshly chopped
1 tsp.	Thyme, freshly chopped
1 tsp.	Rosemary, freshly chopped
½ tsp.	Oregano, freshly chopped
1 ea.	Bay Leaf, whole
To Taste	Sea Salt
To Taste	Black Pepper, cracked
½ c.	Pinot Noir
¼ c.	Extra Virgin Olive Oil
3-(2 oz.) each	Lamb Shank
1 Tbl.	Olive Oil
As Needed	Rosemary, whole

Method:
1. Combine the garlic, herbs, wine and oil in a steel pan.
   Add lamb shanks, cover with plastic wrap and refrigerate overnight.
2. Sauté lamb shanks in olive oil, remove from pan and keep warm.
3. Arrange white bean and tomato garlic puree on entrée plate with lamb shanks on top.
   Arrange mango apple sauce and garnish with fresh rosemary.

White Bean and Tomato Garlic Puree:

6 oz.	White Navy Beans, cooked
¼ tsp.	Thyme, freshly chopped
½ ea.	Bay Leaf, whole
1 ea.	Shallot, diced small
3 cl.	Garlic, minced
To Taste	Sea Salt
To Taste	White Pepper, ground
1 Tbl.	Water, cold
¼ c.	Plum Tomatoes-skin, core & seeds removed & diced small

Method:
1. In a small pot, add the white navy beans, herbs, shallot, garlic, salt, white pepper and water.
   Simmer for 5 minutes and pass through a fine mesh strainer.
2. Fold in tomatoes and keep warm.

Mango Apple Sauce:

½ c.	Mango-peeled, seed removed & diced small
2 Tbl.	Cortland Apple-core & skin removed, small diced
1 Tbl.	Orange Juice

Method:
1. In a small pot, add the mango, Cortland apple and orange juice. Simmer for 5 minutes, pass through a fine mesh strainer and keep warm.

☙

∾

Mini Lamb Shanks with Rosemary Mint Sauce And White Beans

3 Tbl.	Extra Virgin Olive Oil
As Needed	Buckwheat Flour, sifted
10 oz.	Lamb Shank
½ c.	Carrot, diced small
1½ c.	Celery, diced small
1 c.	Onion, diced small
3 cl.	Garlic, minced
Pinch	Rosemary, freshly chopped
Pinch	Thyme, freshly chopped
Pinch	Parsley, freshly chopped
1 Tbl.	Curry, ground
½ Tbl.	Cumin, ground
1 Tbl.	Tomato Paste
3½ c.	Beef Stock, cold
To Taste	Sea Salt
To Taste	Black Pepper, ground

Method:
1. Dredge Lamb Shank in flour, shake off excess and sauté in olive oil until golden brown.
   Remove from pan and keep warm.
2. Degrease pan, sauté vegetables, add herbs and tomato paste. Stir in stock, let boil and simmer for 10 minutes.
3. Add lamb back into the pan with a lid and simmer for 1 hour.

Rosemary Mint Sauce:

2½ c.	Lamb Liquid
1 Tbl.	Rosemary, freshly chopped
2 Tbl.	Mint Jelly
1 Tbl.	Roux, warm
To Taste	Sea Salt
To Taste	Black Pepper, ground

Method:
1. In a sauce pot, add liquid, rosemary, mint jelly, bring to a boil and simmer for 10 minutes.
2. Whisk in roux and simmer to a smooth consistency. Season to taste and strain sauce.

White Beans:

1 c.	Navy White Beans, cooked
¼ c.	Chicken Stock, cold
Pinch	Thyme, freshly chopped
To Taste	Sea Salt
To Taste	Black Pepper, ground
As Needed	Spinach, julienne

Method:
1. In a small sauce pot, heat the navy white beans, stock and thyme. Place contents in cuisinart and blend to a smooth consistency.
2. Fold in the fresh spinach.

∾

∾

Roasted Lamb with Mint Hollandaise Sauce, Served with Parsley Couscous and Grilled Asparagus

3#	Lamb with bone-in, whole
Pinch	Rosemary, freshly chopped
Pinch	Thyme, freshly chopped
Pinch	Oregano, freshly chopped
To Taste	Sea Salt
To Taste	Black Pepper, ground
12 ea.	Asparagus, grilled for 3 minutes with olive oil
1½ c.	Couscous, cooked
3 Tbl.	Parsley, freshly chopped
4 ea.	Plum Tomatoes-skin, core & seeds removed & sliced, marinated in Italian dressing for 20 minutes

Method:
1. Roast lamb in a 275ºF oven for 1½ hours or desired doneness. Remove lamb and let rest for 20 minutes.
2. Slice portion on entrée plate.
3. Fold in parsley to couscous and serve with lamb.
4. Arrange asparagus, sliced tomatoes and mint hollandaise sauce on entrée plate.

For Mint Hollandaise Sauce:

½ oz.	White Vinegar
3 ea.	Black Peppercorns, whole
2 Tbl.	Riesling
1 Tbl.	Mint, freshly chopped
2 ea.	Egg Yolks
8 oz.	Clarified Butter, melted
To Taste	Tabasco
To Taste	Sea Salt

Method:
1. Place vinegar, pepper, water, mint in a sauce pot and reduce.
   Strain liquid into a steel bowl with the egg yolks.
   Whisk under a double boiler until ribbon stage.
2. Slowly add the butter to a thick consistency.
3. Season to taste.

Sautéed Lamb Cutlets, Served with Bacon and Savoy Cabbage

6 oz.	Lamb, sliced into cutlets & pounded out
As Needed	Buckwheat Flour, sifted
Pinch	Rosemary, freshly chopped
Pinch	Thyme, freshly chopped
Pinch	Oregano, freshly chopped
To Taste	Sea Salt
To Taste	Black Pepper, ground
3 Tbl.	Extra Virgin Olive Oil

Method:
1. Season lamb and dredge in flour.
2. Sauté lamb on both sides until golden brown and arrange on entrée plate.

4 oz.	Savoy Cabbage, sliced thinly
1 oz.	Bacon, cooked & finely chopped
To Taste	Sea Salt
To Taste	Black Pepper, cracked
½ tsp.	Sesame Seeds
½ tsp	Thyme, finely chopped

Method:
1. Sauté savoy cabbage until tender and season to taste. Incorporate bacon, sesame seeds, thyme into cabbage and arrange on entrée plate.

Rosemary Mint Brown Sauce:

¼ c.	Brown Sauce
1 Tbl.	Rosemary, freshly chopped
2 Tbl.	Mint Jelly
To Taste	Sea Salt
To Taste	Black Pepper, ground
½ tsp.	Rosemary & Mint, finely chopped

Method:
1. In a sauce pot, add brown sauce, rosemary, mint jelly, bring to a boil and simmer for 5 minutes.
   Season to taste and strain sauce.
2. Garnish with fresh herbs.

~

APPETIZERS

Chicken Galantine with a Persimmon Sauce
178
Crabcakes on a Bed of Julienne Spinach with an Herb Mustard Aioli
180
Crabmeat Tuna Soufflés
182
**Mini Quiche with Choice Bits of Mushrooms,
Carrots, Broccoli, Pancetta or Cheese**
183
**Roasted Garlic, Tomato Basil and Provolone
Cheese on French Italian Bread**
184
**Rolled Eggplant Stuffed with Goat Cheese and Lump Crabmeat,
Served with Fresh Plum Tomatoes**
185
Salmon Terrine with Avocado and Shrimp, Served with a Kiwi Fig Sauce
186
Shrimp and Crabmeat Pouches
188
Uncle Paul's Fresh Herb Tomato Sauce
189

~

Chicken Galantine with a Persimmon Sauce

Persimmon Sauce:

1 ea.   Persimmons, skin removed
1 Tbl. Orange Juice

Method:
1. Place ingredients in cuisinart and blend to a smooth consistency.
2. Refrigerate until ready to use.

Yellow Pepper Sauce:

¼ ea.   Yellow Pepper-roasted, skin & seeds removed
To Taste Tabasco

Method:
1. Place yellow pepper in blender and mix to a smooth consistency.
2. Refrigerate until ready to use.

2 ea.   Chicken Tenderloin, sinew removed
1 ea.   Seaweed Sheet
24 oz. Chicken Breast-skin reserved & meat diced
2 ea.   Egg, whole
16 oz. Half & Half, cold
1 tsp. Thyme, freshly chopped
½ tsp. Basil, freshly chopped
½ tsp. Chives, freshly chopped
¼ tsp. Parsley, freshly chopped
¼ tsp. Black Peppercorns, coarsely chopped
¼ tsp. Pink Peppercorns, coarsely chopped
To Taste Sea Salt
1 Tbl. Black Olives, diced
3 Tbl. Proscuitto Ham, diced

Method:

1. Wrap chicken tenderloin in seaweed with water and freeze for 1 hour.
2. In a cuisinart, add diced chicken and pulse blend a few times.
   Add egg, pulse blend again and add herbs.
   Slowly add half & half, while blending the mixture in a steady stream.
   Place mixture in a steel bowl.
   Fold in the peppercorns, salt, black olives and proscuitto.
3. Working with plastic wrap folded on a flat surface, place the skin on the bottom.
   Place the mixture on the skin evenly and then the tenderloin in the middle.
   Form with plastic wrap until completely shaped into a roll.
   Plastic wrap the entire chicken again and then use foil wrap to cover chicken completely.
4. Place in a 160°F water bath until the internal temperature is 135°F.
   Remove chicken from water bath and let cool for 1 hour.
   Place chicken in refrigerator until ready for service.
5. Remove wrap and slice thin on salad plate.
6. Serve with persimmon sauce and garnish with roasted yellow pepper sauce.

∾

Crabcakes on a Bed of Julienne Spinach with an Herb Mustard Aioli

Crabcakes:

1 Tbl.	Extra Virgin Olive Oil
1 tsp.	Celery, finely chopped
1 Tbl.	Red Pepper, finely chopped
1 tsp.	Dill, freshly chopped
1 tsp.	Chives, freshly chopped
1 tsp.	Parsley, freshly chopped
¼ c.	Pinot Grisgio
5 oz.	Lump Crabmeat
¼ c.	Shrimp Stock, cold
2 Tbl.	Cream Cheese
To Taste	Old Bay Seasoning
To Taste	Sea Salt
To Taste	White Pepper, ground
As Needed	Bread Crumbs
As Needed	Extra Virgin Olive Oil
1 c.	Spinach, stems removed & julienne

Method:
1. In a sauté pan, sweat celery and red pepper in olive oil.
   Add herbs, deglaze with wine and reduce until liquid is almost gone.
   Let mixture cool and add in a steel bowl.
2. Add crabmeat, stock, cream cheese, bread crumbs and mix well.
   Season appropriately and form into two round shapes.
3. Sauté crabcakes in olive oil on both sides until golden brown.
   Serve with julienne of spinach and herb mustard aioli.

Herb Mustard Aioli:

3 ea.	Egg Yolks
2 cl.	Garlic, minced
2 Tbl.	Pinot Grisgio
3 Tbl.	Dijon Mustard
¼ tsp.	Old Bay Seasoning
2 tsp.	Dill, freshly chopped
1 tsp.	Thyme, freshly chopped
1 tsp.	Parsley, freshly chopped
6 oz.	Extra Virgin Olive Oil

Method:
1. Place yolks, garlic and wine in a steel bowl.
   Whisk under a low flame until fluffy, being careful not to scramble egg yolks.
   Let cool in refrigerator for 5 minutes.
2. Remove from refrigerator and place contents in a blender.
3. Add mustard, herbs and pulse blend.
   In a steady stream, add olive oil and blend to a smooth consistency.

∽

Crabmeat Tuna Soufflés

1 Tbl.	Butter, softened
2 cl.	Garlic, minced
1 Tbl.	Scallion, white only & finely chopped
1 ea.	Bay Leaf, whole
2 ea.	Peppercorn, crushed
1 c.	Milk, cold
2 Tbl.	Butter, cut into bits
1 ea.	Shallots, minced
4 Tbl.	Buckwheat Flour, sifted
3 ea.	Egg Yolks
8 oz.	Lump Crabmeat
2 oz.	Solid White Tuna, flaked
1 Tbl.	Locatelli Cheese, shaved
½ tsp.	Dill, finely chopped
Pinch	Old Bay Seasoning
5 ea.	Egg Whites, whipped

Method:
1. Rub butter around soufflé bowl and place in refrigerator for 5 minutes.
2. Place garlic, scallion, bay leaf, peppercorn, milk in a small pot and heat contents.
3. In another pot, melt the butter, shallots and then add flour to form a roux.
   Slowly add the heated milk and whisk to a smooth consistency.
   Whisk in the yolks and fold in crabmeat, tuna, locatelli cheese, dill and season.
4. Fold in the egg whites to a smooth consistency and place in soufflé bowl.
5. Bake in a 375°F oven for 30 minutes.

∽

∽

Mini Quiche with Choice Bits of Mushrooms, Carrots, Broccoli, Pancetta or Cheese

3 c.	All-Purpose Flour, sifted
¼ c.	Buckwheat Flour, sifted
1 Tbl.	Chives, freshly chopped
1 Tbl.	Red Wine Vinegar
1 tsp.	Sea Salt
9 oz.	Butter, cut into bits
1 ea.	Egg, whole
¼ c.	Water, cold

Method:
1. In a cuisinart, mix the flour, chives, vinegar, salt and butter. Add the egg and pulse the mixture.
2. Slowly add the water until a ball is formed.

2 c.	Half & Half, cold
3 ea.	Eggs, medium
Pinch	Nutmeg, ground
To Taste	Sea Salt
To Taste	White Pepper, ground
8 oz.	Swiss Cheese, grated fine
2 Tbl.	Butter, cold
3 Tbl.	Button Mushrooms, finely chopped
3 Tbl.	Carrots, finely chopped
3 Tbl.	Broccoli, finely chopped
3 Tbl.	Pancetta, finely chopped

Method:
3. In a steel bowl, add eggs and whisk for 1 minute. Add half & half slowly and then add nutmeg, salt and pepper. Stir in 2 ounces of grated cheese.
4. Butter molds and place in the refrigerator for 5 minutes. Add grated cheese and one type of vegetable in each mold.
5. Place egg mixture in molds two thirds of the way up.
6. Bake in a 350ºF oven for 15 minutes or until an inserted toothpick comes out clean.

∽

∾

Roasted Garlic, Tomato Basil and Provolone Cheese on French Italian Bread

4 slices	French Italian Bread, sliced & lightly toasted
1 bulb	Roasted Garlic
1 Tbl.	Extra Virgin Olive Oil
2 ea.	Plum Tomatoes-skin, core & seeds removed, diced small
1 Tbl.	Basil, freshly chopped
3 Tbl.	Shiraz
To Taste	Sea Salt
To Taste	Black Pepper, ground
2 ea.	Provolone Cheese, cut into strips
1 tsp.	Parsley & Basil, freshly chopped

Method:
1. Place bulb of garlic in a roasting pan and rub olive oil around bulb. Place in oven and roast until tender, approximately 45 minutes.
2. In a sauté pan, add tomatoes, basil, reduce and deglaze with wine. Season to taste and let cool for 3 minutes.
3. Rub bread with roasted garlic and lightly toast. Add tomato mixture on top of toast. Place provolone cheese on top and grill until melted.
4. Garnish with fresh herbs.

∾

∽

Rolled Eggplant Stuffed with Goat Cheese and Lump Crabmeat, Served with Fresh Plum Tomatoes

1 ea.	Eggplant, ends peeled & sliced thin
As Needed	Extra Virgin Olive Oil
1 ea.	Egg, whole
4 oz.	Goat Cheese
1 oz.	Lump Crabmeat
½ tsp.	Oregano, freshly chopped
¼ tsp.	Thyme, freshly chopped
To Taste	Sea Salt
To Taste	Black Pepper, ground
6 ea.	Plum Tomatoes-skin, core & seeds removed, diced medium
½ tsp.	Parsley & Basil, freshly chopped
As Needed	Asiago Cheese, shaved

Method:
1. Grill eggplant on both sides, let cool and set aside.
2. In a steel bowl, add egg, goat cheese, lump crab meat, herbs and season. Place cheese mixture on top of eggplant and roll up into a round. Arrange eggplant in a baking dish with diced tomatoes.
3. Bake in a 350°F oven for 30 minutes.
4. Arrange eggplant on entrée plate, Asiago cheese and garnish with fresh herbs.

∽

∽

Salmon Terrine with Avocado and Shrimp, Served with a Kiwi Fig Sauce

Avocado and Shrimp:

1 Tbl.	Extra Virgin Olive Oil
1 tsp.	Garlic, minced
1 tsp.	Shallots, minced
2 Tbl.	Pinot Grisgio
1 tsp.	Parsley, freshly chopped
¼ ea.	Avocado, small diced
4 oz.	Shrimp-peeled, de-veined & diced small
1 ea.	Egg, whole
1 oz.	Heavy Cream, cold

Method:
1. In a sauté pan, sweat the garlic and shallots in olive oil.
   Deglaze with wine, add parsley, let cool, place in a bowl with the avocado and shrimp.
   Mix well and place in refrigerator for 20 minutes.
2. In a cuisinart, add mixture and pulse blend a few times.
   Add egg, blend mixture and slowly add the heavy cream.
3. Place mixture on plastic wrap, shape until a roll is formed and freeze for 1 hour.

14 oz.	Salmon, raw filet
To Taste	Sea Salt
½ tsp.	Dill, freshly chopped
Pinch	Parsley, freshly chopped
Pinch	Cayenne Pepper, ground
1 ea.	Eggs, whole
9 oz.	Heavy Cream
3 Tbl.	Capers
3 Tbl.	Sun Dried Tomatoes, finely chopped
As Needed	Extra Virgin Olive Oil

Method:
1. In a cuisinart, add salmon, herbs and pulse blend a few times.
    Add egg and mix well.
    Slowly add the heavy cream, blend well and place mixture in bowl.
    Fold in capers and sun dried tomatoes.
2. Line terrine with olive oil and place half of the Salmon mixture on the bottom.
    Take out avocado shrimp roll, unwrap and place on bottom of Salmon mixture.
    Place the rest of the Salmon mixture on top.
3. Bake in a 160ºF water bath at an internal temperature of 135ºF.
    Remove from oven, let cool for 1 hour and place in the refrigerator overnight.
4. Remove wrap, slice thinly and serve with kiwi fig sauce.

Kiwi Fig Sauce:

> *1 ea.* Kiwi, skin removed
> *1 ea.* Fig, skin removed

Method:
1. Place ingredients in blender and blend to a smooth consistency.

༺༻

∾

Shrimp and Crabmeat Pouches

As Needed	Wonton Sheets
¼#	Shrimp-peeled, de-veined & ground
¼#	Lump Crabmeat
1 Tbl.	Soy Sauce
1 tsp.	Garlic, minced
1 Tbl.	Extra Virgin Olive Oil
2 oz.	Goat Cheese
2 Tbl.	Chicken Stock, cold
¼ tsp.	Sea Salt
¼ tsp.	White Pepper, ground
1 ea.	Scallions, minced
2 c.	Savoy Cabbage, julienne & steamed for 2 minutes
1 tsp.	Cornstarch, sifted
1 Tbl.	Riesling
2 tsp.	Cornstarch, in a little water
As Needed	Olive Oil

Method:
1. In a steel bowl, add the shrimp, crabmeat, soy sauce, garlic and olive oil. Add the goat cheese, chicken stock, salt, pepper, scallions, cabbage, cornstarch and wine.
2. Shape and fill wontons with the mixture and seal with a little cornstarch in water.
   Place in freezer for 10 minutes.
3. Deep fry to a light golden brown.
   Let pouches drain on paper towel.

∾

∾

Uncle Paul's Fresh Herb Tomato Sauce

2 oz.	Extra Virgin Olive Oil
3 cl.	Garlic, minced
¾ c.	Onions, minced
½ c.	Carrots, diced small
½ c.	Celery, diced small
½ ea.	Roasted Red Bell Pepper, diced small
2 Tbl.	Basil, freshly chopped
1 tsp.	Parsley, freshly chopped
1 tsp.	Thyme, freshly chopped
2 ea.	Bay Leaf, whole
¾ tsp.	Oregano, freshly chopped
½ tsp.	Mint, freshly chopped
½ tsp.	Fennel Seed, whole
¼ tsp.	Rosemary, freshly chopped
¼ tsp.	Red Pepper Flakes
6 oz.	Anchovy Fillets, chopped
¼ c.	Brandy
½ c.	Shiraz
½ c.	Pancetta, diced small
¾ c.	Tomato Puree
3½ qts.	Plum Tomatoes, whole
½ c.	Water, cold
¼ c.	Locatelli cheese grated
To Taste	Black Pepper, ground
To Taste	Sea Salt

Method:
1. In a large sauce pot, sweat the garlic, onions and vegetables.
2. Add herbs, anchovies, pancetta and deglaze with brandy, add wine and let reduce.
   Stir in tomato puree, and tomatoes.
   Add water, Locatelli cheese, season to taste, bring to a boil and simmer for three hours.
3. Season to taste and strain.

∾

PASTA

Artichoke, Button Mushroom and Basil Cream Sauce,
Served with Cheese Tortellini
193

Black Pepper Fettuccine with a Proscuitto Herb Goat Cheese Sauce,
Served with Asparagus Tips
195

Cheese Tortellini with a Sun Dried Tomato and Crab Cream Sauce,
Served over a Bed of Fresh Spinach and Garnished with
Roasted Red Pepper Coulis
196

Chicken Tenders with an Herb Artichoke Caper Sauce,
Served with Fettuccine and Garnished with Herbs and Parmesan Cheese
198

Four Vegetable Lasagna Smothered in a Rich Style Tomato Sauce
199

Grilled Lemon Chicken with a Tomato, Olive and Leek Sauce,
Served with Fettuccine
200

Grilled Skewered Shrimp and Scallops with a
Goat Cheese Dill Sauce, Served over Fettuccine
201

Langoustines and Lobster Claw with an Herb, Garlic and
Tomato Port Cream Sauce, Served with Fettuccine
204

Linguini and Clams with Bits of Lobster, Garnished with
Julienne of Smoked Salmon
205

Lobster Ravioli with a Spicy Tomato Beurre Blanc Sauce,
Served with Spaghetti Squash
206

Lump Crabmeat and Marinated Tomatoes, Served with Chive Angel Hair,
Belgium Endive and Garnished with Pine Nuts
208

Marinated Grilled Tiger Shrimp with Angel Hair Pasta
209

Oven Baked Chicken Breast Topped with a Plum Tomato Herb Salsa,
Layered with Fresh Mozzarella Cheese and Served with Linguini
210
Penne Pasta with an Herb Tomato Vodka Sauce
211
Penne Pasta with a Jalapeño, Mustard and Pancetta Cream Sauce
212
Penne Pasta Tossed in a Gorgonzola Cream Sauce
213
Poached Salmon with Tomato Pasta, Smoked Salmon
And Caviar, Served with an Herb Salmon Sauce
214
Sautéed Tiger Shrimp in a Sun Dried Tomato and Goat Cheese
Cream Sauce, Served with Angel Hair
216
Seafood of King Crab, Scallops and Shrimp with a Roasted Jalapeno
Dill Spaetzli in a Spicy Tomato Beurre Blanc Sauce
217
Shrimp, Feta and Fresh Tomato, Served with Fettuccine
219

ᗧ

༉

Artichoke, Button Mushroom and Basil
Cream Sauce, Served with Cheese Tortellini

8 ea.	Tortellini
1 Tbl.	Plum Tomato-skin, core & seeds removed, julienne
1 Tbl.	Basil, freshly chopped
1 Tbl.	Parsley, freshly chopped
1 Tbl.	Asiago Cheese, shaved
3 ea.	Spinach, julienne
2 ea.	Artichokes, sliced thin

Method:
1. Place tortellini in boiling salted water and let simmer for 5 minutes.
2. On salad plate, add tortellini with artichoke, button mushroom & basil cream sauce.
   Garnish with tomatoes, herbs, Asiago cheese, spinach and artichokes.

Artichoke, Button Mushroom & Basil Cream Sauce:

3 Tbl.	Extra Virgin Olive Oil
3 ea.	Button Mushrooms-cleaned, stems removed & diced small
1 Tbl.	Carrot, peeled & medium diced
1 Tbl.	Celery, minced
1 tsp.	Garlic, minced
1 Tbl.	Shallots, minced
1 tsp.	Thyme, freshly chopped
1 tsp.	Basil, freshly chopped
3 Tbl.	Chardonnay
½ c.	Chicken Stock, cold
3 ea.	Artichoke Hearts, julienne
¼ c.	Half & Half, hot
To Taste	Sea Salt
To Taste	White Pepper, ground

Method:

1. In a sauce pot, sauté mushrooms in olive oil.
   Sweat vegetables, garlic and shallots.
2. Add herbs, deglaze with wine, add chicken stock, artichokes and let simmer.
   Reduce by one-half, add half & half and reduce again to a smooth consistency.
3. Strain sauce, season to taste and place over tortellini.

∾

෨

Black Pepper Fettuccine with a Proscuitto Herb Goat Cheese Sauce, Served with Asparagus Tips

8 oz.	Fettuccine, cooked in boiling salted water
½ tsp.	Black Pepper, cracked
1 Tbl.	Plum Tomatoes-skin, core & seeds removed, diced medium
6 ea.	Asparagus Tips, steamed for 2 minutes
1 Tbl.	Chives & Parsley, freshly chopped
1 Tbl.	Locatelli Cheese, grated

Proscuitto Herb Goat Cheese Sauce:

1 Tbl.	Extra Virgin Olive Oil
2 cl.	Garlic, minced
1 tsp.	Shallots, minced
1 tsp.	Thyme, freshly chopped
1 tsp.	Basil, freshly chopped
1 tsp.	Parsley, freshly chopped
2 Tbl.	Pinot Grisgio
1 Tbl.	Roux, warm
½ c.	Chicken Stock, cold
1¼ c.	Half & Half, hot
1 Tbl.	Proscuitto Ham, julienne
To Taste	Sea Salt
To Taste	Black Pepper, ground
2 Tbl.	Goat Cheese, fresh

Method:
1. In a sauce pot, sweat the garlic and shallots in olive oil.
   Add herbs, deglaze with wine, add stock, bring to a boil and let simmer for 10 minutes.
   Whisk in roux, stir in half & half, reduce again and strain sauce.
2. Incorporate goat cheese in sauce, add proscuitto and season to taste.
3. Toss pasta with black pepper and arrange on entrée plate with sauce.
   Garnish with tomatoes, asparagus tips, fresh herbs and Locatelli cheese.

෨

෮ঌ

Cheese Tortellini with a Sun Dried Tomato and Crab Cream Sauce, Served over a Bed of Fresh Spinach and Garnished with Roasted Red Pepper Coulis

Roasted Red Pepper Coulis:

1 ea.	Red Pepper, whole
1 tsp.	Jalapeño Pepper, roasted
1 ea.	Shallots, minced
2 tsp.	Cilantro, freshly chopped
1 tsp.	Parsley, freshly chopped
1 Tbl.	Chardonnay
3 Tbl.	Chicken Stock, cold
To Taste	Tabasco

Method:
1. Roast pepper on an open flame until black.
   Place in a sealed container for 20 minutes, remove skin, core, seeds and medium dice pepper.
2. In a sauce pot, add shallots, herbs and deglaze with wine.
   Add peppers, chicken stock and a dash of Tabasco.
   Simmer for 2 minutes, let cool and blend until smooth.
3. Strain sauce into a bottled container.

Sun Dried Tomato and Crab Cream Sauce:

3 Tbl.	Extra Virgin Olive Oil
2 Tbl.	Leeks, white part only & minced
½ cl.	Garlic, minced
¼ tsp.	Thyme, freshly chopped
¼ tsp.	Basil, freshly chopped
¼ c.	Sherry
¼ c.	Chicken Stock, cold
¼ c.	Half & Half, warm
1 tsp.	Roux, warm
3 Tbl.	Lump Crab Meat, crumbled

Method:
1. In a sauté pan, sweat the onions and garlic in olive oil.
   Add herbs, deglaze with wine, add stock and reduce by one-half.
   Stir in the half & half and reduce again by one-half.
2. Whisk in roux to a smooth consistency and simmer for 2 minutes.
3. Strain sauce into a sauce pot and stir in lump crab meat.

6 ea.	Cheese Tortellini, cooked in boiling salted water
¼ c.	Spinach-stems removed, washed & julienne
As Needed	Parsley, freshly chopped

Method:
1. Place tortellini on bed of spinach.
2. Ladle cream sauce on top.
   Garnish with roasted pepper sauce and fresh parsley.

‿

Chicken Tenders with an Herb Artichoke Caper Sauce, Served with Fettuccine and Garnished with Herbs and Parmesan Cheese

3 ea.	Chicken Strips, pounded out slightly
As Needed	Buckwheat Flour, sifted
3 Tbl.	Extra Virgin Olive Oil
1 tsp.	Garlic, minced
1 tsp.	Shallots, minced
¼ tsp.	Oregano, freshly chopped
¼ tsp.	Thyme, freshly chopped
¼ tsp.	Parsley, freshly chopped
3 Tbl.	Vermouth
½ c.	Chicken Stock, cold
1 Tbl.	Roux, warm
4 ea.	Artichokes, quarters
1 tsp.	Capers, whole
To Taste	Sea Salt
To Taste	White Pepper, ground
8 oz.	Fettuccine, cooked in boiling salted water
½ tsp.	Chives & Parsley, freshly chopped
As Needed	Parmesan Cheese, shaved

Method:
1. Dredge chicken in flour and shake off excess.
   Sauté until golden brown on both sides in olive oil, take out and keep warm.
2. In the same pan, sauté the garlic and shallots.
   Add herbs, deglaze with wine, add stock and reduce.
   Whisk in roux to a smooth consistency.
3. Add artichokes, capers and season to taste.
4. Place Fettuccine on entrée plate and add chicken.
   Garnish with fresh herbs and parmesan cheese.

‿

෩

Four Vegetable Lasagna Smothered in a Rich Style Tomato Sauce

4 ea.	Zucchini, sliced thin
4 ea.	Yellow Squash, sliced thin
6 ea.	Carrots, sliced thin
As Needed	Extra Virgin Olive Oil
1 bg.	Spinach, washed & stems removed
3½#	Ricotta Cheese
4 ea.	Eggs, whole
1 tsp.	Sea Salt
1 Tbl.	Parsley, freshly chopped
1 Tbl.	Oregano, freshly chopped
1 tsp.	Thyme, freshly chopped
1 tsp.	Basil, freshly chopped
10 ea.	Lasagna Sheets, cooked in boiling salted water
½#	Locatelli Cheese, grated
1#	Mozzarella Cheese, shredded
1½ qts.	Uncle Paul's Tomato Sauce

Method:
1. Brush vegetables with olive oil, grill and let cool.
2. Steam spinach, let cool and coarsely chop.
   Mix the spinach, ricotta cheese, eggs, salt and fresh herbs in a steel bowl.
3. Place the sauce down first, lasagna and ricotta cheese mixture.
   Sprinkle with Locatelli and mozzarella cheese.
   Repeat layers with the sauce at the end.
4. Bake in a 350ºF oven for 35 minutes.

෩

∾

Grilled Lemon Chicken with a Tomato, Olive and Leek Sauce, Served with Fettuccine

8 oz.	Chicken-skin & fat removed, pounded out slightly
To Taste	Sea Salt
To Taste	Black Pepper, ground
To Taste	Poultry Seasoning, ground
3 Tbl.	Lemon Juice, squeezed
1 tsp.	Garlic, minced
½ ea.	Leek-white part only, cut into rounds
¼ tsp.	Thyme, freshly chopped
¼ tsp.	Basil, freshly chopped
¼ tsp.	Parsley, freshly chopped
3 Tbl.	Vermouth
½ c.	Chicken Stock, cold
2 ea.	Plum Tomatoes-skin, core & seeds removed, julienne
2 Tbl.	Black Olives, cut in half
2 Tbl.	Green Olives, cut in half
3 Tbl.	Butter, cold
To Taste	Sea Salt
To Taste	Black Pepper, ground
4 oz.	Fettuccine, cooked in boiling salted water
2 Tbl.	Parsley & Basil, freshly chopped
½ ea.	Cucumber, peeled & small diced

Method:
1. Season chicken with salt, black pepper, poultry seasoning and add
2. lemon juice.
   Let rest for 20 minutes.
   Grill chicken, cut into strips and keep warm.
3. In a sauté pan, add garlic, leeks, herbs and sweat.
   Deglaze with wine, add stock and reduce.
   Add tomatoes, olives and reduce.
4. Whisk in butter and season to taste.
5. In an entrée bowl, place sauce on top of fettuccine and lay chicken on top.
   Garnish with fresh herbs and cucumber.

∾

∽

Grilled Skewered Shrimp and Scallops with a Goat Cheese Dill Sauce, Served over Fettuccine

2 ea.	Bay Scallops, mussels removed & sliced in one-half
4 ea.	Shrimp-peeled, de-veined & tail on
As Needed	Extra Virgin Olive Oil
1 ea.	Skewer, soaked in water for 10 minutes
¼ c.	Italian Vinaigrette

Method:
1. Place shrimp on skewer, then scallop and repeat layers. Marinate in Italian vinaigrette overnight.
2. Brush seafood with olive oil and grill until proper doneness. Set aside and keep warm.

Goat Cheese Dill Sauce:

1 Tbl.	Extra Virgin Olive Oil
1 cl.	Garlic, minced
1 Tbl.	Shallots, minced
1 tsp.	Dill, freshly chopped
¼ tsp.	Cilantro, freshly chopped
¼ tsp.	Thyme, freshly chopped
¼ tsp.	Parsley, freshly chopped
Pinch	Old Bay Seasoning
¼ c.	Riesling
1 Tbl.	Lemon Juice, freshly squeezed
½ c.	Shrimp Stock, cold
1 c.	Half & Half, hot
1 Tbl.	Roux, warm
To Taste	Sea Salt
To Taste	White Pepper, ground
¼ c.	Goat Cheese
4 oz.	Fettuccine, cooked in boiling salted water
1 Tbl.	Chives & Dill, freshly chopped
As Needed	Goat Cheese

1. In a sauté pan, sweat the garlic and shallots in olive oil.
   Add herbs, deglaze with wine, add lemon and reduce until
   liquid is almost gone.
   Stir in stock, reduce by one-half, add half & half and reduce
   again by one-half.
2. Incorporate roux, season to taste, strain into another saucepot and
   blend in goat cheese.
3. Place fettuccine, seafood and sauce on entrée plate.
   Garnish with fresh herbs and goat cheese.

Shrimp Stock:

1½#	Shrimp Shells
3 Tbl.	Extra Virgin Olive Oil
1 c.	Onion, medium dice
2 Tbl.	Garlic, minced
1 ea.	Plum Tomatoes-skin, core & seeds removed, diced medium
2 Tbl.	Paprika, ground
1 ea.	Bay Leaf, whole
1 Tbl.	Thyme, freshly chopped
1 Tbl.	Old Bay Seasoning
½ Tbl.	Oregano, freshly chopped
1 Tbl.	Thyme, freshly chopped
1 Tbl.	Parsley, freshly chopped
¼ c.	Brandy
1½ gal.	Water, cold
To Taste	Sea Salt
To Taste	Black Pepper, ground

Method:
1. In a soup pot, add shrimp shells with the olive oil.
   Stir occasionally under medium high heat until shells turn color.
2. Add onion, garlic, tomato and herbs.
3. Deglaze with brandy.
   Add water, let boil and simmer for 30 minutes.
4. Strain and let cool.

∾

Langoustines and Lobster Claw with an Herb, Garlic and Tomato Port Cream Sauce, Served with Fettuccine

2 c.	Shrimp Stock, cold
½ c.	Half & Half, hot
1 tsp.	Lemon Juice, freshly squeezed
2 Tbl.	Roux, warm
½ c.	Langoustines, peeled
3 Tbl.	Port
To Taste	Sea Salt
To Taste	Pink Peppercorns, cracked
2 Tbl.	Parmesan Cheese, grated
¼ c.	Plum Tomatoes-skin, core & seeds removed, julienne
4 oz.	Fettuccine, cooked in boiling salted water
As Needed	Parsley, freshly chopped
As Needed	Cilantro, freshly chopped
1 ea.	Lobster Claw, warm

Method:

1. In a sauce pot, add wine, garlic, herbs and reduce until almost gone.
   Add shrimp stock and reduce by one-half.
   Stir in half & half, lemon and reduce again by one-half.
   Whisk in roux, simmer for 5 minutes and strain into sauce pot
   of the langoustines.
2. Separately in a sauce pot, sauté langoustines and deglaze with wine.
   Season with salt, pink peppercorns and parmesan cheese.
   Stir in tomatoes.
3. On a large oval plate, add sauce on top of Fettuccine.
   Garnish with fresh herbs and lobster claw.

∾

∽

Linguini and Clams with Bits of Lobster, Garnished With Julienne of Smoked Salmon

6 ea.	Little Neck Clams
3 Tbl.	Extra Virgin Olive Oil
1 cl.	Garlic, minced
1 tsp.	Shallots, minced
¼ tsp.	Jalapeño, roasted
1 tsp.	Parsley, freshly chopped
½ tsp.	Cilantro, freshly chopped
½ tsp.	Thyme, freshly chopped
½ tsp.	Oregano, freshly chopped
3 Tbl.	Vodka
As Needed	Clam Juice, from clams
3 Tbl.	Lobster, diced small
2 Tbl.	Roux, warm
4 oz.	Linguini, cooked in boiling salted water
½ tsp.	Cilantro & Chives, whole
1 oz.	Smoked Salmon, julienne
As Needed	Locatelli Cheese, shaved

Method:
1. Open clams, place in a steel bowl and refrigerator.
2. In a sauté pan, sweat the garlic and shallots in olive oil.
   Add jalapeno pepper, herbs and deglaze with vodka.
   Stir in clam juice, add lobster and let simmer.
3. Whisk in the roux and let reduce.
   Stir in clams and let simmer.
4. In an entrée bowl, arrange linguini and clam sauce.
   Garnish with fresh herbs, smoked salmon and Locatelli cheese.

∽

∾

Lobster Ravioli with a Spicy Tomato Beurre Blanc Sauce, Served with Spaghetti Squash

Spicy Tomato Beurre Blanc Sauce:

1 cl.	Garlic, minced
1 Tbl.	Extra Virgin Olive Oil
1 ea.	Shallots, minced
Pinch	Basil, freshly chopped
Pinch	Oregano, freshly chopped
Pinch	Thyme, freshly chopped
1 oz.	Jerez Wine
3 ea.	Plum Tomatoes-skin, core & seeds removed, diced medium
Pinch	Red Pepper Flakes
To Taste	Sea Salt
2 oz.	Butter-whole, cubed & left cold

Method:
1. Sweat the garlic and shallots in olive oil.
   Add herbs and deglaze with wine.
   Stir in tomatoes, red pepper flakes and reduce by one-half.
2. Let cool, place in blender and mix until smooth.
   Strain in another sauté pot, heat contents and season to taste.
3. Whisk in cold butter a little at a time.

Lobster Ravioli:

3 oz.	Lobster meat, chopped
6 oz.	Ricotta Cheese
1 tsp.	Parsley, freshly chopped
¼ tsp.	Oregano, freshly chopped
1 ea.	Egg, whole
To Taste	Sea Salt
To Taste	Black Pepper, ground
¼#	Pasta Sheet

Method:
1. In a steel bowl, mix together the lobster, ricotta cheese, egg, salt and black pepper.
2. Cut pasta into two inch squares.
   Place mixture in the center of pasta sheet and cover with other layer. Shape ravioli's by pinch sides together.
3. Cook ravioli's in boiling salted water for 2 minutes.
4. Serve with tomato beurre blanc sauce and spaghetti Squash.

Spaghetti Squash:

1 oz.	Spaghetti Squash, steamed
½ tsp.	Butter, whole
To Taste	Sea Salt

Method:
1. Shape spaghetti squash in a round on plate.

෧෧

ᕣᕤ

Lump Crabmeat and Marinated Tomatoes, Served with Chive Angel Hair, Belgium Endive and Garnished with Pine Nuts

Lump Crabmeat & Marinated Tomatoes:

1 Tbl.	Extra Virgin Olive Oil
1 cl.	Garlic, minced
1 ea.	Shallots, minced
¼ tsp.	Basil, freshly chopped
¼ tsp.	Oregano, freshly chopped
¼ c.	Champagne
3 ea.	Plum Tomatoes-skins, core & seeds removed, julienne
¼ c.	White Wine Vinaigrette
6 oz.	Claw Crabmeat
To Taste	Sea Salt
To Taste	Black Pepper, cracked

Method:
1. Sauté the garlic and shallots in olive oil.
   Add herbs, champagne and reduce until almost gone.
2. Cool mixture, add the rest of the ingredients and toss.
3. Season to taste and keep chilled.

6 oz.	Chive Angel Hair-cooked in boiling salted water & cooled quickly
3 leaves	Belgium Endive, garnish
As Needed	Pine Nuts
As Needed	Cilantro & Parsley, freshly chopped

Method:
1. Arrange angel hair around entrée plate.
   Place Belgium Endive on sides of pasta and in the middle.
2. Lightly toss crabmeat mixture and place in center.
3. Garnish with pine nuts and fresh herbs.

ᕣᕤ

Marinated Grilled Tiger Shrimp with Angel Hair Pasta

1 ea. Bay Leaf, whole
½ tsp. Thyme, whole
2 cl. Garlic, coarsely chopped
Pinch Hot Pepper Flakes
¼ c. Extra Virgin Olive Oil
3 ea. Tiger Shrimp-peeled, de-veined & tail on
1 ea. Wood Skewer, soaked in water for 20 minutes
1 Tbl. Extra Virgin Olive Oil
1 cl. Garlic
1 ea. Shallots, finely chopped
2 Tbl. Celery, finely chopped
1 tsp. Basil, freshly chopped
¼ c. Riesling
3 oz. Shrimp Stock
4 oz. Angel Hair Pasta, cooked in boiling salted water
As Needed Sea Salt
As Needed Black Pepper, ground
1 tsp. Dill & Chives, freshly chopped

Method:
1. In a stainless steel pan, add the bay leaf, thyme, garlic, hot pepper flakes and olive oil.
   Skewer tiger shrimp and place in pan.
   Marinate shrimp overnight.
2. Grill shrimp and keep warm.
3. Sauté garlic, shallots and celery in oil.
   Add basil, deglaze with wine and add stock.
   Reduce for one minute and season to taste.
4. Arrange angel hair pasta, shrimp and sauce on entrée plate.
   Garnish with herbs.

◠◡

Oven Baked Chicken Breast Topped with a Plum Tomato Herb Salsa, Layered with Fresh Mozzarella Cheese And Served with Linguini

2-(8 oz.) each	Chicken Breasts-skin & sinew removed
To Taste	Sea Salt
To Taste	Black Pepper, cracked
¼ c.	Buckwheat Flour, sifted
3 Tbl.	Extra Virgin Olive Oil
3 Tbl.	Pinot Noir
5 oz.	Plum Tomatoes-skin, core & seeds removed, diced medium
5 oz.	Leeks, white part only & medium diced
¼ tsp.	Garlic, minced
Pinch	Basil, freshly chopped
Pinch	Oregano, freshly chopped
Pinch	Thyme, freshly chopped
2 ea.	Mozzarella Cheese, freshly sliced into strips
6 oz.	Linguini, cooked in boiling salted water
To Taste	Sea Salt
To Taste	White Pepper, ground
2 Tbl.	Extra Virgin Olive Oil
As Needed	Locatelli Cheese, shaved
1 tsp.	Parsley & Chives, freshly chopped

Method:

1. Season chicken, dredge in flour and shake off excess.
   Sauté until golden brown on both sides in olive oil, remove from pan and keep warm.
2. In the same pan, deglaze with wine.
   Add tomatoes, leeks, garlic, herbs and simmer for 7 minutes.
3. On a baking dish, place tomato salsa on chicken and top with mozzarella cheese strips. Bake until cheese is melted.
4. Serve with linguini tossed with salt, pepper and olive oil.
   Garnish with shaved Locatelli cheese and fresh herbs.

◠◡

⌒

Penne Pasta with an Herb Tomato Vodka Sauce

12 oz.	Penne Pasta, cooked in boiling salted water
3 Tbl.	Extra Virgin Olive Oil
1 cl.	Garlic, minced
1 Tbl.	Shallots, minced
1 tsp.	Celery, finely chopped
1 Tbl.	Basil, freshly chopped
½ tsp.	Thyme, freshly chopped
½ tsp.	Oregano, freshly chopped
4 oz.	Vodka
10 oz.	Uncle Paul's Tomato Sauce, hot
3 oz.	Half & Half, hot
As Needed	Parmesan Cheese, grated
As Needed	Sea Salt
As Needed	Black Pepper, cracked
3 ea.	Basil, whole for garnish

Method:
1. In a sauce pot, sweat the garlic, shallots and celery in olive oil.
   Add herbs, deglaze with 2 ounces of vodka, add tomato sauce
   and half & half.
   Simmer sauce for 7 minutes.
   Stir in 2 ounces of vodka, parmesan cheese and season to taste.
2. Place pasta in sauté pot with some of the sauce and mix well.
3. In an entrée bowl, add pasta with sauce on top.
   Garnish with fresh basil leaves.

⌒

∽

Penne Pasta with a Jalapeño, Mustard and Pancetta Cream Sauce

8 oz.	Penne Pasta, cooked in boiling salted water
3 Tbl.	Extra Virgin Olive Oil
2 cl.	Garlic, minced
½ tsp.	Thyme, freshly chopped
½ tsp.	Parsley, freshly chopped
3 Tbl.	Chardonnay
2 c.	Chicken Stock, cold
6 oz.	Half & Half, hot
2 Tbl.	Roux, warm
4 oz.	Cream cheese, chopped
8 oz.	Mild White American cheese, diced small
1 tsp.	Dijon Mustard
½ ea.	Jalapeño Pepper, seeds removed & minced
¼ c.	Pancetta, diced small
1 Tbl.	Parsley & Thyme, freshly chopped
½ ea.	Green Scallion, finely chopped

Method:
1. In a sauce pot, sweat the garlic and shallots in olive oil.
    Add herbs, deglaze with wine, add chicken stock and reduce by one-half.
    Stir in half & half and reduce.
2. Whisk in roux and incorporate the cheese a little at a time.
    Add mustard, Jalapeño pepper and pancetta.
3. Garnish with herbs and scallions.

∽

∾

Penne Pasta Tossed in a Gorgonzola Cream Sauce

2 Tbl.	Extra Virgin Olive Oil
½ ea.	Leek-white part only & minced
1 cl.	Garlic, minced
½ tsp.	Thyme, freshly chopped
½ tsp.	Basil, freshly chopped
3 Tbl.	Chardonnay
½ c.	Chicken Stock, cold
¼ c.	Half & Half, hot
As Needed	Parmesan Cheese, grated
3 Tbl.	Gorgonzola Blue Cheese, crumbled
To Taste	Sea Salt
¼ tsp.	Black Pepper, cracked
4 oz.	Penne Pasta, cooked in boiling salted water
2 Tbl.	Chives & Parsley, freshly chopped
½ ea.	Green Scallions, finely chopped

Method:
1. In a sauté pan, sweat the leeks and garlic in olive oil.
   Add herbs, deglaze with wine, add chicken stock and reduce.
   Stir in half & half, reduce again and add parmesan cheese.
2. Incorporate the gorgonzola cheese a little at a time.
   Season to taste and toss with penne pasta.
3. Garnish with fresh herbs and green scallions.

∾

$\backsim$

Poached Salmon with Tomato Pasta, Smoked Salmon And Caviar, Served with an Herb Salmon Sauce

Tomato Pasta:

2¾ c.	Semolina, finely ground
¼ c.	Wheat Flour, sifted
4 ea.	Eggs, whole
1 Tbl.	Extra Virgin Olive Oil
As Needed	Sea Salt & Black Pepper, ground
2½ Tbl.	Sun Dried Tomatoes, minced

Method:
1. Place contents in mixer, knead for 3 minutes and let rest for 15 minutes in refrigerator.
2. Roll out pasta thinly and cut into desired shapes. Cook pasta in boiling salted water.

For the Salmon:

4 oz.	Fresh Salmon Fillet, cut into 3 slices
½ c.	Water, cold

Method:
1. Poach Salmon in boiling salted water, with a pinch of thyme, parsley and 1 bay leaf.
Keep warm and reserve one-half cup salmon stock for sauce.

Garnish:

2 Tbl.	Extra Virgin Olive Oil
4 oz.	Zucchini, julienne
½ ea.	Red Pepper, julienne
1 tsp.	Caviar, Red & Black
1 oz.	Smoked Salmon, diced
3 ea.	Chives, whole

Method:
1. Sauté zucchini and red pepper in olive oil.
2. Garnish with caviar, add fresh and smoked salmon on entrée plate.

Herb Salmon Sauce:

2 Tbl.	Extra Virgin Olive Oil
1 cl.	Garlic, minced
¼ c.	Shallots, minced
½ c.	Salmon stock, strained
4 tsp.	Dill, freshly chopped
1 tsp.	Parsley, freshly chopped
Pinch	Hot Pepper Flakes
½ c.	Half & Half, hot
1 ea.	Plum Tomatoes-skin, core & seeds removed, diced small
½ ea.	Green Scallion, chopped

Method:
1. Sauté garlic and shallots in olive oil, add herbs, salmon stock and reduce by one-half.
2. Add half & half, reduce again by one-half, add tomatoes, scallion and simmer for 5 minutes.
   Strain sauce and arrange on entrée plate with tomato pasta.

෧ා

༄

Sautéed Tiger Shrimp in a Sun Dried Tomato and Goat Cheese Cream Sauce, Served with Angel Hair

3 ea.	Tiger Shrimp-peeled, de-veined & tail on
As Needed	Extra Virgin Olive Oil

Method:
1. Sauté shrimp and keep warm.

Sun Dried Tomato and Goat Cheese Cream Sauce:

2 Tbl.	Extra Virgin Olive Oil
1 tsp.	Garlic, minced
2 ea.	Shallots, minced
3 ea.	Sun Dried Tomatoes
½ tsp.	Basil, freshly chopped
½ tsp.	Thyme, freshly chopped
½ tsp.	Cilantro, freshly chopped
3 Tbl.	Sherry
½ c.	Shrimp Stock, cold
1 tsp.	Jalapeño Pepper, roasted
¼ c.	Half & Half, hot
½ tsp.	Lemon Juice, freshly squeezed
1 tsp.	Roux, warm
3 Tbl.	Goat Cheese, crumbled
4 oz.	Angel Hair Pasta, cooked in boiling salted water
Garnish	Parsley & Chives, freshly chopped

Method:
1. In the same sauté pan, sweat the garlic and shallots in olive oil.
   Add tomatoes and herbs.
   Deglaze with wine, add shrimp stock, roasted jalapeño and reduce by one-half.
2. Stir in half & half, lemon, whisk in roux and let simmer for 2 minutes.
   Remove from stove and stir in goat cheese.
3. Place sauce over angel hair and arrange shrimp on top.
   Garnish with fresh herbs.

༄

෧෨

Seafood of King Crab, Scallops and Shrimp with a Roasted Jalapeno Dill Spaetzli in a Spicy Tomato Beurre Blanc Sauce

Spicy Tomato Beurre Blanc Sauce:

3 Tbl.	Extra Virgin Olive Oil
1 cl.	Garlic, minced
1 ea.	Shallots, minced
Pinch	Basil, freshly chopped
Pinch	Oregano, freshly chopped
Pinch	Thyme, freshly chopped
1 oz.	Sherry
3 ea.	Plum Tomatoes-skin, core & seeds removed, diced medium
Pinch	Red Pepper Flakes
To Taste	Sea Salt
2 oz.	Butter-whole, cubed & left cold

Method:
1. In a sauté pan, sweat the garlic and shallots in olive oil.
   Add herbs and deglaze with wine.
   Stir in tomatoes, add red pepper flakes and reduce by one-half.
2. Let cool, place in cuisinart and strain in sauté pot.
3. Heat contents and season to taste.
   Whisk in cold butter a little at a time.

෧෨

∾

Roasted Jalapeño Dill Spaetzli:

8 oz.	All-Purpose Flour, sifted
4 oz.	Buckwheat Flour, sifted
3 ea.	Eggs, whole
3 Tbl.	Milk, whole
2 Tbl.	Dill, freshly chopped
To Taste	Sea Salt
¼ tsp.	Jalapeño Pepper, roasted & minced
To Taste	Nutmeg, freshly ground
3 c.	Water
3 Tbl.	Extra Virgin Olive Oil

Method:
1. In a bowl, add flour, eggs, milk, dill, salt, jalapeño and mix well. Drop spaetzli in boiling salted water.
2. Remove and let cool in a steel pan.

½ c.	Spicy Tomato Beurre Blanc
¼ c.	Alaskan King Crab, crumbled
¼ c.	Sea Scallops, mussels removed
¼ c.	Shrimp-peeled & de-veined

Method:
1. Sauté sea scallops and shrimp in olive oil, remove and keep warm.
2. In the same pan, sauté spaetzli in olive oil, add tomato beurre blanc, then toss with seafood.

∾

∽

Shrimp, Feta and Fresh Tomato, Served with Fettuccine

4 ea.	Shrimp-peeled, de-veined & tail on
2 Tbl.	Extra Virgin Olive Oil
1 cl.	Garlic, minced
1 tsp.	Shallots, minced
½ tsp.	Basil, freshly chopped
½ tsp.	Thyme, freshly chopped
1 tsp.	Parsley, freshly chopped
3 Tbl.	Vodka
½ c.	Chicken Stock, cold
¼ c.	Half & Half, hot
1 Tbl.	Butter, cold
2 oz.	Feta Cheese, diced small
2 ea.	Plum Tomatoes-skin, core & seeds removed, julienne
½ tsp.	Pink Peppercorns, cracked
To Taste	Sea Salt
4 oz.	Fettuccine, cooked in boiled salted water
Garnish	Green Scallion, chopped
1 Tbl.	Cilantro & Parsley, freshly chopped

Method:
1. Sauté shrimp quickly in olive oil, remove and keep warm.
2. In the same sauté pan, sweat the garlic and shallots.
   Add herbs, deglaze with vodka, add chicken stock and reduce by one-half.
3. Stir in half & half, reduce and whisk in butter.
   Add feta cheese, tomatoes and season to taste.
4. Place fettuccine on oval plate, place mixture on top and arrange shrimp around plate.
   Garnish with green scallions and fresh herbs.

∽

∽

PORK

Cabbage Rolls with Potatoes, Green Peppers,
Smothered in a Tomato Sauce
222
Lean Kielbasa with Fresh Herbs, Served with Red Beet Horseradish
224
Pork Chops Stuffed with an Apple Bread Stuffing,
Served with an Apple Walnut Pecan Raisin Chutney
225
Roast Pork Tenderloin with a Mushroom, Spinach and Feta Cheese
Stuffing, Served with a Marsala Wild Mushroom Sauce
227
Sautéed Sausage, Black Beans and White Rice with Garden Fresh Peas,
Served with Steamed Clams and Shrimp
229
Sliced Porketta with Black Pepper Egg Fettuccine
230

∽

∾

Cabbage Rolls with Potatoes, Green Peppers, Smothered in a Tomato Sauce

For Cabbage:

1 hd.	Savoy Cabbage, center core removed
3 Tbl.	White Vinegar
1 Tbl.	Sea Salt

Method:
1. Place cabbage in a large pot with enough water to cover. Add white vinegar and salt.
2. Bring to a boil and simmer until cabbage is soft. Remove from stove and let cool overnight.

1½#	Mild Sausage, ground
1½#	Sirloin Beef, ground
1¼#	Veal, ground
1 Tbl.	Oregano, freshly chopped
1 tsp.	Thyme, freshly chopped
½ tsp.	Basil, freshly chopped
3 Tbl.	Parsley, freshly chopped
¼ tsp.	Poultry Seasoning, ground
To Taste	Sea Salt
To Taste	Black Pepper, ground
3 cl.	Garlic, minced
4 ea.	Eggs, whole
3¼ c.	White Rice, uncooked
1 tsp.	Sea Salt
1½ ea.	Green Pepper-core & seeds removed, sliced thin
1 ea.	Red Potato-skins removed & medium diced
2 qt.	Uncle Paul's Tomato Sauce

Method:

1. In a mixer, add sausage, beef, veal, herbs, garlic, eggs and mix thoroughly.
    Cook white rice with salt, let cool, add to mixture and blend well.
2. Place mixture in cabbage leaf, fold up firmly and place in a baking dish.
    Add peppers, potatoes and tomato sauce on top of cabbage rolls.
3. Place in a 350ºF oven for one hour.

∾

Lean Kielbasa with Fresh Herbs, Served with Red Beet Horseradish

5#	Pork Butt, ground fine
3#	Pork Fat, ground fine
2½#	Deer Meat, ground fine
6 cl.	Garlic, coarsely chopped
¼ c.	Sea Salt
1½ Tbl.	Marjoram, ground
2 Tbl.	Oregano, freshly chopped
2 Tbl.	Thyme, freshly chopped
1 Tbl.	Parsley, freshly chopped
½ Tbl.	Fennel, finely ground
1 Tbl.	Whole Allspice, whole & coarsely crushed
1 Tbl.	Black Pepper, whole & coarsely crushed
As Needed	Pig Casings
As Needed	Red Beet Horseradish, prepared

Method:
1. Combine all ingredients in a large mixer and blend well.
   Place in refrigerator for four hours.
2. Stuff mixture inside pig casings.
3. Place kielbasa in boiling water until proper doneness.
   Remove kielbasa, slice thin and serve with red beet horseradish.

∾

༨

Pork Chops Stuffed with an Apple Bread Stuffing, Served with an Apple Walnut Pecan Raisin Chutney

Apple Walnut Raisin Chutney:

2 tsp.	Light Brown Sugar
½ tsp.	White Balsamic Vinegar
1 Tbl.	Clover Honey
2 Tbl.	Golden Raisins
Pinch	Cinnamon, ground
Pinch	Nutmeg, ground
1½ c.	Orange Juice
½ ea.	Orange Peel, julienne
¾ c.	Chicken Stock, cold
3 ea.	Apples-core & skin removed, diced small
¼ c.	Walnuts, coarsely chopped
¼ c.	Pecans, coarsely chopped
As Needed	Cornstarch in water

Method:
1. Combine all ingredients, except for the apples and cornstarch. Bring to a boil, simmer for 15 minutes and thicken sauce to a medium consistency.
2. Add apples and simmer for another 3 minutes.

3 Tbl.	Extra Virgin Olive Oil
2 cl.	Garlic, minced
¼ c.	Onions, diced small
¼ c.	Celery, diced small
Pinch	Thyme, freshly chopped
Pinch	Poultry Seasoning, ground
1½ c.	Chicken Stock, cold
1 ea.	Apple-core & skin removed, finely chopped
8 ea.	White bread, crusts removed & cut into medium diced cubes

4 ea. Pork Chops, with bone removed
To Taste Sea Salt
To Taste Black Pepper, ground
As Needed Poultry Seasoning, ground

Method:

1. Place chicken stock, bones of pork and simmer for 10 minutes.
   Remove bones, clean and reserve on entrée plate for presentation.
2. In a sauté pan, sweat the garlic, onions, celery in olive oil, add herbs, stock and let cool.
   In a steel bowl, add mixture, apples, bread, mix well and season to taste.
   Cut a slit on the inside of pork making a pocket and fill with stuffing mixture.
3. Season pork and bake in a 350°F oven until proper doneness.
4. Arrange pork, apple raisin chutney and pork bone on entrée plate.

❦

∾

Roast Pork Tenderloin with a Mushroom, Spinach and Feta Cheese Stuffing, Served with a Marsala Wild Mushroom Sauce

Marsala Wild Mushroom Sauce:

1 Tbl.	Extra Virgin Olive Oil
1 ea.	Shallots, minced
1 cl.	Garlic, minced
1 tsp.	Oregano, freshly chopped
¼ tsp.	Marjoram, freshly chopped
¼ tsp.	Rosemary, freshly chopped
½ tsp.	Thyme, freshly chopped
½ tsp.	Parsley, freshly chopped
½ c.	Shitake Mushrooms, julienne
¼ c.	Marsala
2 c.	Beef Stock, cold
2 Tbl.	Roux, warm
To Taste	Sea Salt
To Taste	Black Pepper, ground

Method:
1. In a sauté pan, sweat the shallots and garlic in olive oil.
   Add herbs, mushrooms, wine and reduce until liquid is almost gone.
2. In a separate sauce pot, add the beef stock, bring to a boil, simmer and whisk in the roux.
   Reduce to a medium consistency and strain into herb mushroom mixture.
3. Simmer for 3 minutes and season to taste.

2 ea.	Pork Tenderloin, fat & sinew removed
To Taste	Sea Salt
To Taste	Black Pepper, ground
½#	Button Mushrooms-washed, stems removed & sliced

4 oz.	Spinach-steamed, drained with no moisture & chopped fine
3 oz.	Feta Cheese, crumbled
To Taste	Sea Salt
To Taste	Black Pepper, ground
Pinch	Thyme, freshly chopped
Pinch	Poultry Seasoning, ground
Pinch	Rosemary, freshly chopped
As Needed	Butcher's Twine

Method:

1. Cut pork lengthwise, pound out slightly and season.
2. Sauté mushrooms until liquid is completely gone, place in cuisinart and chop fine.
   In a steel bowl, add the mushrooms, spinach, feta and mix well.
3. Place mixture on two thirds of pork and roll up.
   Tie up pork tenderloin and place in roasting pan.
   Season pork tenderloin and roast in a 350ºF oven until proper doneness.
4. Let pork rest for 10 minutes, slice on bias and arrange on plate with mushroom sauce.

࿇

√

Sautéed Sausage, Black Beans and White Rice with Garden Fresh Peas, Served with Steamed Clams and Shrimp

1 Tbl.	Extra Virgin Olive Oil
1½[#]	Sweet Italian Sausage
1 ea.	Onions, sliced
3 cl.	Garlic, minced
1 tsp.	Thyme, freshly chopped
1 tsp.	Oregano, freshly chopped
¼ tsp.	Cilantro, freshly chopped
2 Tbl.	Parsley, freshly chopped
1½ c.	White Rice, uncooked
½ tsp.	Sea Salt
4½ c.	Chicken Stock, cold
¼ tsp.	Black Pepper, cracked
4 ea.	Plum Tomatoes-skin, core & seeds removed, diced large
1 ea.	Hot Cherry Peppers, minced
1[#]	Black Beans, precooked
½ c.	Peas, fresh
6 ea.	Clams, steamed
6 ea.	Shrimp-peeled, de-veined with tail on& steamed

Method:
1. In a sauté pot, add the oil, sausage and cook until proper doneness.
   Rough cut sausage into medium diced cubes and set aside.
2. In the same sauté pot, sauté onions, garlic and add herbs.
   Mix in white rice, salt, add stock and bring to a boil.
   Simmer mixture until rice is cooked.
3. Stir in sausage, tomatoes, hot cherry peppers, black beans and peas.
4. Arrange rice on an oval entrée plate.
   Garnish around plate with clams and shrimp.

√

∾

Sliced Porketta with Black Pepper Egg Fettuccine

¼ c.	Extra Virgin Olive Oil
5 cl.	Garlic, minced
3#	Pork Butt, boneless
1 Tbl.	Parsley, freshly chopped
1 Tbl.	Oregano, freshly chopped
1½ tsp.	Fennel Seed, whole
1 Tbl.	Dill, freshly chopped
1 Tbl.	Thyme, freshly chopped
1 tsp.	Mint, freshly chopped
As Needed	Black Pepper, freshly cracked
As Needed	Sea Salt
As Needed	Butcher's Twine
¼ c.	Brandy
½ c.	Shiraz wine
3 qts.	Uncle Paul's Tomato Sauce
1 ea.	Bay Leaf, whole
1#	Black Pepper Egg Fettuccine, cooked in boiling salted water
As Needed	Locatelli cheese grated
As Needed	Parsley & Thyme, freshly chopped

Method:
1. Add extra virgin olive oil around pork, rub herbs and season to taste. Wrap pork with butcher's twine cover with plastic wrap and refrigerator overnight.
2. In a large sauce pot, sauté porketta on all sides very quickly.
3. Deglaze with brandy, add shiraz and let reduce.
   Add herb tomato sauce, let boil and simmer for 2 hours.
4. Remove porketta, slice thinly and serve with black pepper fettuccine. Serve with Locatelli cheese and garnish with fresh herbs.

∾

~

SALADS

Chicken Salad with Red and White Seedless Grapes with
Pecans And Walnuts, Served in a Giant Croissant
232
Guacamole Salad with Kiwi, Tomatoes and Hearts of Romaine
233
Half Roasted Duck Breast Salad served with Italian Marmalade
Vinaigrette Over Boston Bibb Lettuce
234
Marinated Bow Tie Noodles with Portabella Mushrooms,
Roasted Red Peppers and Fresh Spinach
236
Marinated Oriental Salad with Rice Noodles,
Served with a Ginger Sesame Vinaigrette
237
Plum Tomatoes with Black Olives and Red Onions
Garnished with Asiago Cheese, Toasted Pine Nuts and
Smoked Salmon
238
Tiger Shrimp in a Portabella Oil Vinaigrette, Served with
Portabella Mushrooms and Marinated Tomatoes
239

~

∽

Chicken Salad with Red and White Seedless Grapes with Pecans And Walnuts, Served in a Giant Croissant

10 oz.	Chicken-skin & sinew removed
6 ea.	Red Seedless Grapes, cut in half
6 ea.	White Seedless Grapes, cut in half
4 ea.	Walnuts, coarsely chopped
4 ea.	Pecans, coarsely chopped
½ tsp.	Thyme, freshly chopped
1 tsp.	Parsley, freshly chopped
3 Tbl.	Mayonnaise
1 tsp.	Buttermilk Ranch Vinaigrette
1 Tbl.	Blue Cheese, crumbled
1 ea.	Giant Croissant
¼ ea.	Red Pepper-roasted, skin & seeds removed, julienne
As Needed	Strawberries, stems on
As Needed	Blackberries

Method:
1. Steam chicken and let cool.
   Dice chicken and place in a steel bowl.
2. Combine chicken with grapes, walnuts, pecans and herbs.
   Mix in mayonnaise, buttermilk ranch vinaigrette, blue cheese and blend until smooth.
3. Slice croissant in half and place chicken salad on bottom half of croissant.
   Place roasted red pepper on top of chicken salad.
4. Serve with sliced fresh fruit.

∽

∾

Guacamole Salad with Kiwi, Tomatoes and Hearts of Romaine

1 cl.	Garlic, minced
3 Tbl.	Riesling
1 Tbl.	Lime Juice, freshly squeezed
2 Tbl.	Cream Cheese, very soft
½ c.	Mayonnaise
1 ea.	Green Scallion, minced
1 Tbl.	Pimentos, minced
2 ea.	Avocados-skin & seed removed, diced small
2 Tbl.	Cilantro, freshly chopped
1 Tbl.	Parsley, freshly chopped
To Taste	Sea Salt
To Taste	Black Pepper, ground
To Taste	Tabasco Sauce
3 c.	Romaine Hearts, washed & cut
3 ea.	Plum Tomatoes-skin, core & seeds removed, julienne
2 ea.	Kiwi, skins removed & quartered

Method:
1. Place garlic and wine in sauce pot, reduce and let cool.
2. In a steel bowl, add the garlic, lime juice, cream cheese, mayonnaise and blend.
   Fold in the scallions, pimentos and avocados.
   Add herbs and season to taste.
3. Arrange romaine hearts, tomatoes, kiwi and guacamole salad on a salad plate.

∾

∽

Half Roasted Duck Breast Salad served with Italian Marmalade Vinaigrette Over Boston Bibb Lettuce

Italian Marmalade Vinaigrette:

¾ c.	Orange Marmalade
½ tsp.	Oyster Sauce
2 Tbl.	Sherry
1 tsp.	Ginger, grated
1 cl.	Garlic, minced
1 ea.	Shallots, minced
1 tsp.	Parsley, freshly chopped
½ tsp.	Thyme, freshly chopped
½ tsp.	Oregano, freshly chopped
½ Tbl.	Orange Zest

    ¼ c. Italian Vinaigrette
To Taste Sea Salt
To Taste Black Pepper, ground

Method:
1. Combine all ingredients and rest for 20 minutes.

    1 ea. Roasted Duck, split in one-half & grilled quickly on both sides
As Needed Eggplant, ends removed & sliced thin
As Needed Olive Oil
1 ea. Boston Bibb Lettuce, cut into quarters

Method:
1. Arrange duck, eggplant and boston bibb lettuce on entrée plate.
2. Serve with Italian marmalade vinaigrette.
   Garnish with thinly sliced orange skin.

ೲ

Marinated Bow Tie Noodles with Portabella Mushrooms, Roasted Red Peppers and Fresh Spinach

½#	Bow Tie Noodles-cooked in boiling salted water
¼#	Portabella Mushrooms, steamed & cut into large strips
1 ea.	Red Pepper-roasted, skin & seeds removed, cut into large strips
¼ c.	Italian Vinaigrette
½ tsp.	Oregano, freshly chopped
½ tsp.	Thyme, freshly chopped
½ tsp.	Parsley, freshly chopped
To Taste	Sea Salt
To Taste	Black Pepper, ground
As Needed	Spinach Leaves, stems removed & julienne

Method:

1. In a steel bowl, add bow tie noodles, portabella mushrooms and red pepper.
   Toss with Italian vinaigrette, herbs and season to taste.
2. Arrange fresh cut spinach and marinated noodles around oval entrée plate.

ೲ

⌒⌒

Marinated Oriental Salad with Rice Noodles, Served with a Ginger Sesame Vinaigrette

Ginger Sesame Vinaigrette:

1 Tbl.	Ginger, freshly grated
2 Tbl.	Soy sauce
½ c.	Italian White Balsamic Vinaigrette
¼ c.	Sesame Oil

Method:
1. Whisk ingredients to a smooth consistency.

6 oz.	Chicken Breasts-steamed until proper doneness, cooled & julienne
½ ea.	Carrots-steamed, cooled & julienne
½ ea.	Zucchini, julienne
½ ea.	Yellow squash, julienne
3 ea.	Red Oak Leaf Lettuce
1 pkg.	Rice Noodles, cooked in boiled salted water
1 tsp.	Sesame seeds
4 ea.	Pickled Ginger
1 Tbl.	Scallions, bias cut

Method:
1. In a bowl, add chicken, vegetables and toss with vinaigrette.
2. Arrange lettuce on plate with rice noodles in the middle.
   Place chicken and vegetables around rice noodles.
   Garnish with sesame seeds, pickled ginger and scallions.

⌒⌒

∽

Plum Tomatoes with Black Olives and Red Onions Garnished with Asiago Cheese, Toasted Pine Nuts

And Smoked Salmon

6 ea.	Plum Tomatoes-skin, core & seeds removed, cut in half
4 ea.	Plum Yellow Tomatoes-skin, core & seeds removed, cut in half
¼ c.	Basil, freshly julienne
1 tsp.	Thyme, freshly chopped
½ tsp.	Oregano, freshly chopped
To Taste	Black Pepper, cracked
1 ea.	Red Onion, sliced thin
½ c.	Black Olives, cut in half
As Needed	Red Oak Lettuce, chopped
½ c.	Italian Balsamic Vinaigrette
¼ c.	Asiago Cheese, shaved
¼ c.	Pine Nuts, toasted
2 oz.	Smoked Salmon, cut into strips

Method:
1. In a steel bowl combine the tomatoes, herbs, red onion and olives. Toss ingredients with vinaigrette.
2. Place red oak lettuce on salad plate and arrange marinated ingredients in center.
   Garnish with Asiago cheese, pine nuts and smoked salmon.

∽

❧

Tiger Shrimp in a Portabella Oil Vinaigrette, Served with Portabella Mushrooms And Marinated Tomatoes

Portabella Oil Vinaigrette:

1 ea.	Portabella-stems removed, grill on both sides & place in cuisinart
¾ c.	Extra Virgin Olive Oil
1 tsp.	Dijon Mustard
2 Tbl.	Sherry Vinegar
1 tsp.	Parsley, freshly chopped
½ tsp.	Oregano, freshly chopped
½ tsp.	Thyme, freshly chopped
To Taste	Sea Salt
To Taste	Black Pepper, cracked

Method:
1. Strain portabella juice and using one-half of a cup.
2. Whisk in remaining ingredients together and refrigerate for 1 hour.

3 ea.	Tiger Shrimp-peeled, de-veined & tail on
1 ea.	Portabella Mushroom-stem removed
½ c.	Portabella Oil Vinaigrette
3 cl.	Garlic, minced
As Needed	Plum Tomatoes-skin, core & seeds removed, julienne
1 Tbl.	Basil & Parsley, freshly chopped

Method:
1. In a steel container, add the portabella oil vinaigrette, shrimp, portabella mushrooms and garlic.
   Place in refrigerator and marinate overnight.
2. Grill shrimp, mushrooms, set aside and keep warm.
   Thinly slice portabella mushrooms.
3. In a steel bowl, toss the tomatoes, fresh herbs some of the vinaigrette.
   Marinate in refrigerator for 30 minutes.
4. Arrange marinated tomatoes, mushrooms and shrimp on salad plate.

❧

~

SEAFOOD

Blackened Salmon with a Toasted Pecan Cream Sauce, Served with Fettuccini And Garnished with Roasted Shallots
244

Breaded Dover Sole with Avocado and Roasted Red Pepper Mango Coulis, Garnished with Toasted Almonds
246

Ceviche of Tuna, Swordfish and Asparagus Tossed in a Ginger And Sesame Oil Vinaigrette, Served with Bibb Lettuce
248

Clams Casino with a Peach Essence
250

Cod Roulade Laced with Bits of Shrimp and Capers, Served On a Bed of Romaine with an Herb Mango Coulis
251

Dover Sole Francaise in a Pine Nut and Pistachio Crust, Served with a Lemon Caper Salsa
252

Filet of Dover Sole, Filled with Bay Scallops and Shrimp In a Riesling Herb Dill Cream Sauce, Garnished with Bits of Mango
254

Flounder in a Crabmeat Stuffing Laced in Tuna And Cucumber, Served with an Artichoke Sauce
256

Fried Calamari with a Spicy Yellow Tomato Sauce, Served with Spaghetti Zucchini
258

Grilled Halibut and Rounds of Sautéed Leeks with a Tequila Lime Butter, Served with Fresh Julienne Spinach
260

Grilled Shrimp with a White Bean Puree' and Peach Mango Chutney
261

Grilled Snapper with a Southern Comfort Lime Butter, Served with a Warm White Bean Tomato Salsa
263

*Grilled Swordfish, Served with a Spicy Roasted Red Pepper Beurre Blanc
And Garnished with Mango's and Peaches*
265
*Grilled Twin Filets of Trout, Served with a Cucumber and Roasted
Pepper Salsa, Garnished with Roasted Red and Yellow Pepper Coulis*
267
Hardy Style Fisherman's Seafood in a Tomato Saffron Broth
269
*Jumbo Shrimp Stuffed with Herb Goat Cheese,
Served with a Spicy Yellow Tomato Coulis*
271
Marinated Grilled Jumbo Shrimp, Served with Open Brie and Caviar
273
*Marinated Grilled Soft Shell Crabs with Grilled Eggplant,
Artichoke and Zucchini Medley*
274
*Marinated Grilled Wild Caught Salmon on a Bed of Steamed Spinach And
Spaghetti Squash, Served with Portabella Mushrooms And a
Mixture of Red and Yellow Peppers*
276
*Mesquite Grilled Tuna with Sun Dried Tomato Herb Butter, Served with
Asparagus, Black Beans and Yellow Plum Tomatoes,
Garnished with Shaved Asiago*
278
*New Zealand Garlic Mussels with a Spicy Tomato and
Green Pepper White Rice Timbale*
280
*Poached Filet of Dover Sole Filled with a Red Pepper Snapper Mousse,
Served with Asparagus Coulis*
281
Poached Halibut and Morels in a Shitake Mushroom Herb Broth
283
*Poached Salmon with a Crabmeat Filling, Served with a
Sherry Dill Cream Sauce and Garnished with Prawns and Scallops*
285
*Poached Salmon and Roasted Yellow Pepper Mousse Wrapped in a Layer
of Salmon Skin, Served with Bibb Lettuce and a Mango Peach Coulis*
287
*Poached Sea Bass in a Rich Broth of Vegetables
And Wild Mushrooms*
289

*Red Snapper Medallions, Served with an Herb Crayfish Sauce
And Garnished with Sliced Red Potatoes*
291
*Red Snapper with Oyster Shitake Mushrooms and Artichoke Hearts,
Served with Asparagus Tips*
293
*Salmon Filet with an Herb Feta Cheese Spinach Stuffing, Served with a
Spicy Plum Tomato Cream Sauce and Garnished with Toasted Pine Nuts*
294
*Sautéed and Seared Swordfish Rolled in Tuna and Asparagus with
Four Peppercorns, Served with a Champagne Wild Flower
Honey and Ginger Sauce*
296
*Sautéed Buckwheat Soft Shell Crabs,
Served with a Pear Mango Champagne Chutney*
298
*Sautéed Dover Sole with a Pineapple, Coconut and Mandarin
Orange Salsa, Garnished with Sliced Avocado*
299
*Scallops on a Bed of Roasted Garlic, Herb and Sun Dried Tomato Sauce,
Garnished with Julienne of Spinach*
300
*Seared Tuna with a Warm Marinated Corn, Plum Tomato,
And Cilantro Salsa, Served with Herb Risotto*
301
Shrimp Broth with Fresh Herbs
303
Shrimp Stuffed with Crabmeat, Served with a Lemon Garlic Cream Sauce
304
*Smoked Shrimp and Scallops with Julienne of Cucumbers And Mixed
Salad Greens, Served with a Pineapple Orange Mint Chutney*
306
*Summer Chilled Red Snapper with Tortellini Salad,
Served with a White Bean Dill Dressing*
308
*Summer Pan Seared Sea Scallops with Fresh Mixed Beans,
Button Mushrooms and Garnished with Tomato Basil Salsa*
310
Tuna Carpaccio with Fresh Herbs
311

∾

Blackened Salmon with a Toasted Pecan Cream Sauce, Served with Fettuccini And Garnished with Roasted Shallots

6 oz.	Salmon, skin off
As Needed	Old Bay Seasoning
As Needed	Sea Salt
As Needed	Black Pepper, ground
1½ c.	Water, cold

Method:
1. Season salmon on one side.
   In a sauté pan, heat on high and blacken salmon on the seasoned side.
2. Turn salmon over and add stock.
   Finish cooking in a 350ºF oven until proper doneness.

Toasted Pecan Cream Sauce:

1 Tbl.	Extra Virgin Olive Oil
1 cl.	Garlic, minced
1 Tbl.	Shallots, minced
½ tsp.	Dill, freshly chopped
½ tsp.	Cilantro, freshly chopped
½ tsp.	Thyme, freshly chopped
½ tsp.	Parsley, freshly chopped
¼ tsp.	Old Bay Seasoning
½ c.	Riesling
1 Tbl.	Lemon Juice, freshly squeezed
1½ c.	Salmon Stock, from Blacken Salmon
½ c.	Pecans, toasted & chopped
1 c.	Half & Half, hot
1 Tbl.	Roux, warm
To Taste	Sea Salt
To Taste	Black Pepper, ground

4 oz.   Fettuccini, cooked
1 Tbl.   Chives & Dill, whole
3 ea.   Shallots, roasted
As Needed   Pecans, roasted

Method:
1. In a sauté pan, sweat the garlic and shallots in olive oil.
   Add herbs, deglaze with wine, add lemon, stock, pecans and reduce by one-half.
   Stir in half & half and reduce again by one-half.
2. Whisk in roux, season to taste and strain lobster sauce.
3. Arrange fettuccini, blacken salmon and toasted pecan cream sauce on entrée plate.
   Garnish with herbs and roasted shallots.

∽

Breaded Dover Sole with Avocado and Roasted Red Pepper Mango Coulis, Garnished with Toasted Almonds

Avocado Coulis:

½ ea.	Avocado-skin & seed removed & diced medium
1 tsp.	Cilantro, freshly chopped
3 Tbl.	Half & Half, cold

Method:
1. Combine ingredients in a cuisinart and blend to a smooth consistency. Place avocado coulis in a refrigerator.

Roasted Red Pepper Mango Coulis:

½ ea.	Red Pepper, whole
1 ea.	Shallots, minced
1 tsp.	Cilantro, freshly chopped
1 Tbl.	Riesling
¼ c.	Chicken Stock, cold
To Taste	Tabasco
To Taste	Sea Salt
½ ea.	Mango, diced small

Method:
1. Roast red pepper on an open flame until black.
   Place in a sealed container for 20 minutes, remove skin, core, seeds and medium dice pepper.
2. In a sauce pot, add shallots, herbs and deglaze with wine.
   Add diced peppers, chicken stock and a dash of Tabasco.
   Let reduce by one-half, let cool, add mango and blend to a smooth consistency.
3. Strain sauce into a bottled container.

Breaded Sole:

8 oz.	Dover Sole, bones removed
To Taste	Sea Salt
To Taste	White Pepper, ground
As Needed	Buckwheat Flour, sifted
1 ea.	Egg, whole & whisk in 1 Tbl. water
¼ c.	Bread Crumbs
1 tsp.	Parsley, freshly chopped
1 tsp.	Dill, freshly chopped
1 Tbl.	Extra Virgin Olive Oil
As Needed	Sliced Almonds, toasted

Method:
1. Combine bread crumbs together with parsley.
2. Season fish, dredge in flour and shake excess off. Dip in egg mixture and then in crumb mixture. Sauté sole in olive oil.
3. Arrange sole and sauces on entrée plate.
4. Garnish with toasted almonds.

☙

Ceviche of Tuna, Swordfish and Asparagus Tossed in a Ginger And Sesame Oil Vinaigrette, Served with Bibb Lettuce

2 oz.	Swordfish, sliced thin
1 tsp.	Extra Virgin Olive Oil
2 oz.	Tuna Loin, cut small
3 ea.	Asparagus-peeled & cut small
2 Tbl.	Ginger, shaved & cut small
1 Tbl.	Parsley, Dill & Chives-freshly chopped
1 Tbl.	Sesame Oil
2 tsp.	Soy Sauce
1 tsp.	Wild Flower Honey
2 Tbl.	Champagne
To Taste	Black Pepper, cracked
As Needed	Bibb Lettuce
As Needed	Sesame Seeds

Method:
1. Sauté the swordfish in olive oil, remove and let cool.
    Cut into small portions and place in a steel bowl.
2. Add tuna, asparagus, ginger, herbs, sesame oil and soy sauce.
    Drizzle in wild flower honey and add champagne.
    Toss lightly and arrange on salad plate with Bibb lettuce.
3. Garnish with sesame seeds.

∽

Clams Casino with a Peach Essence

12 ea.	Clams, on half shell
3 Tbl.	Extra Virgin Olive Oil
1 Tbl.	Butter, whole
2 cl.	Garlic, minced
½ ea.	Red Pepper, minced
¼ ea.	Green Pepper, minced
3 ea.	Shallots, minced
½ tsp.	Parsley, freshly chopped
½ tsp.	Thyme, freshly chopped
¼ tsp.	Oregano, freshly chopped
1 tsp.	Lemon, freshly squeezed
3 Tbl.	Riesling
To Taste	Tabasco
2 ea.	Peach-skin & pit removed, minced

Method:
1. Place clams on baking dish.
2. In a sauté pan, heat the olive oil and butter.
   Sweat the garlic, peppers and shallots.
   Add herbs, lemon, deglaze with wine and add Tabasco.
   Incorporate peaches into mixture.
3. Place a small mixture on each of the clams.
   Bake in a 350ºF oven for 7 minutes.

∽

~

Cod Roulade Laced with Bits of Shrimp and Capers, Served On a Bed of Romaine with an Herb Mango Coulis

Cod Roulade:

1 Tbl.	Extra Virgin Olive Oil
1 ea.	Shallots, minced
1 cl.	Garlic, minced
¼ tsp.	Parsley, freshly chopped
¼ tsp.	Dill, freshly chopped
2 Tbl.	Champagne
4 oz.	Cod, diced small
1 ea.	Egg, whole
4 oz.	Half & Half, cold
2 oz.	Shrimp-peeled, de-veined & diced small
2 Tbl.	Capers, whole

Method:
1. In a sauté pan, sweat the shallots and garlic in olive oil.
   Add herbs, champagne and let reduce.
2. Blend the cod in a cuisinart, add the egg and blend again.
   Add slowly the half & half and blend to a smooth consistency.
3. Fold in shrimp and herb reduction.

Herb Mango Coulis:

¼ c.	Champagne
¼ c.	Mango, diced small
1 tsp.	Parsley, freshly chopped
½ tsp.	Cilantro, freshly chopped

Method:
1. In a small pot, add all the ingredients and simmer for 3 minutes.
   Let cool and strain in a squirt bottle.
   As Needed Romaine, julienne

Method:
1. Arrange romaine, cod roulade and herb mango coulis on salad plate.

~

Dover Sole Francaise in a Pine Nut and Pistachio Crust, Served with a Lemon Caper Salsa

8 oz.	Dover Sole, bones removed
To Taste	Cayenne Pepper, ground
As Needed	Buckwheat Flour, sifted
2 ea.	Eggs, whole
1 Tbl.	Locatelli Cheese, grated
1 tsp.	Parsley, freshly chopped
½ tsp.	Honey Wheat Germ, ground
3 Tbl.	Pine Nuts, ground
3 Tbl.	Pistachios, ground
2 Tbl.	Water, cold
As Needed	Extra Virgin Olive Oil

Method:
1. Season fish, dredge in flour and shake off excess.
2. In a steel bowl, whisk together the egg and cheese.
   Fold in the parsley, honey wheat germ, pine nuts, pistachios and water.
   Dip sole in mixture and fry in oil until golden brown.
3. Remove sole and keep warm.

Lemon Caper Salsa:

1 Tbl.	Extra Virgin Olive Oil
1 cl.	Garlic, minced
1 tsp.	Shallots, minced
3 Tbl.	Pinot Grisgio
½ c.	Fish Stock, cold
1½ Tbl.	Lemon Juice, freshly squeezed
1 tsp.	Lemon Zest
½ tsp.	Parsley, freshly chopped
½ tsp.	Chives, freshly chopped
1 tsp.	Capers, whole
1 Tbl.	Butter, whole
As Needed	Pine nuts
As Needed	Pistachios
As Needed	Dill, whole

Method:
1. In the same sauté pan, sweat the garlic and shallots in olive oil.
2. Deglaze with wine, add fish stock, lemon and reduce by one-half.
   Add herbs, capers and whisk in butter.
3. Arrange sole and lemon caper beurre blanc sauce on entrée plate.
   Garnish with pine nuts, pistachios and fresh dill.

$\backsim$

Filet of Dover Sole, Filled with Bay Scallops and Shrimp In a Riesling Herb Dill Cream Sauce, Garnished with Bits of Mango

Riesling Herb Dill Cream Sauce:

3 Tbl.	Extra Virgin Olive Oil
4 oz.	Shallots, minced
2 cl.	Garlic, minced
1 tsp.	Dill, freshly chopped
½ tsp.	Parsley, freshly chopped
½ tsp.	Cilantro, freshly chopped
¼ c.	Riesling
2 tsp.	Lemon Juice, freshly squeezed
1 c.	Fish Velouté, hot
To Taste	Sea Salt
To Taste	Tabasco

Method:
1. In a sauté pan, sweat the garlic and shallots in olive oil.
   Add herbs, deglaze with wine, add lemon juice, velouté and reduce.
2. Strain sauce and season to taste.

For the Sole:

12 oz.	Dover Sole, bones removed
To Taste	Sea Salt
To Taste	White Pepper, ground
2 ea.	Toothpicks
8 ea.	Bay Scallops, mussels removed
6 ea.	Shrimp-peeled, de-veined & tail on
½ c.	Riesling
3 oz.	Butter, clarified
¼ ea.	Mango, diced small
1 tsp.	Chives & Dill, freshly chopped

Method:
1. Slice sole lengthwise and season.
   Wrap sole until pocket is formed and insert toothpick in place.
2. Add scallops and rearrange three shrimp for each sole.
3. Drizzle wine and clarified butter on sole.
   Place bits of mango in center of sole.
   Bake in a 350°F oven for 12 minutes.
4. Arrange sole and Riesling herb dill cream sauce on entrée plate.
   Garnish with fresh herbs.

༄

Flounder in a Crabmeat Stuffing Laced in Tuna And Cucumber, Served with an Artichoke Sauce

Artichoke Sauce:

1 Tbl.	Extra Virgin Olive Oil
1 Tbl.	Leeks, sliced
1 tsp.	Garlic, minced
½ tsp.	Thyme, freshly chopped
½ tsp.	Parsley, freshly chopped
¼ c.	Riesling
¼ tsp.	Tarragon, freshly chopped
1 c.	Chicken Stock, cold
½ c.	Artichoke Hearts
1 Tbl.	Butter, cold
To Taste	Sea Salt
To Taste	Black Pepper, ground

Method:
1. In a sauté pan, sweat the leeks and garlic in olive oil.
   Add herbs, deglaze with wine and reduce by one-half.
   Stir in chicken stock, add artichokes and reduce again by one-half.
2. Remove from stove, strain, heat again and whisk in cold butter.
3. Season to taste.

Crabmeat Stuffing:

12 oz.	Cream Cheese
½ c.	Celery, minced
1 bn.	Scallions, minced
1 Tbl.	Parsley, freshly chopped
16 oz.	Lump Crabmeat
3 Tbl.	Buttermilk Ranch Vinaigrette
To Taste	Tabasco
To Taste	Cayenne Pepper, ground

Method:
1. Combine all ingredients in a steel bowl and mix until smooth.

> *7 oz.* Flounder, bones removed
> *As Needed* Toothpicks
> *1 ea.* Cucumber-peeled, seeds removed &
> thinly cut into long strips
> *4 oz.* Tuna, thinly cut into long strips

Method:
1. Slice flounder lengthwise, wrap until pocket is formed and insert toothpick in place.
   Stuff with crabmeat stuffing and bake in a 350°F oven for 10 minutes.
2. Take flounder out and let rest for one minute.
   Lace tuna and cucumber around flounder.
3. Serve with Artichoke sauce.

∾

Fried Calamari with a Spicy Yellow Tomato Sauce, Served with Spaghetti Zucchini

Spicy Yellow Tomato Sauce:

1 Tbl.	Extra Virgin Olive Oil
1 cl.	Garlic, minced
1 ea.	Shallots, minced
4 ea.	Yellow Plum Tomatoes-skin, core & seeds removed, diced medium
2 Tbl.	Cilantro, freshly chopped
1 Tbl.	Jalapeño, seeds removed & minced
3 Tbl.	Brandy
To Taste	Sea Salt
To Taste	Black Pepper, ground

Method:
1. In a sauté pan, sweat the garlic and shallots in olive oil.
   Add herbs, jalapeño, deglaze with brandy and add yellow tomatoes.
2. Season to taste and simmer for 10 minutes.
3. Strain tomato sauce.

Calamari:

¼ c.	Cornmeal
¼ c.	Buckwheat Flour, sifted
¼ c.	Bread Crumbs
1 tsp.	Thyme, freshly chopped
1 tsp.	Oregano, freshly chopped
½ tsp.	Parsley, freshly chopped
8 oz.	Squid, cleaned & sliced
¼ c.	All-Purpose Flour, sifted
1 ea.	Egg, whole & whisk in 1 Tbl. water
As Needed	Olive Oil

Method:
1. Combine the cornmeal, buckwheat, bread crumbs and herbs in a steel bowl.
2. Coat squid with flour, then egg mixture and then in crumb mixture. Deep fry squid until golden brown.
3. Serve with a spicy yellow tomato sauce and spaghetti zucchini.

Spaghetti Zucchini:

1 Tbl.	Olive Oil
1 ea.	Yellow Zucchini, julienne
1 ea.	Green Zucchini, julienne
1 cl.	Garlic, minced
½ tsp.	Oregano, freshly chopped

Method:
1. Sauté zucchini with garlic in olive oil very quickly for 1 minute. Add fresh oregano and toss again.

෴

∽

Grilled Halibut and Rounds of Sautéed Leeks with a Tequila Lime Butter, Served with Fresh Julienne Spinach

Tequila Lime Butter:

4 oz.	Butter, whole
½ oz.	Tequila
½ oz.	Lime Juice, freshly squeezed
1 tsp.	Lemon Juice, freshly squeezed
To Taste	Tabasco
1 Tbl.	Cilantro, freshly chopped

Method:
1. Soften butter to room temperature.
   Combine all ingredients in a mixing bowl and blend to a smooth consistency.
2. Roll up in plastic wrap and freeze for 30 minutes.

Grilled Halibut:

8 oz.	Halibut, bones removed
2 Tbl.	Extra Virgin Olive Oil
½ c.	Leeks, white only and sliced in rounds
¼ c.	Spinach, julienne
As Needed	Corn, steamed
As Needed	Plum Tomatoes-skin, core & seeds removed, diced small

Method:
1. Rub olive oil on halibut and grill on both sides until proper doneness.
2. Sweat leeks in a sauté pan in olive oil.
3. Place spinach on entrée plate and arrange halibut appropriately.
   Arrange the sautéed leeks and tequila lime butter.
   Garnish with corn and plum tomatoes.

∽

∽

Grilled Shrimp with a White Bean Puree' and Peach Mango Chutney

Peach Mango Chutney:

½ c. Peach-skin & pit removed, diced small
½ c. Mango-skin & pit removed, diced small

Method:
1. Place one quarter of a cup peaches and one quarter of a cup mango in a cuisinart.
2. Blend to a smooth consistency and fold in remaining fruit.

White Bean Puree:

6 ea. Shrimp-peeled, de-veined & tail on
¾ c. Extra Virgin Olive Oil
2 cl. Garlic, sliced
1 ea. Bay Leaf, whole
¼ c. White Balsamic Vinegar
1 c. Navy White Beans, cooked
1½ c. Shrimp Stock, from shrimp shells
½ tsp. Thyme, freshly chopped
1 ea. Bay Leaf, whole
1 cl. Garlic, minced
1 c. Celery, diced small
To Taste Sea Salt
To Taste Black Pepper, ground
2 Tbl. Dill & Chives, freshly chopped

Method:
1. In a steel bowl, add shrimp, olive oil, garlic, bay leaf and white balsamic vinegar.
   Place in refrigerator and marinate for one hour.
2. In a sauce pot, add beans, shrimp stock, herbs, garlic and celery.
   Bring ingredients to a boil and let simmer for 15 minutes.
   Take out bay leaf, place in cuisinart and blend to a smooth consistency.

262 | PAUL'S KITCHEN

3. Grill shrimp and keep warm.
   Arrange shrimp, white bean puree and peach mango
   chutney appropriately.
4. Garnish with fresh herbs.

∾

Grilled Snapper with a Southern Comfort Lime Butter, Served with a Warm White Bean Tomato Salsa

1 tsp.	Extra Virgin Olive Oil
8 oz.	Snapper, bones removed
To Taste	Sea Salt
To Taste	Cayenne Pepper, ground
¼ c.	Fish Stock

Method:
1. Rub olive oil on snapper, grill appropriately and keep warm.
2. Season and place in a sauté pan with fish stock.
   Finish cooking in a 350°F oven until proper doneness.

Southern Comfort Lime Butter:

4 oz.	Butter, whole
½ oz.	Southern Comfort
½ oz.	Lime Zest, freshly chopped
1 tsp.	Lemon Juice, freshly squeezed
To Taste	Tabasco
½ tsp.	Cilantro, freshly chopped
½ tsp.	Parsley, freshly chopped

Method:
1. Soften butter to room temperature.
2. Combine all ingredients in a large bowl and blend to a smooth consistency.
   Roll up in plastic wrap and freeze for 30 minutes.

White Beans:

1 c.	White Beans, cooked
1 cl.	Garlic, minced
1 ea.	Onion, minced
1 tsp.	Thyme, freshly chopped
1 Tbl.	Parsley, freshly chopped

1 ea.	Bay Leaf, whole
3½ c.	Chicken Stock, cold
To Taste	Sea Salt
To Taste	Black Pepper, ground

Method:
1. Bring ingredients to a boil and let simmer for 15 minutes.
2. Remove from burner and discard bay leaf.
   Place in refrigerator to cool completely.

Tomato Salsa:

1½ c.	Plum Tomatoes-skin, core & seeds removed, diced small
½ c.	Green Scallions, diced small
3 cl.	Garlic, minced
3 Tbl.	Cilantro, freshly chopped
2 Tbl.	Parsley, freshly chopped
1 Tbl.	Thyme, freshly chopped
¼ tsp.	Cumin, ground
1 ea.	Jalapeño Pepper, roasted with seeds removed & minced
3 Tbl.	Lime Juice, freshly squeezed
To Taste	Capers, whole
To Taste	Black Pepper, ground

Method:
1. Combine all ingredients and place in refrigerator for 15 minutes.
   Fold in white beans with tomato salsa.
2. In a sauce pot, stir white bean tomato salsa mixture on low flame for1 minute.
3. Place white bean tomato salsa and grilled snapper on entrée plate.
   Garnish appropriately with southern comfort lime butter.

∽

Grilled Swordfish, Served with a Spicy Roasted Red Pepper Beurre Blanc and Garnished with Mango's and Peaches

Spicy Roasted Red Pepper Beurre Blanc:

1 ea.	Red Pepper, whole
1 cl.	Garlic, minced
1 ea.	Shallots, minced
½ tsp.	Cilantro, freshly chopped
½ tsp.	Parsley, freshly chopped
3 Tbl.	Riesling
2 oz.	Chicken Stock, cold
Pinch	Red Pepper Flakes
To Taste	Tabasco
3 Tbl.	Butter-whole, cubed & left cold
3 Tbl.	Mango, seed removed & diced small
3 Tbl.	Peach, seed removed & diced small

Method:
1. Roast pepper on an open flame until black.
   Place in a sealed container for 20 minutes, remove skin, core and seeds.
   Medium dice pepper and set aside.
2. In a sauce pot, add garlic, shallots, herbs, wine and let reduce.
   Add peppers, chicken stock and red pepper flakes.
   Season with Tabasco and simmer for 5 minutes.
3. Let cool and blend to a smooth consistency.
   Strain sauce into a sauce pot, heat and whisk in cold butter a little at a time.

1 ea.	Swordfish, skin on
1 Tbl.	Extra Virgin Olive Oil
¼ c.	Vermouth
1 tsp.	Parsley & Chives, freshly chopped

Method:

1. Rub olive oil on swordfish and grill on one side making a criss-cross shape.
    In a sauté pan, add the swordfish and wine.
    Place in a 325ºF oven until proper doneness.
2. Arrange swordfish and pepper beurre blanc sauce on entrée plate.
3. Garnish with mango, peaches and fresh herbs.

ᶜⱽ

∽

Grilled Twin Filets of Trout, Served with a Cucumber and Roasted Pepper Salsa, Garnished with Roasted Red and Yellow Pepper Coulis

For the Trout:

8 oz.	Trout, skin on and bones removed
¼ c.	Italian vinaigrette
To Taste	Sea Salt
To Taste	Black Pepper, ground

Method:
1. Place trout in steel pan with vinaigrette and marinate for 30 minutes.
2. Grill until proper doneness, set aside and keep warm.
3. Arrange trout and salsa on entrée plate.
   Garnish with roasted red and yellow pepper coulis.

Cucumber and Roasted Red Pepper Salsa:

¼ c.	Cucumber, no seeds & diced small
1 Tbl.	Celery, diced small
3 Tbl.	Roasted Red Pepper, diced small
3 Tbl.	Roasted Yellow Pepper, diced small
½ tsp.	Cilantro, freshly chopped
½ tsp.	Oregano, freshly chopped
½ tsp.	Thyme, freshly chopped
To Taste	Sea Salt
To Taste	Black Pepper, ground
2 Tbl.	Italian vinaigrette

Method:
1. Add all ingredients in a steel bowl and mix thoroughly.
   Place in refrigerator for 10 minutes.

Roasted Red and Yellow Pepper Coulis:

1 ea.	Red Pepper, whole
1 oz.	Shallots, minced
½ tsp.	Cilantro, freshly chopped
½ tsp.	Parsley, freshly chopped
3 Tbl.	Riesling
2 oz.	Chicken Stock, cold
To Taste	Tabasco

Method:

1. Roast pepper on an open flame until black.
   Place in a sealed container for 20 minutes, remove skin, core and seeds.
   Medium dice pepper and set aside.
2. In a sauce pot, add shallots, herbs, wine and let reduce.
   Add peppers in sauce pot with chicken stock and a dash of Tabasco.
   Simmer for 2 minutes, let cool and blend to a smooth consistency.
3. Strain sauce into a bottled container.
4. For the yellow pepper coulis, replace red pepper with yellow pepper.

∽

∾

Hardy Style Fisherman's Seafood in a Tomato Saffron Broth

Tomato Saffron Broth:

2 Tbl.	Extra Virgin Olive Oil
½ Tbl.	Carrot, diced small
½ Tbl.	Onion, diced small
½ Tbl.	Celery, diced small
½ Tbl.	Green Pepper, diced small
2 tsp.	Saffron
1 tsp.	Old Bay Seasoning
1 ea.	Bay Leaf, whole
1 tsp.	Thyme, freshly chopped
½ tsp.	Oregano, freshly chopped
½ tsp.	Parsley, freshly chopped
1 c.	Riesling
1 Tbl.	Lemon Juice, freshly squeezed
6 c.	Fish Stock, cold
½ c.	Plum Tomatoes-skin, core & seeds removed, diced medium
To Taste	Sea Salt

Method:

1. In a sauce pot, sauté vegetables in olive oil, add herbs, deglaze with wine and reduce by one-half.
   Add lemon juice, fish stock, tomatoes and season.
2. Simmer for 20 minutes and strain broth.

3 Tbl.	Extra Virgin Olive Oil
3 ea.	Shrimp-peeled, de-veined & tail on
4 ea.	Bay Scallops, mussels removed
4 ea.	Mussels, cleaned
4 ea.	Little Neck Clams
4 ea.	Crab Claws
2 cl.	Garlic, minced

1 Tbl.	Shallots, minced
½ tsp.	Thyme, freshly chopped
1 tsp.	Parsley, freshly chopped
½ c.	Brandy
Pinch	Red Pepper Flakes
3 c.	Tomato Saffron Broth
To Taste	Sea Salt
1 c.	Arborio Risotto, cooked
1 Tbl.	Green Scallions, bias cut
1 tsp.	Parsley, freshly chopped

Method:

1. In a large sauce pot, sauté seafood quickly in olive oil.
   Add garlic, herbs, deglaze with brandy, add broth, simmer for 7
   minutes and season to taste.

2. On an entrée platter, arrange seafood around a timbale of risotto rice.
   Garnish with scallions and parsley.

୭~

༄

Jumbo Shrimp Stuffed with Herb Goat Cheese, Served with a Spicy Yellow Plum Tomato Coulis

Spicy Yellow Plum Tomato Coulis:

1 cl.	Garlic, minced
1 ea.	Shallots, minced
1 Tbl.	Extra Virgin Olive Oil
Pinch	Basil, freshly chopped
Pinch	Oregano, freshly chopped
Pinch	Thyme, freshly chopped
¼ c.	Pinot Grisgio
3 ea.	Yellow Plum Tomatoes-skin, core & seeds removed, diced small
½ ea.	Jalapeño, roasted, seeds removed & minced
To Taste	Sea Salt

Method:
1. In a sauté pan, sweat the garlic and shallots in olive oil. Add herbs and deglaze with wine. Stir in tomatoes, jalapeño and reduce by one-half.
2. Let cool, place in cuisinart and strain in sauce pot.
3. Heat contents and season to taste.

4 ea.	Jumbo Shrimp-peeled, de-veined, slit lengthwise & tail on
1 cl.	Garlic, minced
1 ea.	Shallots, minced
2 tsp.	Extra Virgin Olive Oil
1 tsp.	Cilantro, freshly chopped
1 tsp.	Parsley, freshly chopped
3 oz.	Goat Cheese
1 oz.	Cream Cheese
1 ea.	Egg Yolk

3 Tbl.   Vodka

1 tsp.   Cilantro & Dill, freshly chopped

Method:

1. In a sauté pan, sweat the garlic and shallots in olive oil.
    Add herbs and let cool.
2. In a steel bowl, add cooled mixture, goat cheese, cream cheese, egg
    yolk and mix well.
    Stuff shrimp with mixture and place in a sauté pan.
3. Bake in a 350ºF oven for 8 minutes.
    Remove from oven and flambé with Vodka.
4. Arrange stuffed shrimp and spicy yellow plum tomato coulis on
    entrée plate.
    Garnish with fresh herbs.

∽

Marinated Grilled Jumbo Shrimp, Served with Open Brie and Caviar

4 ea.	Jumbo Shrimp-peeled, de-veined, slit lengthwise & tail on
2 ea.	Wooden Skewer
½ c.	Extra Virgin Olive Oil
¼ c.	Pineapple Juice, freshly squeezed
¼ c.	Grapefruit Juice, freshly squeezed
½ tsp.	Parsley, freshly chopped
½ tsp.	Cilantro, freshly chopped
¼ c.	Champagne
To Taste	Black Pepper, cracked
6 oz.	Brie, slit from center making 8 cuts & melted butter rubbed on top
As Needed	Black & Red Caviar
As Needed	Parsley, freshly chopped
As Needed	Champagne

Method:
1. Insert wooden skewer in each of the shrimp.
   In a steel pan, add olive oil, pineapple juice, grapefruit, herbs, champagne and black pepper.
   Place in refrigerate overnight.
2. Grill shrimp until proper doneness.
3. Wrap brie in double foil wrap and leave space on top for brie to expand.
   Place on grill until the skin opens up.
   Remove from foil and place chopped parsley around brie.
4. Arrange on entrée plate the shrimp, brie and black and red caviar.
   Place a glass of champagne on the side.

∽

∾

Marinated Grilled Soft Shell Crabs with Grilled Eggplant, Artichoke and Zucchini Medley

Marinated Grilled Soft Shell Crabs:

1 tsp.	Lemon Juice, freshly squeezed
1 Tbl.	Capers, whole
½ c.	Extra Virgin Olive Oil
3 Tbl.	White Balsamic Vinegar
3 Tbl.	Riesling
1 ea.	Scallion, minced
1 ea.	Jalapeno Pepper, roasted & minced
½ tsp.	Basil, freshly chopped
½ tsp.	Dill, freshly chopped

½ tsp.	Tarragon, freshly chopped
½ tsp.	Thyme, freshly chopped
2 cloves	Garlic, minced
6 ea.	Soft Shell Crabs, gills removed

Method:

1. Add all ingredients into a steel pan and marinate crabs for overnight.
2. Grill soft shell crabs until proper doneness, set aside and keep warm.

1 ea.	Eggplant, sliced thin on bias
2 ea.	Zucchini, sliced thin on bias
½ c.	Artichokes, quartered
3 Tbl.	Italian Vinaigrette
½ tsp.	Oregano, freshly chopped
½ tsp.	Thyme, freshly chopped
To Taste	Sea Salt
To Taste	Black Pepper, ground
1 tsp.	Cilantro & Parsley, freshly chopped

Method:

1. Grilled vegetables until proper doneness.
   Toss vegetables, herbs and Italian vinaigrette in a steel bowl.
   Season to taste.
2. Place crabs and grilled vegetables on oval plate.
   Garnish appropriately.

∾

Marinated Grilled Wild Caught Salmon on a Bed of Steamed Spinach And Spaghetti Squash, Served with Portabella Mushrooms And a Mixture of Red and Yellow Peppers

Marinated Grilled Wild Caught Salmon:

1 pt.	Italian Vinaigrette
4-(6 oz.) each	Salmon Filet, skin & bones removed
¼ c.	Chardonnay
1 cl.	Garlic, minced
2 ea.	Shallots, minced
1 tsp.	Oregano, freshly chopped
½ tsp.	Dill, freshly chopped
¼ tsp.	Mint, freshly chopped
½ tsp.	Thyme, freshly chopped

½ tsp.   Parsley, freshly chopped
1 ea.   Bay Leaf, whole
To Taste   Sea Salt
To Taste   Black Pepper, crushed

Method:
1. In a steel container, add the Italian Vinaigrette, garlic, herbs and salmon. Marinate for two days.
2. Grill salmon until proper doneness. Place salmon on spinach.

Spaghetti Squash:

2 oz.   Spaghetti Squash, steamed
½ tsp.   Butter, whole
To Taste   Sea Salt

Method:
1. Steam spaghetti squash until proper doneness. Scrap out squash with a fork, add butter and season to taste.
2. Shape spaghetti squash in a round on entrée plate.

Steamed Spinach:

¼ c.   Spinach, loosely packed

Method:
1. Steam spinach quickly. Place on spaghetti squash.

Portabella Mushrooms with Red and Yellow Peppers:

¼ c.   Portabella Mushrooms, sliced
½ cl.   Garlic, minced
1/8 c.   Red Pepper, julienne
1/8 c.   Yellow Pepper, julienne
1 Tbl.   Chardonnay

Method:
1. Sauté mushrooms, add garlic and peppers.
2. Deglaze with chardonnay, let reduce, keep warm and place on salmon.

❦

∽

Mesquite Grilled Tuna with Sun Dried Tomato Herb Butter, Served with Asparagus, Black Beans and Yellow Plum Tomatoes, Garnished with Shaved Asiago

Sun Dried Tomato Herb Butter:

4 oz.	Butter, whole
8 oz.	Sun Dried Tomatoes, in olive oil & minced
1 Tbl.	Parsley, freshly chopped
1 Tbl.	Thyme, freshly chopped
1 tsp.	Tomato Juice
To Taste	Black Pepper, ground

Method:
1. Soften butter to room temperature.
   Blend ingredients together, shape with a pastry tip on wax paper and place in refrigerator.

Mesquite Grilled Tuna:

1 oz.	Extra Virgin Olive Oil
1 cl.	Garlic, sliced
1 Tbl.	Basil, freshly chopped
1 Tbl.	Parsley, freshly chopped
1 tsp.	Thyme, freshly chopped
1 Tbl.	Rosemary, freshly chopped
1 ea.	Bay Leaf, whole
5 oz.	Yellow Fin Tuna
As Needed	Apple Chips, place on coals inside grill

Method:
1. Combine ingredients, place in steel pan and marinate tuna in refrigerator for 30 minutes.
2. Grill tuna quickly on both sides and keep tuna medium rare.

Asparagus, Black Beans and Yellow Plum Tomatoes:

3 ea.	Asparagus-peeled, blanched & cut on bias
1 oz.	Black Beans, cooked
5 ea.	Yellow Plum Tomatoes, cut in quarters
1 Tbl.	Extra Virgin Olive Oil
½ oz.	Balsamic Vinegar
½ tsp.	Oregano, freshly chopped
½ tsp.	Thyme, freshly chopped
½ tsp.	Cilantro, freshly chopped
To Taste	Whole Black Pepper, cracked
1 oz.	Sun Dried Tomato Butter
As Needed	Asiago Cheese, shaved

Method:
1. Combine in a steel bowl the asparagus, black beans and yellow plum tomatoes.
   Make vinaigrette, toss lightly and arrange on entrée plate.
2. Arrange tuna, sun dried tomato herb butter and garnish with Asiago cheese.

⁌

∽

New Zealand Garlic Mussels with a Spicy Tomato and Green Pepper White Rice Timbale

6 ea.	New Zealand Mussels
¼ c.	Vermouth
4 cl.	Garlic, minced
3 ea.	Shallots, minced

Method:
1. In a sauté pot, combine ingredients and bring to a boil.
   Simmer for two minutes with lid slightly closed.

Spicy Tomato and Yellow Pepper White Rice Timbale:

1 Tbl.	Onion, diced small
1 Tbl.	Extra Virgin Olive Oil
½ c.	White Rice, uncooked
1 tsp.	Thyme, freshly chopped
½ tsp.	Oregano, freshly chopped
Pinch	Red Pepper Flakes
½ tsp.	Old Bay Seasoning
1½ c.	Chicken Stock, cold
½ ea.	Yellow Pepper-core & seeds removed & diced medium
½ ea.	Plum Tomatoes-skin, core & seeds removed, diced medium
To Taste	Sea Salt
1 Tbl.	Butter, cold

Method:
1. In a sauce pot, add onion, oil, white rice and herbs.
   Heat contents, mix thoroughly and add chicken stock.
   Let boil and simmer until rice is 80% done.
2. Add yellow peppers, tomatoes and simmer for anther 5 minutes.
   Stir in butter and season to taste.
3. Place Rice in center of entrée bowl.
   Arrange mussels around sides with some of the garlic on each mussel.

∽

~

Poached Filet of Dover Sole Filled with a Red Pepper Snapper Mousse, Served with Asparagus Coulis

Asparagus Coulis:

8 ea.	Asparagus, peeled & diced small
1 cl.	Garlic, minced
1 ea.	Shallots, minced
2 tsp.	Extra Virgin Olive Oil
1 tsp.	Parsley, freshly chopped
½ c.	Chicken Stock, cold

Method:
1. In a sauté pan, sweat the garlic and shallots in olive oil.
    Add parsley, chicken stock and simmer until asparagus is tender.
2. Place in cuisinart, blend until smooth.

Red Snapper Mousse:

6 oz.	Red Snapper Fillets, diced medium
1 oz.	Roasted Red Pepper, diced medium
1 ea.	Egg Yolk
1 tsp.	Capers, whole
1 tsp.	Parsley, freshly chopped
Pinch	Old Bay Seasoning
½ c.	Half & Half, cold

Method:
1. Blend in a cuisinart the red snapper fillets and roasted red pepper. Add egg, capers, parsley and blend well.
2. Slowly add the half and half to a smooth consistency.

1 oz.	Butter, whole
2 ea.	Shallots, minced
4 ea.	Dover Sole, cut lengthwise
To Taste	Sea Salt
To Taste	Black Pepper, ground
1 c.	Pinot Grisgio
As Needed	Leek, cut into long thin strips
As Needed	Roasted Red Pepper Coulis, place in bottled container
1 tsp.	Parsley & Dill, freshly chopped

Method:
1. Rub butter on bottom of poaching pan with shallots on top.
2. Season fish and wrap sole to form a pocket for the red snapper mousse. Fill sole with mousse and Insert a large toothpick to hold contents in place.
Wrap leeks around sole and add wine.
3. Place in a sauté pan and let simmer.
Finish cooking in a 350°F oven for 7 minutes.
4. Serve with asparagus and roasted red pepper coulis. Garnish with fresh herbs.

∽

Poached Halibut and Morels in a Shitake Mushroom Herb Broth

Shitake Mushroom Herb Broth:

1½#	Shitake Mushrooms, julienne
2 ea.	Shallots, minced
1 ea.	Bay leaf, whole
2 ea.	Black Peppercorns, whole
3 Tbl.	Sea Salt
1 Tbl.	Parsley, freshly chopped
3 c.	Water

Method:
1. Combine ingredients in a sauce pot.
   Bring to a boil and let simmer for 1 hour.
2. Strain and place in a sauce pot for poaching halibut.

1 ea.	Sea Scallop, mussel removed
1 tsp.	Extra Virgin Olive Oil
8 oz.	Halibut, bones removed
1 ea.	Shallots, minced
½ c.	Fish Stock, cold
1 tsp.	Sea Salt
To Taste	Black Pepper, ground
½ tsp.	Lemon juice, freshly squeezed
½ c.	Shitake Mushroom Herb Broth
4 oz.	Morels, whole
1 tsp.	Dill, freshly chopped
As Needed	Cilantro, whole leaves

Method:
1. Sauté scallop in olive oil until golden brown, set aside and keep warm.
2. Poach Halibut in shallots, fish stock, salt, black pepper and lemon until proper doneness.

3. Separately, simmer Morels in shitake mushroom herb broth for 5 minutes.
4. Arrange the halibut, morels and scallop in entrée bowl.
    Add shitake mushroom herb broth.
    Garnish with fresh herbs.

∞

Poached Salmon with a Crabmeat Filling, Served with a Sherry Dill Cream Sauce and Garnished with Prawns and Scallops

Sherry Dill Cream Sauce:

1 cl.	Garlic, minced
1 ea.	Shallots, minced
1½ tsp.	Dill, freshly chopped
½ tsp.	Thyme, freshly chopped
½ tsp.	Parsley, freshly chopped
¼ c.	Sherry
½ ea.	Lemon Juice, freshly squeezed
1 c.	Shrimp Stock, cold
2 c.	Half & Half, hot
1 oz.	Roux, warm
To Taste	Sea Salt
To Taste	Black Pepper, ground

Method:
1. In a sauce pot, add the garlic, shallots, herbs, wine and lemon juice. Bring to a boil and simmer ingredients until liquid is almost gone.
2. Add shrimp stock, let simmer and reduce by one-half.
3. Stir in half & half, let reduce again by one-half and whisk in roux. Simmer for 15 minutes on low heat, strain and season to taste.

Poached Salmon:

1 ea.	Salmon, bones & skin removed
2 ea.	Prawns-de-veined, head & tail on
2 ea.	Sea Scallops, mussels removed
3 Tbl.	Cream Cheese
1 Tbl.	Buttermilk Ranch Vinaigrette
1 Tbl.	Half & Half, cold
½ tsp.	Dill, freshly chopped

Pinch	Old Bay Seasoning
3 oz.	Lump Crabmeat
1 tsp.	Celery, minced
As Needed	Fish Stock, cold
3 Tbl.	Plum Tomatoes-skin, core & seeds removed, diced medium
1 Tbl.	Dill & Parsley, freshly chopped

Method:
1. Butterfly salmon by making a pocket for the seafood filling.
2. In a steel bowl, mix the cream cheese, ranch vinaigrette and half & half to a smooth consistency.
   Blend together the dill, old bay, celery and crabmeat.
3. Fill salmon pocket with seafood mixture.
   Garnish with scallops and prawns.
4. Poach salmon in fish stock until proper doneness.
5. Place salmon on entrée plate with sherry dill cream sauce.
   Garnish with plum tomatoes and fresh herbs.

෴

Poached Salmon and Roasted Yellow Pepper Mousse Wrapped in a Layer of Salmon Skin, Served with Bibb Lettuce and a Mango Peach Coulis

Poached Salmon & Yellow Pepper Mousse:

6 oz.	Salmon Fillets, diced medium & reserve skin
1 oz.	Roasted Yellow Pepper, diced medium
1 ea.	Egg Yolk
1 tsp.	Capers, whole
1 tsp.	Parsley, freshly chopped
Pinch	Old Bay Seasoning
½ c.	Half & Half, cold
As Needed	Bibb Lettuce

Method:
1. Blend in a cuisinart the red snapper fillets and roasted red pepper. Add egg, capers, parsley and blend well.
2. Slowly add the half and half to a smooth consistency.
3. Place salmon skin on bottom of plastic wrap and then add a thin layer of mousse.
Wrap in plastic wrap and shape into a roll.
Plastic wrap the entire mixture again and then use foil wrap to cover completely.
Place in a 160ºF salted water bath until the internal temperature is 135ºF.
4. Remove from water bath, let cool and place in refrigerator until
5. ready to use.
Unmold, slice thinly and serve with bibb lettuce and mango peach coulis.

Mango Peach Coulis:

¼ c.   Mango-skin & pit removed, diced small
¼ c.   Peach-skin & pit removed, diced small
1 tsp.   Cilantro, freshly chopped

Method:
1. Place mango and peaches in a cuisinart.
2. Blend to a smooth consistency.

∽

Poached Sea Bass in a Rich Broth of Vegetables And Wild Mushrooms

1 Tbl.	Extra Virgin Olive Oil
1 cl.	Garlic, minced
1 tsp.	Shallots, minced
½ c.	Water, cold
½ c.	Pinot Grisgio
1 tsp.	Parsley, freshly chopped
6 oz.	Sea Bass, bones removed
To Taste	Sea Salt
To Taste	Black Pepper, cracked
4 ea.	Asparagus, peeled

¼ c.	Carrot, peeled & julienne
1 oz.	Oyster Mushrooms, washed
1 oz.	Enoli Mushrooms, washed
1 tsp.	Dill & Parsley, freshly chopped

Method:

1. In a poaching pan, add olive oil, garlic, shallots, water, wine and parsley.
   Season sea bass, place in poaching pan and simmer until
   proper doneness.
   Remove sea bass and keep warm.
   Strain poaching liquid in another sauce pot.
2. Add carrots, asparagus and simmer for 1 minute.
   Toss mushrooms in and simmer for 30 seconds.
3. In an entrée bowl, add sea bass, vegetables and broth.
   Garnish with fresh herbs.

‿

∽

Red Snapper Medallions, Served with an Herb Crayfish Sauce And Garnished with Sliced Red Potatoes

Red Snapper Mousse:

12 oz.	Red Snapper Fillets, diced large
2 ea.	Egg, whole
1 Tbl.	Capers, whole
2 Tbl.	Parsley, freshly chopped
Pinch	Old Bay Seasoning
¾ c.	Half & Half, cold
As Needed	Chives, garnish
As Needed	Red Potato, skin on
As Needed	Extra Virgin Olive Oil

Method:
1. In a cuisinart, pulse blend the red snapper fillets.
   Add the eggs one at a time, then add the capers and herbs.
   Slowly add the half & half to a smooth consistency.
2. Wrap in plastic wrap and shape into a roll.
   Plastic wrap the entire mixture again and then use foil wrap to cover completely.
   Place in a 160°F salted water bath until the internal temperature is 135°F.
3. Remove from water bath, let cool and place in refrigerator until ready to use.
   Unmold, slice thinly and serve with crayfish sauce on bottom of entrée bowl.
4. Criss-cross potato on mandolin, fry until crispy and garnish around bowl.

Herb Crayfish Sauce:

3 Tbl.	Extra Virgin Olive Oil
14 oz.	Crayfish, whole
1 sm.	Carrot, cut into diamond shapes
2 Tbl.	Leek, diced small
1 ea.	Celery, cut into diamond shapes
1 cl.	Garlic, minced
2 Tbl.	Parsley, freshly chopped
1 tsp.	Thyme, freshly chopped
1 tsp.	Cilantro, freshly chopped
2 oz.	Vodka
½ c.	Vermouth
1 Tbl.	Plum Tomatoes-skin, core & seeds removed, julienne
1½ c.	Half & Half, hot
To Taste	Sea Salt
To Taste	Black Pepper, ground

Method:
1. In a sauté pan, sauté crayfish in olive oil.
   Sauté vegetables, add garlic and herbs.
2. Flambé with Vodka, add wine and reduce by one-half.
3. Stir in tomatoes, add half & half, simmer and reduce to a smooth consistency. Season to taste.

⤳

Red Snapper with Oyster Shitake Mushrooms and Artichoke Hearts, Served with Asparagus Tips

10 oz.	Red Snapper Fillet, skin & bones removed
To Taste	Sea Salt
To Taste	Black Pepper, ground
As Needed	Buckwheat Flour, sifted
3 Tbl.	Parmesan Cheese, grated
1 tsp.	Parsley, freshly chopped
1 ea.	Egg, whole
1 Tbl.	Water, cold
5 Tbl.	Extra Virgin Olive Oil
2 oz.	Oyster Mushrooms, quartered
1 oz.	Shitake Mushrooms, julienne
4 ea.	Asparagus, peeled & cut on bias
3 ea.	Artichoke Hearts, quartered
1 Tbl.	Lemon Zest
1 Tbl.	Cilantro & Parsley, freshly chopped
1 oz.	Brandy
2 oz.	Butter, whole
1 tsp.	Dill & Chives, freshly chopped

Method:
1. Whip the egg, water, parmesan cheese and parsley together.
2. Season snapper, dredge in flour, shake off excess then dip in egg mixture.
   Sauté red snapper in of olive oil until proper doneness, remove from pan and keep warm.
3. In the same sauté pan, sauté mushrooms in olive oil.
   Toss in asparagus and sauté for 1 minute.
   Add artichokes, lemon zest, herbs and flambé with brandy.
   Whisk in the butter.
4. Arrange red snapper and medley mixture on entrée plate.

⤳

Salmon Filet with an Herb Feta and Spinach Stuffing, Served with a Spicy Plum Tomato Cream Sauce and Garnished with Toasted Pine Nuts

Spicy Plum Tomato Cream Sauce:

1 cl.	Garlic, minced
1 ea.	Shallots, minced
1 Tbl.	Extra Virgin Olive Oil
Pinch	Basil, freshly chopped
Pinch	Oregano, freshly chopped
Pinch	Thyme, freshly chopped
1 oz.	Pinot Noir
4 ea.	Plum Tomatoes-skin, core & seeds removed & diced small
½ ea.	Jalapeño, seeds removed & minced
¼ c.	Heavy Cream, hot
To Taste	Sea Salt

Method:
1. In a sauté pan, sweat the garlic and shallots in olive oil. Add herbs and deglaze with wine.
2. Stir in tomatoes, jalapeño and reduce.
3. Let cool, place in cuisinart and strain in sauce pot. Heat sauce, stir in cream and simmer for 3 minutes. Season to taste.

Herb Feta and Spinach Stuffing:

6 oz.	Feta Cheese
3 oz.	Spinach-steamed, drained & chopped
½ tsp.	Cilantro, freshly chopped
½ tsp.	Thyme, freshly chopped
To Taste	Sea Salt
To Taste	Black Pepper, ground

Method:
1. Combine ingredients together and season to taste.

4 ea.	Salmon Filet, cut wide & thin
To Taste	Sea Salt
To Taste	White Pepper, ground
As Needed	Toothpicks
½ c.	Fish Stock
1 Tbl.	Pine Nuts, toasted
1 tsp.	Parsley, freshly chopped

Method:
1. Season salmon and place one filet on bottom, then stuffing mixture. Place other filet on top and hold together with toothpicks.
2. Transfer salmon to sauté pan with fish stock and let simmer. Place in a 350ºF oven until proper doneness.
3. Arrange salmon and spicy plum tomato cream sauce on entrée plate. Garnish with toasted pine nuts and fresh parsley.

༄

❧

Sautéed and Seared Swordfish Rolled in Tuna and Asparagus with Four Peppercorns, Served with a Champagne Wild Flower Honey and Ginger Sauce

2 ea.	Swordfish, cut thinly
2 oz.	Tuna Loin, skin & bones removed
3 ea.	Asparagus-peeled, steam for 1 minute & reserve tips
1 Tbl.	Extra Virgin Olive Oil
1 tsp.	Black, Green, White & Pink Peppercorns-ground fine
¼ c.	Champagne
1 Tbl.	Wild Flower Honey
2 tsp.	Ginger, grated
1 ea.	Shallots, minced

½ cl.   Garlic, minced
1 tsp.   Dill & Parsley, freshly chopped
As Needed   Ginger, shaved

Method:
1. Lay the swordfish on a flat surface, place tuna loin down with asparagus and roll up tightly.
   Wrap up with butchers twine to hold together.
   Place olive oil in a sauté pan and sear swordfish quickly on all sides.
   Remove from pan and roll in ground peppercorns.
2. In the same sauté pan, add champagne and reduce by one-half.
   Add wild flower honey, ginger, shallots and garlic.
   Reduce again and strain sauce
3. Slice swordfish diagonally and arrange on salad plate.
   Serve with champagne wild flower honey and ginger sauce.
   Garnish with fresh herbs, shaved ginger and asparagus tips.

∾

Sautéed Buckwheat Soft Shell Crabs, Served with a Pear Mango Champagne Chutney

Pear Mango Chutney:

½ c.	Pear-skin, pit removed & diced small
½ c.	Mango-skin, pit removed & diced small
¼ c.	Champagne

Method:
1. Place one quarter of a cup peaches and one quarter of a cup mango in a cuisinart.
   Blend to a smooth consistency.
2. In a sauce pot, add fruit, champagne and reduce for 5 minutes.
   Let ingredients cool in a steel bowl.
3. Fold in remaining fruit.

As Needed	Buckwheat Flour, sifted
1 tsp.	Garlic, minced
½ tsp.	Thyme, freshly chopped
½ tsp.	Parsley, freshly chopped
½ tsp.	Cilantro, freshly chopped
3 Tbl.	Extra Virgin Olive Oil
1 ea.	Soft Shell Crabs, gills removed
1 tsp.	Cilantro & Chives, freshly chopped
½ ea.	Lime, whole & sliced

Method:
1. Mix buckwheat, garlic and herbs together.
2. Dredge soft shell crabs in buckwheat mixture.
   Sauté soft shell crabs in olive oil.
   Drain on paper towel and keep warm.
3. Arrange soft shell crabs and pear mango champagne chutney on entrée plate.
   Garnish with fresh herbs and lime slices.

∾

∾

Sautéed Dover Sole with a Pineapple, Coconut and Mandarin Orange Salsa, Garnished with Sliced Avocado

To Taste	Sea Salt
To Taste	Black Pepper, ground
8 oz.	Dover Sole, bones removed
2 Tbl.	Buckwheat Flour, sifted
1 ea.	Egg, whole
½ c.	Bread Crumbs
3 Tbl.	Extra Virgin Olive Oil
As Needed	Avocado-skin & pit removed, sliced

Method:
1. Season sole, dredge in buckwheat flour and shake excess off.
   Dip sole fillets in egg and then bread crumbs.
   Sauté sole until golden brown in olive oil.
2. Serve with pineapple, mandarin, coconut and orange salsa.
   Garnish with avocado.

Pineapple and Mandarin Orange Salsa:

¼ c.	Pineapple, diced small
¼ c.	Mandarin Oranges
1 Tbl.	Orange Zest
1 Tbl.	Coconut, shredded
1 tsp.	Chives, Parsley & Dill-freshly chopped
1 Tbl.	Grand Marne

Method:
1. Add all ingredients in a steel bowl and toss lightly.
2. Serve with sole.

∾

∽

Scallops on a Bed of Roasted Garlic, Herb and Sun Dried Tomato Sauce, Garnished with Julienne of Spinach

3 ea.	Sea Scallops, mussels removed
1 Tbl.	Extra Virgin Olive Oil
¼ c.	Riesling
½ tsp.	Basil, freshly chopped
½ tsp.	Parsley, freshly chopped
½ tsp.	Thyme, freshly chopped
¼ c.	Sun Dried Tomatoes, julienne
3 cl.	Roasted Garlic
½ c.	Chicken Stock, cold
1 Tbl.	Butter, whole
To Taste	Sea Salt
To Taste	Black Pepper, ground
¼ c.	Spinach, fresh & julienne

Method:
1. Sauté scallops in olive oil, remove from pan and keep warm.
2. In the same sauté pan, deglaze with wine, add herbs and reduce. Add sun dried tomatoes, garlic and chicken stock.
3. Reduce by one-half and whisk in cold butter. Season to taste.
4. Arrange sauce on bottom with scallops on top. Garnish with fresh spinach.

∽

∽

Seared Tuna with a Warm Marinated Corn, Plum Tomato, And Cilantro Salsa, Served with Herb Risotto

Seared Tuna Steak:

1 Tbl.	Extra Virgin Olive Oil
10 oz.	Tuna Steak
To Taste	Sea Salt
To Taste	Black Pepper, cracked

Method:
1. Season tuna steak.
2. In a sauté pan, add olive oil and sear tuna quickly on both sides. Keep tuna medium rare.

Warm Marinated Corn, Plum Tomato and Cilantro Salsa:

2 Tbl.	Corn, steamed for 2 minutes
2 Tbl.	Celery, diced small
1 Tbl.	Plum Tomato-skin, core & seeds removed, diced small
1 Tbl.	Red Onion, diced small
½ tsp.	Cilantro, freshly chopped
½ tsp.	Thyme, freshly chopped
To Taste	Sea Salt
To Taste	Black Pepper, ground
1 tsp.	White Balsamic Vinegar
1 Tbl.	Extra Virgin Olive Oil

Method:
1. Add contents in a steel bowl and mix thoroughly. Sauté contents quickly for 1 minute.

Herb Risotto:

3 Tbl.	Extra Virgin Olive Oil
1 c.	Arborio Rice
1 ea.	Shallots, minced
2½ c.	Chicken Stock, cold
½ tsp.	Thyme, freshly chopped
3 Tbl.	Carrots, diced small
1 Tbl.	Celery, diced small
¼ c.	Parsley, freshly chopped
1 Tbl.	Butter, whole
To Taste	Sea Salt
To Taste	White Pepper, ground

Method:

1. In a sauté pot, stir in the Arborio rice with the olive oil.
   Add shallots, one third of chicken stock, thyme, vegetables, bring to a boil and let simmer.
   Repeat twice with one third more of chicken stock and let reduce.
2. Stir in parsley and butter when rice is almost done.
   Season to taste.
3. Arrange tuna, herb risotto and salsa on entrée plate.

∽

Shrimp Broth with Fresh Herbs

4 c.	Shrimp Shells (from about 16 shrimp)
1 ea.	Onion, sliced
1 ea.	Carrot, diced medium
1 rib	Celery, diced medium
½ ea.	Lemon, whole
4 ea.	Bay Leaf, whole
¼ c.	Parsley, freshly chopped
½ tsp.	Basil, freshly chopped
½ tsp.	Thyme, freshly chopped
½ tsp.	Oregano, freshly chopped
2 ea.	Black Peppercorns, whole
1 tsp.	Sea Salt
2 qt.	Water, cold

Method:
1. Combine ingredients in a stock pot.
2. Bring to a boil.
   Let simmer for 45 minutes.
3. Strain broth and let cool in refrigerator.

Shrimp Stuffed with Crabmeat, Served with a Lemon Garlic Cream Sauce

Lemon Garlic Cream Sauce:

1 Tbl.	Extra Virgin Olive Oil
1 cl.	Garlic, minced
1 ea.	Shallots, minced
Pinch	Old Bay Seasoning
½ tsp.	Dill, freshly chopped
½ tsp.	Thyme, freshly chopped
½ ea.	Bay Leaf, whole
¼ c.	Riesling
½ c.	Shrimp Stock, cold
½ c.	Half & Half, hot
½ ea.	Lemon, freshly squeezed
1 Tbl.	Roux, warm
As Needed	Sea Salt
To Taste	White Pepper, ground

Method:
1. In a sauté pan, sweat the garlic and shallots in olive oil.
   Add herbs, deglaze with wine, add shrimp stock and reduce by one-half.
2. Stir in half & half, lemon and reduce again by one-half.
   Whisk in roux and simmer for 5 minutes.
3. Strain sauce and season to taste.

Crabmeat Stuffing:

3 oz.	Lump Crabmeat
1 tsp.	Buttermilk Ranch Vinaigrette
8 ea.	Jumpo Shrimp-peeled, de-veined & tail on
1 Tbl.	Extra Virgin Olive Oil
1 oz.	Vodka

As Needed Pecans, toasted & coarsely chopped
½ tsp. Lemon, julienne
1 tsp. Dill & Chives, freshly chopped

Method:
1. In a steel bowl, mix together the crabmeat and buttermilk ranch vinaigrette.
2. Butterfly the shrimp, pound out slightly and insert toothpicks to prevent curling.
Brush with olive oil and sauté on both sides.
3. Place crabmeat mixture on top and bake in a 350ºF oven for one minute. Remove from oven and flambé with Vodka.
4. Arrange shrimp on entrée plate with lemon garlic cream sauce.
Garnish with toasted pecans, lemon and fresh herbs.

ᑭ

Smoked Shrimp and Scallops with Julienne of Cucumbers And Mixed Salad Greens, Served with a Pineapple Orange Mint Chutney

6 ea.	Shrimp, smoked
8 ea.	Scallops, smoked
½ ea.	Cucumber-peeled, seeds removed & julienne
3 ea.	Seasonal Salad Greens
1 oz.	Light vinaigrette

Method:
1. Arrange lettuce, seafood and cucumber on salad plate.
   Spray lightly with vinaigrette.

Smoked Shrimp & Scallops:

12 ea.	Shrimp-peeled, de-veined & tail on
16 ea.	Scallops, mussels removed
¼ c.	Sherry
3 cl.	Garlic, minced
½ c.	Scallions, diced small
1 tsp.	Dill & Parsley, freshly chopped
2 Tbl.	Sesame Oil

Method:
1. Smoke shrimp and scallops separately until proper doneness.
   Let seafood cool for 10 minutes.
2. In a sauce pot, add wine, garlic and scallions.
   Let simmer, reduce to one-half and cool completely.
3. Place liquid in a steel bowl, add sesame oil and fresh herbs.
   Add cooked seafood and marinate overnight.

Pineapple Orange Mint Chutney:

½ c.	Pineapple, diced small
½ c.	Orange, cut into segments

      1 Tbl. Orange Zest
     ¼ tsp. Mint, freshly chopped

Method:

1. In a steel bowl, add the pineapple and orange segments. Add the orange peel, mint and toss lightly.
2. Serve with salad.

∾

Summer Chilled Red Snapper with Tortellini Salad, Served with a White Bean Dill Dressing

White Bean Dill Dressing:

1 Tbl.	Onions, minced
8 ea.	Capers, minced
1 Tbl.	Dill, freshly chopped
1 Tbl.	Parsley, freshly chopped
1 tsp.	Thyme, freshly chopped
1 cl.	Garlic, minced
1 tsp.	Dijon Mustard
½ tsp.	White Balsamic Vinegar
½ c.	Navy White Beans, blended to a smooth consistency
1 Tbl.	Sour Cream
1 Tbl.	Mayonnaise

Method:
1. Combine all ingredients in a steel bowl and mix to a smooth consistency.

10 oz.	Red Snapper, bones removed
To Taste	Sea Salt
To Taste	Black Pepper, ground
1 cl.	Garlic, minced
1 ea.	Shallots, minced
¼ c.	Riesling
¼ c.	Water, cold
As Needed	Romaine Lettuce
½ c.	Tortellini Pasta salad
1 tsp.	Parsley & Dill, freshly chopped

1. Season red snapper.
2. In a poaching pan, add shallots, garlic, wine and water. Poach snapper with a lid on until proper doneness. Place in refrigerator for 30 minutes.

3. Arrange red snapper, romaine lettuce and tortellini pasta on salad plate.
4. Serve with white bean dill dressing.
   Garnish with fresh herbs.

∾

࿂

Summer Pan Seared Sea Scallops with Fresh Mixed Beans, Button Mushrooms and Garnished with Tomato Basil Salsa

Tomato Basil Salsa:

1 ea.	Plum Tomatoes-skin, core & seeds removed & julienne
2 Tbl	Basil, julienne
4 oz.	Italian Vinaigrette
To Taste	Black Pepper, cracked

Method:
1. Combine ingredients and place in refrigerator for 10 minutes.

4 ea.	Sea Scallops, mussels removed
1 Tbl.	Extra Virgin Olive Oil
1 cl.	Garlic, minced
1 ea.	Shallots, sliced
1 tsp.	Parsley, freshly chopped
¼ c.	Green Beans, cut on bias & steamed for 2 minutes
¼ c.	Yellow Wax Beans, cut on bias & steamed for 2 minutes
¼ c.	Button Mushrooms, stems removed & cut in quarters
2 Tbl.	Italian Vinaigrette

Method:
1. Sauté the scallops in olive oil until golden brown.
   Remove from pan and place in refrigerator for 20 minutes.
2. In a sauté pan, sweat the garlic and shallots in olive oil and let cool.
3. In a steel bowl, add the parsley, mushrooms, garlic and shallots.
   Toss with beans and Italian vinaigrette.
4. Arrange scallops and beans on salad plate.
   Place tomato basil salsa on each scallop.

࿂

෮෨

Tuna Carpaccio with Fresh Herbs

4 oz.	Yellowfin Tuna
As Needed	Black Pepper, cracked
1 tsp.	Extra Virgin Olive Oil
1 Tbl.	Roasted Red Pepper Coulis
1 Tbl.	Green Pesto
½ tsp.	Soy Sauce
1 Tbl.	Italian Vinaigrette
¼ c.	Romaine Lettuce, julienne
1 Tbl.	Pine Nuts, toasted
1 tsp.	Thyme Leaves, whole

Method

1. Season tuna with black pepper.
   In a sauté pan, add oil and sear tuna quickly on all sides keeping tuna rare.
2. Freeze tuna, remove and slice thinly on salad plate.
   Decorate plate with Red Pepper Coulis and Green Pesto.
3. Place soy sauce and vinaigrette in a container.
4. Arrange romaine on plate and add vinaigrette mix.
   Garnish with toasted pine nuts and thyme leaves.

෮෨

∽

SOUPS

Atlantic Sea Scallop Soup with Leeks,
Garnished with Julienne of Spinach
314
Chicken Soup with Garden Spring Vegetables,
Garnished with Tortellini and Fresh Herbs
315
Clam Chowder with Red Skin Potatoes,
White Beans And Plum Tomatoes
316
Cream of Chicken with Fresh Garden Vegetables
317
Deer Stew with Garden Fresh Vegetables and White Potatoes
318
Grilled Asparagus and Mushroom Soup
320
Lamb Stew with Red Skin Potatoes and Turnips
321
Lobster Tomato Broth, Served with Lobster Basil Quenelles
322
Lump Crabmeat, Shrimp and Mushroom Bisque
324

∽

✑

Atlantic Sea Scallop Soup with Leeks, Garnished with Julienne of Spinach

1 cl.	Garlic, minced
1 ea.	Leeks, white part only & diced small
As Needed	Extra Virgin Olive Oil
½ tsp.	Parsley, freshly chopped
½ tsp.	Thyme, freshly chopped
½ tsp.	Cilantro, freshly chopped
1 ea.	Bay Leaf, whole
2 Tbl.	Brandy
3 c.	Fish Stock, cold
2 Tbl.	Roux, warm
2 c.	Half & Half, hot
½#	Sea Scallops, mussels removed & sliced
½ c.	Spinach, loosely packed & julienne
To Taste	Sea Salt
To Taste	Black Pepper, ground

Method:
1. In a soup pot, sweat the garlic and leeks in olive oil.
   Add herbs, bay leaf, deglaze with brandy, add stock and reduce by one-half.
2. Whisk in roux, add half & half and reduce again by one-half.
   Strain into another sauce pot.
3. Separately, grill sea scallops quickly and add to soup.
   Simmer for 6 minutes stirring occasionally.
   Remove bay leaf and discard.
   Blend soup in cuisinart and strain.
4. Stir in spinach and season to taste.

✑

∽

Chicken Soup with Garden Spring Vegetables, Garnished with Tortellini and Fresh Herbs

3 Tbl.	Extra Virgin Olive Oil
½ c.	Carrots, peeled & diced medium
¼ c.	Onions, diced medium
¼ c.	Celery, diced medium
1 Tbl.	Basil, freshly chopped
1 Tbl.	Thyme, freshly chopped
1 tsp.	Tarragon, freshly chopped
1 ea.	Bay Leaf, whole
½#	Chicken Meat, diced medium
3½ qt.	Chicken Stock, cold
6 ea.	Asparagus, peeled & cut on bias
½#	Cheese Tortellini
3 Tbl.	Chives & Parsley, freshly chopped
To Taste	Sea Salt
To Taste	Black Pepper, ground

Method:

1. In a soup pot, sweat the carrots, onions and celery in olive oil.
   Add herbs, bay leaf, chicken meat, 2 cups of the chicken stock
   and let boil while stirring.
   Stir in remaining stock and simmer for 20 minutes.
2. Add tortellini and simmer for 8 minutes.
3. Stir in asparagus and simmer for another 2 minutes.
4. Garnish with fresh herbs.
   Season to taste.

∽

ↀ

Clam Chowder with Red Skin Potatoes, White Beans and Plum Tomatoes

3 Tbl.	Extra Virgin Olive Oil
2 ea.	Carrots, peeled & diced medium
½ c.	Leeks, white part only & diced medium
¼ c.	Celery, diced medium
¼ ea.	Green Pepper, diced medium
2 cl.	Garlic, minced
2 Tbl.	Tomato Paste
1 Tbl.	Parsley, freshly chopped
1 tsp.	Oregano, freshly chopped
1 tsp.	Thyme, freshly chopped
1 ea.	Bay Leaf, whole
½ tsp.	Old Bay Seasoning
½ c.	Riesling
2 qts.	Clam Juice
1½ qt.	Water, cold
4 ea.	Red Potatoes, skin on & diced medium
2 c.	White Navy Beans
2 c.	Plum Tomatoes-skin, core & seeds removed, diced medium
2 c.	Clams, whole
To Taste	Sea Salt
To Taste	Black Pepper, ground

Method:
1. In a soup pot, sweat the vegetables and garlic in olive oil. Stir in tomato paste, add herbs and deglaze with wine.
2. Add clam juice, water, let boil and simmer for 45 minutes.
3. Stir in potatoes and simmer for another 12 minutes. Add white navy beans, tomatoes and clams.
4. Season to taste.

ↀ

Cream of Chicken with Fresh Garden Vegetables

1 ea.	Celery, diced medium
1 ea.	Onion, diced medium
1 cl.	Garlic, minced
3 Tbl.	Extra Virgin Olive Oil
1 tsp.	Tarragon, freshly chopped
1 tsp.	Thyme, freshly chopped
½ tsp.	Cilantro, freshly chopped
1½ qt.	Chicken Stock, cold
3 oz.	Roux, warm
1 c.	Half & Half, hot
1 ea.	Green Zucchini, cut on bias
1 ea.	Yellow Zucchini, cut on bias
½ ea.	Red Pepper, diced medium
2#	Chicken, cooked & diced medium
1 Tbl.	Parsley & Chives, freshly chopped
To Taste	Sea Salt
To Taste	Black Pepper, ground
To Taste	Tabasco

Method:
1. In a soup pot, sweat the celery, onion and garlic in olive oil.
   Add the herbs, one cup of chicken stock and whisk in roux.
2. Stir in the remaining chicken stock and add half & half.
   Bring to a boil, let simmer for 45 minutes and strain into another soup pot.
3. Add chicken, zucchini, red pepper and simmer for another 5 minutes.
4. Garnish with fresh herbs.
   Season to taste.

∾

Deer Stew with Garden Fresh Vegetables And White Potatoes

2½#	Deer Meat, trimmed & cut into 1-inch cubes
As Needed	Buckwheat Flour, sifted
As Needed	Extra Virgin Olive Oil
3 c.	Carrots, peeled & diced large
¾ c.	Celery, diced medium
1 ea.	Leek, diced medium
3 cl.	Garlic, minced
1 ea.	Bay Leaf, whole
1 tsp.	Thyme, freshly chopped
1 tsp.	Oregano, freshly chopped
½ tsp.	Rosemary, freshly chopped
½ tsp.	Marjoram, freshly chopped
1 Tbl.	Parsley, freshly chopped
¼ c.	Brandy
½ c.	Chianti
4½ qts.	Beef Stock, cold
¼ c.	Roux, warm
2 ea.	Idaho Potatoes, peeled & diced large
2 c.	Pea's, whole
3 ea.	Plum Tomatoes-skin, core & seeds removed, diced medium
To Taste	Sea Salt
To Taste	Black Pepper, ground

Method:

1. Dredge meat in flour and shake off excess.
   In a large soup pot, sauté the deer meat a little at a time in olive oil.
   Remove deer meat and keep warm.
2. Stir in vegetables, garlic, herbs, deglaze with brandy, add wine and let reduce.
   Add one cup beef stock and whisk in roux.

Stir in the rest of the beef stock, sautéed meat, bring to a boil and simmer for 45 minutes.

3. Add potatoes and simmer for 8 minutes.
    Stir in pea's, tomatoes and simmer for another 2 minutes.
    Season to taste.

∾

Grilled Asparagus and Mushroom Soup

1 Tbl.	Extra Virgin Olive Oil
1 tsp.	Garlic, minced
½ c.	Celery, diced small
1 ea.	Leeks, white part & diced small
1#	Asparagus-peeled, grilled & diced medium
½#	Button Mushrooms, sliced
½ tsp.	Parsley, freshly chopped
½ tsp.	Thyme, freshly chopped
1 ea.	Bay Leaf, whole
3 Tbl.	Chardonnay
3 Tbl.	Roux, warm
1 c.	Half & Half, hot
6 c.	Chicken Stock, cold
To Taste	Sea Salt
To Taste	Black Pepper, cracked
Dash	Nutmeg, freshly ground
As Needed	Roasted Red Pepper Coulis

Method:
1. In a soup pot, sweat the garlic, celery and leeks in olive oil.
   Stir in the grilled asparagus, mushrooms, herbs and let reduce.
2. Deglaze with wine, add half & half and reduce by one-half.
3. Whisk in roux, add stock and reduce again by one-half.
   Remove bay leaf and discard.
   Blend soup to a smooth consistency, strain and season to taste.
4. Garnish with freshly ground nutmeg.
   Place roasted red pepper coulis in squirt bottle and make a design on top of soup.

∾

⁓

Lamb Stew with Red Skin Potatoes and Turnips

10 oz.	Lamb, diced small
3 Tbl.	Extra Virgin Olive Oil
As Needed	Buckwheat Flour, sifted
1 c.	Carrot, diced small
1 c.	Turnips, skin removed & diced small
½ c.	Celery, diced small
½ c.	Onion, diced small
3 cl.	Garlic, minced
1 tsp.	Parsley, freshly chopped
½ tsp.	Rosemary, freshly chopped
½ tsp.	Thyme, freshly chopped
¼ tsp.	Marjoram, freshly chopped
¼ tsp.	Cumin, ground
½ c.	Cabernet Sauvignon
4½ c.	Beef Stock, cold
3 ea.	Red Potato, skin on & diced small
3 ea.	Tomatoes-skin, core & seeds removed, diced small
To Taste	Sea Salt
To Taste	Black Pepper, ground

Method:
1. Dredge lamb meat in flour and shake off excess.
   In a large soup pot, sauté lamb meat a little at a time in olive oil.
2. Stir in vegetables and add herbs.
   Deglaze with wine, add beef stock, let boil and simmer for 45 minutes.
3. Stir in red potatoes and simmer for another 8 minutes.
   Add fresh tomatoes and season to taste.

⁓

∽

Lobster Tomato Broth, Served with Lobster Basil Quenelles

Lobster broth:

1¼#	Lobster shells, crushed
3 Tbl.	Extra Virgin Olive Oil
¼ c.	Brandy
1 Tbl.	Tomato paste
¼ c.	Onion, diced medium
½ c.	Celery, diced medium
½ c.	Carrot, peeled & diced medium
1 cl.	Garlic, minced
2 qt.	Water, cold
2 Tbl.	Sea Salt
2 ea.	Black Pepper, whole
½ tsp.	Old Bay Seasoning
1 Tbl.	Basil, freshly chopped
½ tsp.	Parsley, freshly chopped
½ tsp.	Thyme, freshly chopped
½ c.	Tomato Juice, freshly strained

Method:
1. In a soup pot, add lobster shells in olive oil on medium high heat. Stir shells occasionally for 5 minutes and deglaze with brandy.
2. Add the tomato paste, onion, carrot and garlic.
3. Stir in the water, salt, pepper and herbs.
   Bring broth to a boil, let simmer for 25 minutes, strain and add tomato juice.
4. Simmer for another 15 minutes.

Lobster Basil Quenelles:

1¼#	Lobster, diced small
6 ea.	Basil leaves, freshly chopped
1 ea.	Egg, whole

8 oz.	Half & Half, cold
To Taste	Sea Salt
To Taste	Black Pepper, ground
As Needed	Water
To Taste	Sea Salt
2 qt.	Lobster broth, hot
As Needed	Roasted Yellow Pepper, cut into diamonds

Method:
1. In a Cuisinart, add lobster, basil and pulse chop.
   Add egg and pulse chop again.
   Slowly add half & half in a steady stream, while mixing and season to taste.
2. Shape quenelle and place in boiling salted water.
   Let simmer until proper doneness.
3. In a bowl, add Lobster broth and arrange quenelles.
   Garnish with roasted yellow pepper.

∾

∾

Lump Crabmeat, Shrimp and Mushroom Bisque

16 ea.	Shrimp-shells removed for stock, de-veined & diced small
1#	Button Mushrooms, stems removed & diced medium
1 c.	Onion, diced small
2 ea.	Garlic, minced
3 Tbl.	Extra Virgin Olive Oil
2 Tbl.	Tomato Paste
¼ ea.	Red Pepper, diced small
2 ea.	Bay Leaf, whole
1 tsp.	Dill, freshly chopped
1 tsp.	Old Bay Seasoning
½ tsp.	Parsley, freshly chopped

½ tsp.	Thyme, freshly chopped
½ Tbl.	Oregano, freshly chopped
4 oz.	Brandy
5 oz.	Roux, warm
1 qt.	Shrimp Stock, cold
1 qt.	Half & Half, hot
1#	Lump Crabmeat
To Taste	Sea Salt
To Taste	Black Pepper, ground

Method:

1. In a stock pot, prepare shrimp stock out of shrimp shells and mushroom stems.
2. Separately in a soup pot, sauté mushrooms, garlic and onion in olive oil. Stir in tomato paste, add red pepper, herbs and deglaze with brandy. Add shrimp stock and whisk in roux.
3. Stir in half & half, bring to a boil and let simmer for 15 minutes.
4. Add shrimp, crabmeat and let simmer for 3 minutes. Season to taste.

෨෧

⚙

VEAL

Braised Veal Stuffed with Spinach and Two Cheeses,
Served with Carrot Turnip Bundles and a Shitake
And Chantrelle Mushroom Pinot Noir Sauce
328
Sautéed Veal with a Crawfish Garlic and Basil Salsa,
Served with Egg Fettuccini
331
Sautéed Veal Cutlet and Shrimp Smothered in a
Riesling Button Mushroom Sauce,
Garnished with Plum Tomatoes
332
Veal Scaloppini with a Riesling Reduction Garlic Herb Sauce,
Served with Asparagus and Shaved Parmesan
334
Veal Stuffed with Proscuitto Ham, Mozzarella
And Spinach Served with a Marsala and
Whiskey Wild Mushroom Sauce
336

⚙

∽

Braised Veal Stuffed with Spinach and Two Cheeses, Served with Carrot Turnip Bundles and a Shitake And Chantrelle Mushroom Pinot Noir Sauce

Carrot Turnip Bundles:

1 ea.	Carrot, peeled & julienne
1 ea.	Turnip, peeled & julienne
1 ea.	Leek-green part only, cut lengthwise & steamed for 1 minute

Method:
1. Assemble carrots and turnips around leek.
   Tie carefully in a bow not to break the leek.
2. Steam vegetables for 2 minutes.

8 oz.	Spinach, steamed
1 cl.	Garlic, minced
2 oz.	Pine Nuts, toasted & ground
6 oz.	Feta Cheese
6 oz.	Goat Cheese
2½ #	Veal Shoulder, pounded out
To Taste	Sea Salt
To Taste	Black Pepper, ground
As Needed	Butcher's Twine
As Needed	Extra Virgin Olive Oil
½ c.	Onions, diced medium
½ c.	Celery, diced medium
½ c.	Carrot, diced medium
3 cl.	Garlic, whole
½ c.	Tomatoes-skin & seeds removed & diced medium
2 c.	Pinot Noir
3 c.	Beef Stock, cold

| 1 ea. | 5 sprigs parsley, 3 sprigs Thyme, 3 sprigs Oregano, 3 Bay leaves, 4 Black Peppercorns |
| 1½ tsp. | Sea Salt |

Method:

1. In a steel bowl, mix the spinach, garlic, toasted pine nuts and cheeses together.

   Pound out veal, season, stuff with spinach cheese mixture and tie up with butcher's twine.

   Sauté veal in olive oil and brown on all sides in a braising pot.

2. Remove veal and sauté vegetables for 3 minutes.

   Stir in tomatoes, deglaze with wine and add beef stock.

   Add herbs wrapped in cheesecloth, sea salt and place veal in braising pot.

   Set lid on top and let simmer for 15 minutes turning veal occasionally.

3. Remove veal, let rest for 6 minutes, untie and simmer broth for another 20 minutes.

   Arrange sliced veal on entrée plate with shitake chantrelle mushroom sauce.

   Garnish with carrot and turnip bundles.

Shitake and Chantrelle Mushroom Pinot Noir Sauce:

1 Tbl.	Extra Virgin Olive Oil
1 ea.	Shallots, minced
1 cl.	Garlic, minced
1 tsp.	Oregano, freshly chopped
¼ tsp.	Marjoram, freshly chopped
¼ tsp.	Rosemary, freshly chopped
½ tsp.	Thyme, freshly chopped
½ tsp.	Parsley, freshly chopped
¼ c.	Shitake Mushrooms, julienne
¼ c.	Chantrelle Mushrooms, julienne
¼ c.	Pinot Noir
2 c.	Poaching liquid from veal, strained
2 Tbl.	Roux, warm
To Taste	Sea Salt
To Taste	Black Pepper, ground

Method:
1. In a sauté pan, sweat the shallots and garlic in olive oil.
   Add herbs, mushrooms, deglaze with wine.
2. In a separate sauce pot, add the poaching liquid, bring to a boil and let simmer.
   Whisk in roux, let simmer and reduce to a medium consistency.
   Strain into herb mushroom mixture.
3. Season to taste.

෯

Sautéed Veal with a Crawfish Garlic and Basil Salsa, Served with Egg Fettuccini

2-(3 oz.) each	Veal, pounded out
As Needed	Buckwheat Flour, sifted
To Taste	Sea Salt
To Taste	Black Pepper, ground
6 Tbl.	Extra Virgin Olive Oil
1 ea.	Shallots, minced
1 cl.	Garlic, minced
1 c.	Riesling
1 Tbl.	Basil, freshly chopped
½ tsp.	Thyme, freshly chopped
4 ea.	Crawfish, shells removed & finely chopped
½ c.	Yellow Plum Tomatoes-skin, core & seeds removed, diced medium
5 ea.	Green Olives, minced
2 ea.	Black Olives, minced
½ c.	Chicken Stock, cold
2 Tbl.	Butter, cold
½#	Egg Fettuccini, cooked in boiling salted water
1 tsp.	Basil & Parsley, freshly chopped

Method:
1. Season veal, dredge in flour and shake excess off.
   Sauté in olive oil until golden brown, remove veal and keep warm.
2. In the same pan, sweat the shallots and garlic.
   Deglaze with wine and reduce until almost gone.
3. Add the crawfish, tomatoes, olives and chicken stock.
   Simmer for 7 minutes and whisk in butter.
4. Arrange on oval entrée plate the veal, basil crawfish salsa and egg fettuccini.
   Garnish with fresh herbs.

∾

Sautéed Veal Cutlet and Shrimp Smothered in a Riesling Button Mushroom Sauce, Garnished with Plum Tomatoes

2-(3 oz.) each	Veal Cutlet, pounded out
To Taste	Sea Salt
To Taste	Black Pepper, ground
As Needed	Buckwheat Flour, sifted
As Needed	Extra Virgin Olive Oil
3 ea.	Shrimp-peeled, de-veined & tail on
1 ea.	Plum Tomatoes-skin, core & seeds removed, julienne
1 tsp.	Parsley, freshly chopped
1 tsp.	Oregano, freshly chopped

Method:
1. Season veal, dredge in flour and shake excess off.
   Sauté in olive oil until golden brown, remove veal and keep warm.
2. In the same sauté pan, sauté the shrimp until proper doneness and keep warm.
3. Arrange shrimp on top of veal cutlet.
   Add Riesling button mushroom sauce.
   Garnish with tomatoes and fresh herbs.

Riesling Button Mushroom Sauce:

1 Tbl.	Extra Virgin Olive Oil
¾ c.	Button Mushrooms, stems removed & quartered
2 cl.	Garlic, minced
1 ea.	Shallots, minced
¼ c.	Riesling
½ tsp.	Oregano, freshly chopped
½ tsp.	Thyme, freshly chopped
1 tsp.	Lemon Juice, freshly squeezed
½ tsp.	Lemon Zest

¾ c.   Veal Stock, cold
As Needed   Cornstarch
As Needed   Sea Salt
As Needed   Black Pepper, ground

Method:
1. In the same sauté pan, sauté mushrooms in olive oil.
   Sweat the garlic and shallots.
   Deglaze with wine, add herbs, lemon juice, lemon zest and reduce.
2. Add veal stock and reduce again by one-half.
3. Thicken with cornstarch to a medium consistency.

∾

∽

Veal Scaloppini with a Riesling Reduction Garlic Herb Sauce, Served with Asparagus And Shaved Parmesan

Asparagus and Shaved Parmesan:

4	Asparagus, peeled & bias cut
As Needed	Parmesan Cheese, shaved
To Taste	Black Pepper, cracked

Method:
1. Steam asparagus for 1 minute.
    Toss asparagus with parmesan cheese.

For the Veal:

2-(3 oz.) each	Veal, pounded out
To Taste	Sea Salt
To Taste	Black Pepper, ground
As Needed	Buckwheat Flour, sifted
As Needed	Extra Virgin Olive Oil

Method:
1. Season veal, dredge in flour and shake excess off.
    Sauté in olive oil until golden brown, remove veal and keep warm.

Riesling Reduction Garlic Herb Sauce:

3 Tbl.	Extra Virgin Olive Oil
4 cl.	Garlic, minced
1 ea.	Shallots, minced
½ tsp.	Thyme, freshly chopped
½ tsp.	Parsley, freshly chopped
¼ tsp.	Rosemary, freshly chopped
¾ c.	Riesling
½ c.	Veal Stock, cold

To Taste	Sea Salt
To Taste	Black Pepper, ground
2 Tbl.	Butter, cold
1 tsp.	Cilantro & Chives, freshly chopped
1 tsp.	Pine Nuts, toasted
1 tsp.	Capers

Method:

1. In the same sauté pan, sweat the garlic and shallots in olive oil.
   Add herbs, deglaze with wine and add veal stock.
   Reduce until liquid is almost gone.
2. Strain sauce and whisk in the cold butter.
3. Arrange veal, Riesling garlic herb sauce and asparagus on entrée plate.
   Garnish with fresh herbs, toasted pine nuts and capers.

ᕲᕖ

∾

Veal Stuffed with Proscuitto Ham, Mozzarella And Spinach Served with a Marsala and Whiskey Wild Mushroom Sauce

2-(10 oz.) each	Veal cutlets, pounded out
2 oz.	Spinach-steamed, drained with no moisture & chopped
To Taste	Sea Salt
To Taste	Black Pepper, ground
2 oz.	Proscuitto Ham, sliced thin
4 ea.	Mozzarella Cheese, sliced thin
As Needed	Buckwheat Flour, sifted
2 ea.	Eggs, whole
As Needed	Bread Crumbs with 1 Tbl. Parsley, freshly chopped
As Needed	Olive Oil
1 tsp.	Cilantro & Oregano, freshly chopped

Method:
1. Season veal, add proscuitto, mozzarella and then the spinach. Roll up veal and shape into a round. Dredge veal in flour, egg wash and roll in bread mixture.
2. Deep fry in olive oil until golden brown. Finish baking in a 350°F oven until proper doneness.
3. Remove veal, let rest for 5 minutes and slice veal diagonally on entrée plate. Serve with marsala wild mushroom sauce. Garnish with fresh herbs.

Marsala and Whiskey Wild Mushroom Sauce:

1 Tbl.	Extra Virgin Olive Oil
1 ea.	Shallots, minced
1 cl.	Garlic, minced
½ c.	Shitake Mushrooms, julienne
1 tsp.	Oregano, freshly chopped

½ *tsp.* Thyme, freshly chopped
½ *tsp.* Parsley, freshly chopped
¼ *tsp.* Rosemary, freshly chopped
¼ *c.* Marsala
3 *Tbl.* Scotch Whiskey
1 *c.* Beef Stock, cold
1 *Tbl.* Roux, warm
To Taste Sea Salt
To Taste Black Pepper, ground

Method:
1. Sweat the shallots and garlic in olive oil.
   Sauté shitake mushrooms, add herbs, deglaze with wine, add whiskey and let reduce.
2. Add stock and reduce by one-half.
3. Whisk in roux, let simmer for 15 minutes and strain.
   Season to taste.

~

SEASONINGS

All Purpose Spice Mix
340
Cajun Spice Mix
341
Capri Spice Mix
342
Lemon Oreganato Seasoning
343
Mild Creole Seasoning
344
Parmesan Spice Mix
345
White Spice Dry Seasoning
346
White Spice Marination
347

~

༄

All Purpose Spice Mix

2 Tbl.	Paprika, ground
1 Tbl.	Sea Salt
½ Tbl.	Garlic Powder, ground
½ Tbl.	Onion Powder, ground
½ Tbl.	Cayenne Pepper, ground
½ Tbl.	Thyme, dry
½ Tbl.	Oregano, dry
¼ Tbl.	Black Pepper, ground
¼ Tbl.	White Pepper, ground

Method:
1. Combine ingredients and mix thoroughly.
   Place in a sealed container and label contents.
2. Replace recipes containing salt and pepper with dry seasoning mix.
3. Used for beef, chicken, pork or seafood.

༄

∾

Cajun Spice Mix

4 Tbl.	Paprika, ground
3 Tbl.	Dry Fennel Seed, whole
2½ Tbl.	Poultry Seasoning, ground
2 Tbl.	Sea Salt
2 Tbl.	Old Bay Seasoning
2 Tbl.	Basil, dry
1½ Tbl.	Cayenne Pepper, ground
1 Tbl.	Mint, dry
1 Tbl.	Dill, dry
1 Tbl.	Black Pepper, ground
½ Tbl.	White Pepper, ground
½ Tbl.	Tarragon, ground
½ Tbl.	Garlic Powder, ground
¼ tsp.	Red Pepper Flakes, dry

Method:
1. Combine ingredients and mix thoroughly.
   Place in a sealed container and label contents.
2. Replace recipes containing salt and pepper with dry seasoning mix.
3. Used for beef, chicken, pork or seafood.

∾

ᏀᎧ

Capri Spice Mix

½ *Tbl.*	Basil, dry
3 *Tbl.*	Rosemary, dry
2¾ *Tbl.*	Sea Salt
2 *Tbl.*	Paprika, ground
1 *Tbl.*	Garlic Powder, ground
½ *Tbl.*	Mint, dry
½ *Tbl.*	Poultry Seasoning, ground
½ *Tbl.*	Thyme, dry
¼ *Tbl.*	Dill, dry
½ *tsp.*	White Pepper, ground
½ *tsp.*	Black Pepper, ground
1 *tsp.*	Cayenne Pepper, ground

Method:
1. Combine ingredients and mix thoroughly.
   Place in a sealed container and label contents.
2. Replace recipes containing salt and pepper with dry seasoning mix.
3. Used for beef, chicken or pork.

ᏀᎧ

Lemon Oreganato Seasoning

1 Tbl.   Bread Crumbs
1 Tbl.   Oregano, dry
1 Tbl.   Parsley, dry
1 Tbl.   Lemon Zest
½ Tbl.   Garlic Powder, ground
½ Tbl.   Parmesan Cheese, grated
¼ Tbl.   Basil, dry
As Needed   Extra Virgin Olive Oil

Method:
1. Combine dry ingredients and mix thoroughly.
    Slowly add the olive oil to bind ingredients together.
    Place in a sealed container, label contents and refrigerate.
2. Replace recipes containing salt and pepper with dry seasoning mix.
3. Used for chicken, clams, oysters or seafood.

∾

Mild Creole Seasoning

2½ Tbl.	Paprika, ground
2 Tbl.	Sea Salt
2 Tbl.	Garlic Powder, ground
1 Tbl.	Black Pepper, ground
1 Tbl.	Onion Powder, ground
1 Tbl.	Cayenne Pepper, ground
1 Tbl.	Oregano, dry
1 Tbl.	Thyme, dry

Method:
1. Combine ingredients and mix thoroughly.
   Place in a sealed container and label contents.
2. Replace recipes containing salt and pepper with dry seasoning mix.
3. Used for chicken or seafood.

∾

∽

Parmesan Spice Mix

1¼ Tbl.	Thyme, dry
1¼ Tbl.	Oregano, dry
1 Tbl.	Sea Salt
1 Tbl.	Parsley, dry
1 Tbl.	Basil, dry
1 Tbl.	Poultry Seasoning, ground
1 Tbl.	Garlic Powder, ground
½ Tbl.	Black Pepper, ground
½ Tbl.	White Pepper, ground

Method:
1. Combine ingredients and mix thoroughly.
   Place in a sealed container and label contents.
2. Replace recipes containing salt and pepper with dry seasoning mix.
3. Used for chicken, seafood or veal.

∽

∾

White Spice Dry Seasoning

1 Tbl.   Bread Crumbs
¼ Tbl.   Dry Mustard, ground
¼ Tbl.   Sea Salt
½ tsp.   Garlic Powder, ground
½ tsp.   Lemon Zest, dry
½ tsp.   Onion Powder, ground
½ tsp.   White Pepper, ground

Method:
1. Combine ingredients and mix thoroughly.
    Place in a sealed container and label contents.
2. Replace recipes containing salt and pepper with dry seasoning mix.
3. Used for chicken or seafood.

∾

White Spice Marination

1 Tbl.	Tarragon, dry
1 Tbl.	Basil, dry
2 Tbl.	Old Bay Seasoning
1 Tbl.	Black Pepper, ground
1 Tbl.	Sea Salt
1 Tbl.	Onion Powder, ground
1 Tbl.	Garlic Powder, ground
1 Tbl.	Thyme, dry
1 Tbl.	Rosemary, dry
1 Tbl.	Sage, dry
½ c.	White Wine Vinegar
½ c.	Red Wine Vinegar
1 c.	Tarragon Vinegar
1 Tbl.	Garlic, minced

Method:
1. Combine dry ingredients and mix thoroughly. Add garlic and whisk in vinegars.
2. Used for marinating chicken or seafood.

∽

HOLIDAY COCKTAILS

Dad's Whiskey Sour
350
Mom's White Russian
350
Holiday Vodka Martini
350
Pink Lady Papaya Cocktail
351
Wild Lizzy's Raspberry Watermelon Mojito
351
Uncle Paul's Mango Pineapple Cocktail
352

∽

∾

Dad's Whiskey Sour

2 oz.	Blended Whiskey
½ oz.	Lemon, freshly squeezed
1 Tbl.	Simple Syrup
½ oz.	Cherry Juice
Dash	Orange Juice
As Needed	Ice Cubes
As Needed	Cherries

Method:
Shake blended whiskey, lemon juice, simple syrup, cherry juice, orange juice and ice. Strain into a glass with ice and add a cherry.

∾

Mom's White Russian

As Needed	Ice Cubes
2 oz.	Vodka
½ oz.	Kahlua Liqueur
½ oz.	Coffee Liqueur
1½ Tbl.	Half & Half

Method:
Add ice in a glass and pour in vodka and kahlua.
Drizzle half & half on top, stir and serve.

∾

Holiday Vodka Martini

As Needed	Ice, cubed
3 oz.	Vodka
½ oz.	Vermouth
2 oz.	Olive Juice

As Needed Green Olives with pimentoes
As Needed Toothpicks

Method:
Fill mixing glass with ice, add vodka, vermouth and stir well for 3 minutes. Strain into chilled martini glasses and add 3 olives on a toothpick.

෴

Pink Lady Papaya Cocktail

¾ c. Papaya or Mango, freshly cut in cubes
1 oz. Orange Juice
1 oz. Pink Grapefruit, juice
As Needed Ice, cubed
½ oz. Vodka
2 oz. Southern Comfort

Method:
Combine papaya, orange juice, grapefuit juice and a few ice cubes in a blender and mix until smooth. Add vodka, southern comfort and mix again for 2 minutes. Pour into chilled glasses.

෴

Wild Lizzy's Raspberry Watermelon Mojito

½ c. Raspberry Juice
¼ c. Watermelon juice
¼ oz. Simple Syrup
1 tsp. Lime Juice
2 oz. Vodka
As Needed Ice, cubed
3 ea. Mint, cut into strips

Method:
Combine raspberry, watermelon, simple syrup, lime, vodka and ice in a container. Shake for 3 minutes, strain into a ice filled glass and stir in mint.

෴

❧

Uncle Paul's Mango Pineapple Cocktail

½ ea. Mango, cubed
¼ c. Pineapple Juice
As Needed Ice, cubed
1 oz. Southern Comfort
2 oz. Vodka

Method:
Combine mango, pinapple juice and ice in a blender and mix until smooth.
Add southern comfort, vodka and mix again for 2 minutes. in blender and
mix until smooth. Pour into chilled glasses.

❧

INDEX

APPETIZERS:
chicken galantine 178
crabcakes 180
crabmeat tuna souffles 182
mini quiche 183
roasted garlic, tomato basil on french
italian bread 184
rolled eggplant with goat cheese and
crabmeat 185
salmon terrine with avocado and shrimp 186
shrimp and crabmeat pouches 188
uncle Paul's fresh herb tomato sauce 189
BEEF:
beef tenderloin 29
grilled beef tornadoes 17
grilled skewered beef 15
ground sirloin beef chili 18
marinated grilled beef, shrimp and lobster 19
marinated and grilled london broil 21
prime rib beef 23
roasted angus beef 25
scaloppini of angus beef 27
tenderloin of beef 33
tenderloin of beef medallions 31
three meat and mushroom meat loaf 35
tortilla wrap 36
wellington 13
BREADS:
cinnamon raisin bread 4
french bread rye braids 5
herb brioche 6
herb style pizza bread 8
pineapple and cranberry tea scones 9
CHICKEN:
almond crusted tenders 43
breast of chicken 44
breast of chicken saltimbocca 41

chicken and veal dumplings 55
coconut tenders 61
grilled chicken breast 62
grilled breast wrapped in asparagus 59
marinated grilled chicken breast 65
marinated grilled chicken tenderloins 66
marinated and grilled with dijon mustard 63
marinated strips of chicken 68
roasted 72
roasted herb 75
roasted with apple stuffing 70
roulade with mango and vanilla bean 47
sauteed breast of chicken 77,79
scaloppini 49
tenderloins 46,51,53
wellington 57

COCKTAILS:
dad's whiskey sour, 350
mom's white Russian, 350
holiday Vodka martini, 350
pink lady Papaya, 351
wild Lizzy's raspberry watermelon mojito, 351
uncle Paul's mango pineapple, 352

DESSERTS:
CAKES:
apple crisp 83
banana 84
blackberry forest 85
black walnut and hazelnut 86
blueberry 87
carrot with pineapple, coconut and
walnuts 88
carrot cake with pineapple, raisins and
pecans 89
chocolate black walnut brownies 90
chocolate hazelnut oil, covered with
hazelnuts 92
chocolate walnut souffles 93
coconut orange 94

coffee cake with cream cheese, pineapple, mango filling 95

coffee cake laced with a walnut pistachio filling 97

coffee cake with a pecan walnut topping 99

dark chocolate coconut godiva sabayon 100

disaronno liqueur sponge filled with layers of fruit 102

german chocolate orange with dark chocolate shavings 103

hazelnut and pecan chocolate with dark chocolate ganache 104

moist chocolate brazil nut coffee cake 105

old fashioned pumpkin walnut 107

orange kahlua cocoa 108

pear cinnamon walnut 110

poppy seed 111

pumpkin and acorn squash 112

rhubarb 113

two berry sponge 114

walnut cinnamon apple 115

winter persimmon nut 116

yellow peach and papaya upside down 117

zucchini 118

CHEESECAKE:

baked mango 120

berry jam topped with mixed berries 121

delicate chocolate 122

lime and mandarin orange 123

mini royal persimmon 124

peach ricotta 125

COOKIES and SMALL DESSERTS:

cream cheese raspberry cookies 128

honey wheat chocolate chip cookies 129

crème caramel 130

crepe berry turnovers 131

hazelnut chocolate souffles 133

peach papaya cobbler 134

puff pastry with poppy cream cheese 135

rice pudding with dark sweet raisins 136
strawberries filled with orange cream
cheese 137
DOUGHS:
pie dough with essence of pecans 147
pizza dough with fresh oregano 148
braided sugar raised doughnuts 149
ICING & FROSTING:
caramelized orange sugar 130
chocolate almond marsala sabayon 90
chocolate sabayon 133
chocolate whipped cream 100
chocolate whipped frosting 92
cinnamon walnut frosting 2
cream cheese and coconut frosting 84
lemon cream cheese frosting 88
orange cream cheese frosting 94
rich chocolate kahlua frosting 108
vanilla nutmeg sauce 131
white icing 105
white orange lemon frosting 112
MUFFINS:
blueberry 2
carrot 3
PIES:
acorn squash 140
lime mint cream 141
mini apple and orange marmalade crust 142
sour cream apple pie with disaronno
sauce 144
wild blackberry crust 146
DRESSING:
balsamic 152
caesar 153
ginger sesame 237
italian marmalade 234
italian raspberry marmalade 27
lemon anchovy 154
portabella oil 239
raspberry 155

warm vinaigrette with fresh herbs 65
white bean dill 308
DUCK:
duck cordon bleu 158
breast of duck 160
roasted duck 161
LAMB:
carpaccio 164
pot roast 166
marinated lamb shanks 168
mini lamb shanks 170
roasted 172
sauteed lamb cutlets 174
MARINATE
beef, shrimp & lobster 19
jumbo shrimp 273
marinated london broil 22
marinated grilled soft shell crabs 274
mesquite grilled tuna 278
zucchini & wild mushroom 15
MUSHROOM:
duxelle 13
portabella with red and yellow peppers 277
shitake herb broth 283
PASTA:
angel hair with grilled shrimp 209
angel hair with tiger shrimp, tomato and
goat cheese 216
black pepper egg fettuccine and porketta 230
cheese tortellini 193,196
chive angel hair with lumb crabmeat 208
black pepper fettuccine 195
egg fettuccine 331
fettuccine with chicken tenders 198
fettuccine with grilled lemon chicken 200
fettuccine with langoustines and lobster
claw 204
fettuccine with shrimp, feta and fresh
tomato 219
fettuccine with skewered shrimp and

scallops 201
four vegetable lasagna 199
linguini and clams with bits of lobster 205
linguini with baked chicken and plum
tomatoes 210
lobster ravioli with spaghetti squash 206
penne with vodka sauce 211
penne with jalapeno, mustard and pancetta 212
penne tossed with gorgonzola cream 213
roasted jalapeno dill spaetzli with seafood 217
tomato served with poached salmon 214
PORK:
cabbage rolls smothered in tomato sauce 222
lean kielbasa 224
pork chops stuffed with apple bread 225
roast pork tenderloin stuffed with spinach
and feta 227
sauteed sausage, black beans and white rice 229
sliced porketta with black pepper egg
fettuccine 230
POTATO:
creamy rutabaga potatoes 167
garlic mashed red bliss 73
piped red bliss 49
twice baked 23
RICE:
herb risotto 63,302
scallion wild rice 15
spicy tomato and yellow pepper timbale 280
three pepper risotto 19
SALADS:
chicken with red and white grapes 232
guacamole with kiwi and tomatoes 233
duck breast over boston bibb 234
marinated bow tie noodles with mushrooms
peppers and spinach 236
marinated oriental vegetables and rice
noodles 237
plum tomatoes with olives and toasted
pine nuts 238

tiger shrimp with portabella mushrooms and tomatoes 239
SAUCES:
almond garlic sherry cream 57
apple walnut raisin chutney 225
artichoke 256
artichoke, button mushroom and basil cream 193
artichoke, roasted garlic and tomato 49
asparagus butter 33
basil shiraz cream 44
button mushroom three pepper herb cream 62
champagne wild flower honey and ginger 296
chianti herb reduction 29
crawfish garlic and basil salsa 331
dijon mint horseradish 164
garlic herb port cream 158
garlic herb sherry cream 41
ginger and wild mushroom brown 160
goat cheese dill 202
gorgonzola cream 213
herb artichoke caper 198
herb butter 75
herb caper hollandaise 25
herb crayfish 292
herb, garlic and tomato port cream 204
herb mango coulis 251
herb mustard aioli 181
herb salmon 215
herb tomato hollandaise 32
herb scallop champagne 17
herb tomato vodka 211
horseradish Au Jus 23
kiwi fig 187
jalapeno, mustard and pancetta cream 212
lemon caper salsa 253
lemon caper reduction 60
lemon garlic cream 304
lime vodka cream brown 55
lobster tomato broth 322

mango apple sauce 168
marsala and whiskey wild mushroom 336
marsala wild mushroom 227
mint hollandaise 173
orange veloute brown 162
pan gravy and toasted pine nuts 72
peach mango chutney 261
pear and mango chutney 298
pepper, olive and tomato salsa 77
persimmon sauce 178
pineapple and mandarin orange salsa 299
pineapple mango mint chutney 61
pineapple orange mint chutney 306
plum tomato herb salsa 210
port shitake herb cream brown 14
port wild mushroom 21
pot roast brown 167
proscuitto herb goat cheese 195
riesling button mushroom 332
riesling herb dill cream 254
riesling reduction garlic herb 334
roasted garlic, herb and sun dried tomato 300
roasted garlic, leek and artichoke 75
roasted red pepper mango coulis 246
rosemary mint 171
rosemary mint brown 174
sherry dill cream 285
shitake chanterelle pinot noir 328
shrimp broth with fresh herbs 303
spicy plum tomato cream 294
spicy roasted red pepper beurre blanc 265
spicy tomato beurre blanc 206,217
spicy yellow plum tomato coulis 271
spicy yellow tomato 258
southern comfort lime butter 263
sun dried tomato and crab cream 197
sun dried tomato and goat cheese 216
sun dried tomato port cream 51
tequila lime butter 260
toasted pecan cream 244

tomato basil salsa 310
tomato herb brown sauce 71
tomato, olive and leek 200
tomato saffron broth 269
tomato salsa 264
uncle Paul's fresh herb tomato sauce 189
wild mushroom roasted garlic cream 79
SEAFOOD:
blackened salmon with fettuccine and roasted
shallots 244
breaded sole with avocado and toasted
almonds 246
ceviche of tuna, swordfish and asparagus 248
clams casino with peach essence 250
cod roulade with bits of shrimp and capers 251
dover sole francaise 252
fillet of dover sole with scallops and shrimp 254
flounder in crabmeat stuffing 256
fried calamari 258
grilled halibut and rounds of leeks 260
grilled shrimp with white bean puree 261
grilled snapper 263
grilled swordfish with mango's and peaches 265
shrimp stock 203
grilled twin filets of trout 267
hardy style fisherman's seafood 269
jumbo shrimp stuffed with goat cheese 271
marinated grilled jumbo shrimp 273
marinated grilled soft shell crabs 274
marinated grilled wild caught salmon 276
mesquite grilled tuna with sun dried
tomatoes 278
new zealand garlic mussels 280
poached dover sole filled with red snapper
mousse 281
poached halibut and morels 283
poached salmon with crabmeat filling 285
poached salmon and yellow pepper mousse 287
poached sea bass in a vegetable and wild
mushroom broth 289

red snapper medallions with herb crayfish sauce 291
salmon filet with an herb feta and spinach stuffing 294
sauteed and seared swordfish with tuna and asparagus 296
sauteed buckwheat soft shell crabs 298
sauteed dover sole with pineapple and mandarin salsa 299
scallops on a bed of roasted garlic and sun dried tomato 300
seared tuna with a corn, plum tomato and cilantro salsa 301
shrimp broth with fresh herbs 303
shrimp stuffed with crabmeat, with lemon garlic cream 304
smoked shrimp and scallops with julienne of cucumbers 306
summer chilled red snapper with tortellini salad 308
summer pan seared sea scallops with beans and mushrooms 310
tuna carpaccio with fresh herbs 311

SEASONINGS:
all purpose spice mix 340
cajun spice mix 341
capri spice mix 342
lemon oreganato seasoning 343
mild creole seasoning 344
parmesan spice mix 345
white spice dry seasoning 346
white spice marination 347

SOUPS:
atlantic sea scallop and leek 314
chicken garden spring vegetables 315
clam chowder with red skin potatoes 316
cream of chicken with garden vegetables 317
deer stew with fresh vegetables and white potatoes 318
grilled asparagus and mushroom 320

lamb stew with potatoes and turnips 321
lobster tomato broth with lobster basil
quenelles 322
lumb crabmeat, shrimp and mushroom
bisque 324
shrimp broth with fresh herbs 303
tomato saffron broth 269
STUFFING:
apple bread 70
crabmeat 31,256,304
herb feta and spinach 294
pine nut crust 45
sausage sage 44
wild mushroom 57
VEAL:
braised and stuffed with spinach and two
cheeses 328
sauteed veal with crawfish garlic and basil
salsa 331
sauteed cutlet and shrimp 332
scaloppini with asparagus and shaved
parmesan 334
stuffed with proscuitto, mozzarella and
spinach 336
VEGETABLE:
asparagus and shaved parmesan 334
asparagus juice 33
asparagus coulis 281
carrot turnip bundles 328
corn, cucumber, roasted red pepper salsa 73
cucumber and roasted pepper salsa 267
herb idaho mashed potatoes 75
grilled wild mushrooms & asparagus 30
marinated corn, plum tomato and cilantro
salsa 301
oriental vegetables 68
roasted yellow pepper 67,178,268
roasted red pepper coulis 197,270
seasoned brussels sprouts 22
spaghetti zucchini 258

spaghetti squash 207,277
white beans 171
white bean and tomato garlic puree 169
white bean tomato salsa 263
white bean puree 261

3436610